TEENS FIGHT

ADULT CORRUPTION

R. A. "BUDDY" SCOTT

THIS NOVEL
MUST NOT BE JUDGED
UNTIL THE COMPLETE WORK IS READ.

ALL❁N
PUBLISHING

DEDICATION
THIS NOVEL IS DEDICATED
TO ALL STRONG-WILLED READERS
WHO DARE TO UNRAVEL THE MYSTERIES OF LIFE.

Buddy Scott is also the author of *Relief for Hurting Parents* (ISBN: 0-9637645-0-0):
Copyright © 1989 by Allon Publishing, P.O. Box 804, Lake Jackson, Texas 77566.
To order *Relief for Hurting Parents* or *Teens Fight Adult Corruption*, call: (409) 297-5700.

Unless otherwise noted, Scripture quotations in *Teens Fight Adult Corruption*
are from the *King James Version* of the Holy Bible.

Scripture quotations noted NKJV are from the *New King James Version*.
Copyright © 1979, 1980, 1982, Thomas Nelson, Inc., Publishers.
Used by permission.

Scripture quotations noted TEV are from the *Good News Bible*—
Old Testament: Copyright © American Bible Society 1976;
New Testament: Copyright © American Bible Society 1966, 1971, 1976.
Used by permission.

Scripture quotations noted NIV are from the *Holy Bible: New International Version*.
Copyright © 1973, 1978, 1984, 1987 International Bible Society.
Used by permission of Zondervan Bible Publishers.

Printed in the United States.

Library of Congress Catalog Card Number: 97-94114

ISBN: 0-9637645-2-7

1 2 3 4 5 6 7 8 9 10—07 06 05 04 03 02 01 00 99 98

SCENE 1

Who has an attitude?

ONE

THE PRINCIPAL was mad at his new coach. He said in an obnoxiously gruff voice, "It has come to my attention that you—you, sir, a PE teacher—have been trying to counsel students. That is not appropriate. We have professionals for that purpose. So, butt out! Do you understand, Coach Bright? Leave my students alone!"

A few days into the new school year and his first coaching job after college, Coach John Bright sat nervously in the principal's office at Lincoln High School. Dressed in a tan T-shirt and shorts and with a chrome-plated whistle hanging from his neck, he was totally unprepared for this surprise attack from his new principal. The rude comments erupted from Mr. A. H. Rumley, fifty-nine, who was dressed in a pricey suit and peered at John over skinny black reading glasses from behind a large polished hard-rock maple desk.

The handsome young coach was finding out why the students had renamed their principal, adding a *p* to his last name: Mr. Rumpley. For variety, they also called him Rump Face, or Rump Brain, or Big Rump, or whatever. Rumley's rear was a little oversized for his medium-sized body, but not enough to deserve the titles. The students just like to link his personality with his butt.

Rumley continued griping out the coach, "May I remind you that you were hired to teach kids to play games, not to counsel them? Counseling is out of your league. It's something that licensed professional therapists do. Not you!"

The principal was named after his grandfathers, Alfredo and Henry, one an undertaker and the other a drill sergeant. Someone said that his heritage explained why he was so insensitive and controlling. Right or wrong, politically correct or not, the explanation stuck.

Rumley raged on without giving the coach a chance to explain his side. "Teaching PE does not qualify you to be a counselor," he said hatefully. "I'd advise you to stay out of the personal problems of my students and their families!"

Taking a deep breath and calming down a bit, Rumley continued, "With our head coach out this semester recovering from his car accident, I'm confident that you have more responsibility than you can possibly manage at twenty-three years of age, son, being as young and inexperienced as you are. You had better keep your mind on leading our football team into a winning season. You have a game in seven days. Is your team ready?"

"The season starts two Fridays from now," John politely corrected.

John was in shock. What had made his boss so mad? John had shown concern for several students. He wondered which ones Rumley heard about.

Rumley's secretary, an African-American woman named Ms. Gibson, sat off to one side. Her eyes were glued to her notepad. Her pencil scampered back and forth. Rumley had told her to take notes. John felt outnumbered, two to one.

The principal's cheap comment about John's career hurt deeply. He had been teased about it all through college. A lot of college students seemed to think that only dumb people majored in PE. Business majors would put him down in a teasing way by asking: "How's basket weaving going, John?"

But John was no fool in choosing his career. He liked teenagers, and he loved sports. In coaching, he could be with teens and be around sports.

Coach John Bright was doing well with the students. His players respected him. The girls liked his blond hair and blond eyebrows and adored his aqua-blue eyes. The guys didn't mind that the girls liked him so much because John didn't flirt with the female students. He gave the guys most of his attention, and he had won their approval.

At the moment, the coach's adorable aqua-blue eyes were fixed on an angry man. John remembered the students' nickname for the principal and thought: *I know how he got his name. Big Rump knows how to be a total rear!*

Rumley wouldn't get off his case. He came at John again, "And while we're having our little meeting, I find it necessary to mention an even bigger problem. It has also come to my attention that you have talked about God on my campus."

Rumley leaned back in his fancy chair, placing his hands behind his bushy gray hair, elbows sticking out, making his arms look like elephant ears. He said, "That obviously violates the separation of church and state. That'll get you fired, my boy! Lincoln High School is second to none in the state in progressive ideas, probably one of the most enlightened schools in the whole country. I won't allow you to put my school in jeopardy of being sued. You cannot push your outdated values at this institution."

John sank in his chair and sighed deeply. He just didn't know what to say to Rumley's lecture. He wasn't prepared for what was happening. He hadn't been called into a principal's office since he was in the eleventh grade. He had deserved it then because he was caught making out with his girlfriend behind the stage during a Shakespearean play. They would have gotten away with it except they got so carried away that John forgot to appear on stage for his part. It seems John and his girlfriend had taken *Romeo and Juliet* a little too seriously.

When Rumley thought he'd given his coach enough time to think about being fired, he asked sarcastically, "Am I making myself clear?"

Disgustingly so! John thought.

Realizing Rumley had jumped to conclusions without giving him an opportunity to explain his side of the story, the young coach attempted an offensive move. "Mr. Rumley, do you mind if I ask you who this is about?"

"Russo! Some student named Franco Russo!" the principal snapped as he stayed in his holier-than-thou posture.

John attempted an explanation. "Russo's in my fourth-period class. I noticed that he was depressed yesterday in the gym. I called him aside and asked what was going on. He told me that another live-in had moved in with his mom and was knocking her around in front of him and Crisco. Crisco is his little sister. Franco doesn't know what to do. You know which student Franco is, don't you? He's a junior. He works early mornings at Donut World across the street from the school. I got to know him there this summer. Crisco goes to work with him when she's in town."

"And?" Rumley pressed.

"Well...okay...I called his mom and alerted her to his depression. I asked if there was anything I could—"

Rumley interrupted and growled, "You told her that you would be praying about their situation! Ms. Russo—or whatever the heck her name is now—called me ten minutes ago and gave me a butt chewing. She told me to tell you to keep your nose out of their business and keep your values to yourself. And that's exactly what I'm ordering you to do! You can't get involved in every—"

John interrupted in calm protest, "I can't believe I'm in trouble with you about religion. I don't even go to church—I don't like hanging out with hypocrites. But I'm just very concerned about Franco! What about the little girl?"

Rumley boomed, "Franco's family will have to deal with their own problems! They have to have enough sense to get their own help. But even if they do get counseling, it won't help them much. These people reproduce themselves. You're not experienced enough to know that, are you? You're a rookie coach, not the Rescue Ranger! Stick to physical education! Got it?"

John got louder, too. He said, "You can't ignore those kids! Franco and Crisco are hurting!"

Rumley glared at the new kid on the block who dared to raise his voice at a supervisor. The principal leaned forward, his palms pushing down on his shiny desk, and he firmly said, "You have an attitude problem, son. People with attitudes don't make it at my school. Back off, or you are going to be depressed right beside Franco...because you are not going to have a job!"

Rumley stood up as he spoke louder, "In education these days, you have to close your eyes and teach! The school can't solve everybody's problems!"

Turning up the volume all the way, Rumley thundered, "Just teach! Just coach! Nothing more! Is that clear?!"

John gathered up as much dignity as he could while he moved from his chair to the door. He paused before opening it and sincerely said, almost in a whisper, "I won't ignore my students. You can fire me if you want, but I won't turn away from them when they need me. Kids have always been able to talk to their coaches. This is nothing new or out of line, Mr. Rumley."

Rumley shouted, "With your rebellious attitude, firing you will be a high point in my career!" He pointed a finger at his secretary. "And you can be sure Ms. Gibson's notes will be placed in your permanent employee file!"

John slipped out of the office and closed the door softly so his boss couldn't think he slammed it.

He maneuvered his way through a noisy hallway, crowded with students talking, laughing, shrieking, banging locker doors. A few spoke to him as he dodged his way through.

"Hi, Coach."

"How's it going?"

"See you at practice, Coach."

"Did you get those tests graded?"

John hardly noticed the students or the noise. He was too busy thinking about the principal. *He's a total jerk!* John thought. *I hope I never become as cold and insensitive as Mr. Rumley.*

His thoughts were interrupted by Franco. Franco stopped right in front of the coach's face so John could hear his important announcement above the noise in the hall.

Franco said loudly, "Big Rump's gonna lean on you! My mom called 'im up and cussed 'im out! Sorry, Coach. Thanks for tryin'."

The bell rang. Students dashed into rooms, leaving the hallway nearly deserted and suddenly quiet.

John placed his hand on Franco's shoulder and said, "I just came from Mr. Rumley's office. He has already leaned on me. I'm okay. I survived."

"He didn't fire you?"

"No, you've still got me for fourth period."

"Whoa, that's a big relief!"

"Everything's cool, Franco, except that Mr. Rumley has made a rule that I'm not supposed to talk to you about your problems. I'm supposed to refer you to the school counselor. I'll get you an appointment with her, okay?"

Franco looked down at the floor. "I've been there already. She told me that all she had time to do was work with scheduling and stuff. She gave me a list of counseling places in the community. They cost big bucks—$90 an hour! Each minute costs $1.50. Can you believe that, Coach? What am I supposed to do to get that kind of money? Deal drugs?"

Staring at the papers littering the hallway, Franco continued, "My mom won't help pay for it. She thinks counseling's just a rip-off." With mounting anger, he said, "Rump Brain doesn't need to sweat it. Me and my friends are stronger than adults think. We can figure out things for ourselves. No problem!"

Franco looked up at John. Their eyes met. Moments passed. Franco cooled down. He felt a warm bond with John. "Coach, I can't talk to you?"

Franco's lonely and searching eyes touched John deeply. He thought of his words to Rumley: *You can fire me if you want, but I won't turn away from my students when they need me.*

John squeezed Franco's shoulder, saying, "You bet your boots you can talk to me! I'll meet you at Fifties Burgers tonight at eight. They have carhops. We can sit in my car and talk all you want."

Without replying with words, Franco shook his head yes in small movements.

Moving his hand from Franco's shoulder to his back, John said, "Come on, I'll get you into class without an admit. Your teacher is a friend of mine."

As they walked, John's mind returned to the principal's office. *I used to be blamed for being a strong-willed child,* he thought, *and now I guess I'll be blamed for being a strong-willed coach. Whatever!*

SCENE 2

*The
teens
are full
of surprises*

TWO

JOHN ARRIVED at Fifties Burgers five minutes till eight and parked for about twenty minutes. Maria, his pretty, trim Hispanic wife, was with him. She commented on how the smell of hamburgers made her hungry. She ordered one, but John was too busy looking for Franco's old army jeep to think about food.

John started his car and circled the drive-in twice looking carefully. No jeep. No Franco.

But where was that music coming from? LOUD music—music thudding with bass! Boom! Boom! Kaboom! John felt it pounding inside his body.

Puzzled and disappointed, John pulled out of Fifties, wondering why Franco hadn't shown. Then John noticed Franco's jeep in the mall parking lot across the street. There, in the outer edge of the parking lot, where the overhead lights weren't so bright, were five trucks, a couple of cars, Franco's jeep, and a new motor scooter. The trucks were backed up together to form a circle of tailgates in the shape of a pentagon. A carhop at Fifties Burgers was supposed to have told John where Franco was, but she neglected to do so since she had gotten behind on getting out orders.

Twelve teenagers and a little girl sat on the tailgates, laughing and talking. The open truck doors acted like megaphones, sending music back to the circle of kids from 500-watt sound systems. All the radios were tuned to the same rock station.

John parked his metallic maroon '65 Mustang convertible some distance away, among cars owned by people shopping in the mall. He and Maria stepped out. Before they approached the circle, someone shouted, "Coach John is here! His wife is with him! Remember, we agreed not to cuss in front of him. Let's show some respect."

Another yelled, "And no teen slang. His wife's still trying to learn English."

The teenager's comment was not correct. Maria was bilingual. She could communicate well in both English and Spanish. However, her English had a Spanish accent since Spanish was her native tongue.

Two girls, varsity cheerleaders at Lincoln High School, sprang into the middle of the circle as John and Maria approached. They had worn their new uniforms for the occasion. Their tops and pleated skirts

were purple and gold with white trim. They began leading a special cheer
for John and Maria. Franco's little sister joined them, trying to copy
what they were doing:

> Who you gonna yell for?
> Coach John! Coach John!
>
> Whatta you gonna yell?
> We won't let Rump dump on you!
> We're the ones who'll see you through!
>
> Fire Coach John? No, he will not!
> Bongo Buns can go to pot!
>
> Hey, Coach John! Yeah, you're so fine!
> Thanks for puttin' your neck on the line!
>
> Yea! Yea! Yea, Coach John!!

The girls finished with jumps and high kicks. Everyone waited
to see the coach's reaction.

Daniel, a senior at LHS, took it upon himself to slip into each of
the five trucks and turn down the radios a few decibels.

Smiling as big as a rainbow, but mystified, John asked, "How did
you guys know what went on between me and Mr. Rumley?"

One of the cheerleaders cheerfully announced, "My mom is
Mr. Rumley's secretary!"

John recognized her as Kaprice Gibson and made the connection.

Kaprice pranced proudlike over to John and Maria and said, "Mom
tells me everything because she trusts me. She knows I won't tell anything she says…well, I just tell my friends here, but they can be trusted,
too. Anyway, Mom said you really stood up for us."

Leilani, from Hawaii, the other cheerleader, took over and said
excitedly, "Kaprice told us that her mom told her that you told old Rump
Face that he could fire you if he wanted, but you weren't going to ignore
your students' needs. You have put your job on the line for us. We are so
impressed! Go, Coach!"

Kaprice grabbed John's right hand and lifted it up as she pulled him into the middle of the circle of trucks as if they were in a boxing ring. She exclaimed, "The new coach! He's a keeper!"

John was super thrilled by the way the kids welcomed him into their group. He loved kids, and they were loving him back in a royal way. But even as he celebrated with them, he was feeling insecure. He was asking himself, *Can I perform a balancing act between Mr. Rumley and these kids without falling off into unemployment?*

Franco took John's hand away from Kaprice and began shaking it, saying, "You took the heat for me! Thank you very, very much!"

Then Franco pulled John over to sit beside him on the tailgate of Daniel's Chevy truck. Kaprice jumped up there, too. Maria sat down next to her. Franco hoisted his little sister onto his lap. He said to Maria, "This here is Crisco. She's my number one sister. She flies in from her dad's home for most weekends." John already knew her from Donut World.

"I'm eight. I'm in the third grade," Crisco said, volunteering the answers to the questions adults always ask.

Crisco and Franco didn't match. He was white. Crisco's skin was almost black. The two of them didn't look as if they could be from the same family.

Little Crisco had a glowing personality. As John looked at her, he got a sick feeling at the thought of that cute child, that precious little girl, having to watch her mother get beat up time and again by live-in boyfriends. He wondered what it was doing to her emotional life. In college, John had been taught to label her as an at-risk kid. Not because labels are good, but because school officials want to identify at-risk children and help them avoid the usual spiral downward.

Leilani returned to her boyfriend, Brady. He placed an arm around her, and she snuggled up close to him.

It was a cozy scene, a little like being at summer camp, except for the sound of traffic and city smells. A campfire would have completed the serene setting.

A junior named Ray broke the silence. "Well, Coach, wanna beer? We've poured 'em in Mountain Dew bottles to keep from gettin' busted." The sixteen-year-old motioned to the ice chest in the bed of his truck. Ray always did off-the-wall things. Offering the coach a beer was way out of step with protocol.

John changed the subject fast. He didn't want anything to spoil his party. Ignoring the underage-drinking issue, he said, "Guys, I want to introduce you to my wife, Maria."

Ray brushed back a shock of black hair as his brown eyes gleamed. He held up a beer as if proposing a toast. He tried his best to mimic an Australian accent, but his failure was obvious. He said, "Good day, Maria! Any mate good enough to mate with our new mate is good enough for us."

It seemed as if Ray had already been to the ice chest too many times. John and Maria didn't respond to his crude remark.

John caught Franco's attention and asked how things had gone at home that evening.

"Not bad," Franco answered without optimism, still feeling down. "Crisco and I were home-alone kids after I picked her up from the airport. I think my mom and her boyfriend are out drinking or something. If they are, and they come home polluted, Mom will probably get beat up again tonight."

Ray popped off, "Franco's not the only one here who's got something to be depressed about. Tell him about your problem, Candace!"

"Shut up, Ray!" Candace shrieked, wishing he hadn't run his mouth. She turned to the girl next to her, bent over, and held her stomach.

John couldn't see her face for the long blond hair that fell over it, but it was obvious by her body language that she was mortified by Ray's comment.

Candace turned Ray's comment over in her mind. *Who had been stupid enough to tell Ray? How many people know now?* The very thought made Candace sick to her stomach.

John took the pressure off her. "That's okay, Candace, you don't have to say a word. People shouldn't have to talk until they are ready."

Daniel, the guy who turned down the radios, said, "I'm ready to talk! My parents are totally unfair, and they pry into my business. I'm a senior, but they, uh, they think they can choose my friends!" With a sweeping gesture, he added, "They think these people are, like, bad for me or something!"

Ray bailed off his tailgate into the middle of the circle and got dramatic. "Maybe we are bad for you! Maybe we are the wrong crowd!" Pointing both hands at himself, he confessed, "I drink like a fish."

Then, pointing to the others one at a time, he revealed:

"Terence didn't have enough credits to move up to his senior year.

"Hope called the principal Bongo Buns to his face. Oh, and Hope lives in a youth home. Her dad's a minister. Can you believe that? They're, like, dysfunctional!

"Dale lives on the streets. His brother was a gang member, and he was killed in a turf war.

"We have an underground library of X-rated videos at Fred's house, and we know the addresses of all the porno sites and perverted chat lines on the Internet, and someone in this circle has tapped a neighbor's phone to call phone-sex lines. Who? Who? I wonder who?

"Then there's Franco. Franco's from a crazy family, and his mom runs her mouth at Big Rump and almost gets our new coach fired."

"Enough already!" Leilani warned, trying to push Ray's stop button.

Ray didn't take the hint. Instead he turned on her, "You always have a joint to pass around, Leilani.

"Kyong Suk, is that a cigarette I see in thy hand?

"Shoplifting is a skill most of us have perfected.

"And would all the virgins stand, please? I doubt that there are any virgins on these tailgates.

"Candace's gramps is messin' with her.

"We listen to rock that's so wild it blows our speakers…and our minds!

"Hey! I do believe that we are the wrong crowd!"

Ray jumped into the back of his truck, put his hand to his forehead as if peering into the distance, and said, "Or maybe a carnival is parked near here, and we're the freak show!"

Whirling around to face the opposite direction, being overdramatic, nearly falling down, Ray continued, "Is that a pirate ship I see in the distance? Maybe our ancestors were pirates, and we are genetically doomed to be wrong-crowd types."

"Shut up, you stupid drunk!" Fred yelled.

"Dam it up, dude!" Dale growled. "Or hit the road! Your choice!"

"Ray! How crude! How rude!" exclaimed Kaprice in disgust.

"What is this, *Ray's National Intruder* magazine?" asked Brady angrily. "Is your brain unplugged or what?"

Franco leaned over to John. "You can't believe everything this guy says. He's always hyper, and now he's drunk." Getting louder so Ray could hear him, he said, "Just look at him! He's pathetic!"

Ray protested, "But everyone knew all this stuff already! Well, except Coach John and his mate, and he's proven that he's our friend. Maybe he can do something! You all know there's more I can tell…"

Franco shifted Crisco off his lap and slid off the tailgate with his fists clenched. Looking up at Ray, he threatened, "Look, man, you had better shut up if you know what's good for you! I'm in no mood to put up with your mouth, Ray!"

Crisco began to cry.

"What's your problem?" Ray slurred at the black-haired boy. "Okay, okay, I'll shut up. Sorry." Ray backed away unsteadily and sat down on his ice chest. "What's the big deal?" he muttered. "We all live with it."

Then his voice trailed off as he tried to have the last word, looking at John and Maria. "Welcome to the world of teenagers."

Candace straightened her slender shoulders and said something to everyone, but John had a feeling she was saying her words for him. Even in the dim light, he saw tears pooling in her blue eyes as she spoke. "Ray's wrong," she said. "No one's messing with me. I don't even have a grandfather. They're both…they're both dead. One died of cancer, and the other died of a heart attack or something."

Ray was listening intently to Candace. He watched her lie about her situation. He was terribly disappointed.

As he glanced at his peers, Ray's eyes were met with cold stares, major glaciers. A silent warning was being sounded: *Mess up Candace's lie, and the consequences will be grave.*

John made eye contact with Ray, too. He said, "Ray, it was very wrong of you to mention anything like that. That's nothing to handle lightly." He added a postscript, "And do me a favor. Refer to Maria as my wife, not my mate."

Hope, the minister's daughter living at the youth home, hit Ray where it hurt the most, "Ray, you are hopelessly immature. I definitely can't believe you did that."

Feeling rejected, Ray leaned against the cab of his truck and knew there was no use trying to defend himself. He had blown it. He had blown it, big time.

The coach had seen and heard all he could handle. He and Maria excused themselves, agreeing to join the kids' tailgate party another time.

Engines roared. Music started pounding again. Tires squealed. What had started out to be fun had ended in disaster.

Brady drove Ray's truck home for him. Leilani followed them.

Leilani figured Ray was getting a lecture from Brady all the way home. She thought: *How can Ray be such an idiot when he looks so fine?* "Oh, well!" she said aloud to herself, lighting up a joint.

Brady was wasting his breath. Ray was ignoring his lecture. He was thinking about how miserably he had failed. He was thinking about Candace.

Candace was on her way home, too. Her stepdad's father, Gramps, was living with them. He was a big, strong, and youthful-looking man for his sixty-two years. Gramps had been a community leader and a top executive in a large corporation. Back home, he and his wife have a luxurious house, completely debt free.

Gramps had taken early retirement to enjoy the money he had made and to pursue his interests. His hobby, welding, was one of his interests, and Candace, his favorite stepgrandchild, was the other. He was living with her family for a while to build a patio for them, complete with ornamental iron. At least, that was his excuse for being near Candace.

Welding was a he-man kind of thing to do, and Gramps saw himself as very macho. He entertained himself with his hobby during the day and with his stepgranddaughter during the night.

Candace stayed away from home as much as she could. She joined everything that came along. She was in band, played sports at school, was in the community soccer association, and volunteered to tutor junior high students.

A loving and caring child, Candace would never destroy her mother's home and marriage. That's what Gramps held over her head and warned her would happen if she said anything about their sex. Gramps told Candace, "Do you see how close my son and I are? He'd never believe you over me. Your mom would never believe me over you. So, pow! The marriage would split like a tree that'd been struck by lightning!"

Also, Gramps had bought her a sports car, fully loaded, for her sixteenth birthday. As he handed Candace the keys, he whispered, "This car is a yo-yo. If you run your mouth about our sex or stop takin' care of my needs, the car returns to me." She hated what the car represented, but it gave her a way to stay away from home…and him.

Even more intimidating, the pervert had walked in on Candace and her boyfriend and caught them with his hand inside her zipper. He later told her, "If you ever tell, I'll tell, too, and they'll think you're nothing but a little slut, gettin' some anywhere you can."

Gramps had Candace blackmailed, indebted, and intimidated, like a puppy cornered by an alligator, emotionally trembling in fear, afraid to make a move. His bedroom was on the second floor next to hers. Her mom and stepfather's bedroom was downstairs.

Ray, knowing Gramps would visit Candace's bedroom again that night, began to cry. He couldn't help it; he cried openly as Brady drove him home.

Brady didn't know the real reason he was crying. He thought it was because of his drinking. Brady snorted, "Man, you are nothing but disgusting! Get a life!"

Brady parked Ray's truck and left him in it. Brady scooted into his own truck beside Leilani, took the wheel, and laid rubber.

Ray heard the squealing tires and felt their rejection. He slumped over onto the seat of his truck and cried himself to sleep.

SCENE 3

Who's who among the teens

THREE

JOHN AND Maria drove home with the Mustang's top down. Both were quiet.

John glanced at Maria. He knew she must be as upset over Ray's outburst as he was. Wind whipped her long, thick, black hair. The headlights of an oncoming car accented her naturally dark skin and revealed the intensity of her brown eyes. She was beautiful to John. He admired her sensitive spirit, her integrity.

Maria noticed she had her husband's attention. She spoke over the wind noise. "One of the girls told me why Fred got so upset. He was afraid Ray was going to tell us that Ray's mom and his dad are having an affair."

"Oh, great. Which girl told you that?"

"I don't remember her name. She had dark hair, combed to the side, the really thin girl. She was in black denims and a black T-shirt… the one who's living at the youth home."

"Hope," John suggested. "The one whose father is a minister?"

"That's her," Maria agreed.

Maria slid down in the seat a little, leaned her head onto the seatback, and stared at the starlit sky. The cool breeze felt clean after what they'd heard in the mall parking lot.

John pondered, "I wonder if Mr. Rumley's aware of the seriousness of the problems these kids are facing."

Maria responded matter-of-factly, "Of course not. Kids quit talking when no one's listening."

Nothing more was said on the way home—a ten-minute drive.

At their one-bedroom apartment, John went to the fridge and grabbed a couple of beers for himself. Maria went to the bathroom. They came back together at the couch.

John said, "I need to remember who said what. Too many names came at me too fast. I'm not good with names anyway."

With his elbows on his knees, resting his chin in his hands, he thought out loud, "Ray's the one who blabbed. Fred's the one that shut him up…and Fred's the kids' official porno librarian."

"Some library!" Maria added, chuckled nervously, and changed the subject. "I love the way Dale has his say—the guy from the streets. He's the one who told Ray, 'Dam it up, dude!'"

John shared her amusement, then recalled, "Hope is the minister's daughter who lives at the youth home. The cheerleaders were..." He paused to think.

"Kaprice and Leilani." Maria finished his sentence for him. "Kaprice is Ms. Gibson's daughter, don't forget."

"How could I forget that?" John responded with a wink.

Maria asked, "Are Kaprice and her mom alike?"

"Not really. Ms. Gibson is all business. She's a professional secretary in every sense of the word. She dresses in suits and carries herself like a charm-school graduate. Kaprice is fun loving, almost hyperactive, everywhere at once. Her mom seems a little shy."

Maria probed further, "I was really talking about appearance. I haven't seen Ms. Gibson yet."

"Oh, she has black hair. She's not fat, not skinny either. She's taller than you, but not really tall. I'd say five seven, maybe. She's nice looking...Kaprice is head cheerleader for LHS. She has black hair—"

Maria interrupted, "I know. I saw her, don't forget. Her hair is almost shoulder length, and she has it straightened. I'm glad Kaprice and Leilani are best friends. They're neat together. Both are high on life and outgoing. Leilani has the tan skin and high cheekbones that women would kill for. She's Hawaiian, and I heard the kids pronounce her name Lay-lawn-ee.

"Did you notice, John, that Leilani's long jet-black hair flowed in the breeze while she cheered tonight? Have you noticed that the cheerleaders are pretty, John? Have you noticed they have great figures, John?"

Hoping to avoid Maria's teasing, John returned to calling roll, "Leilani's boyfriend was Brady. We both know which one Candace is. What was that little Asian-American girl's name?"

"Sue something."

"Sue Li?"

"Sue is right, but there's more. Sue Song?"

"Sue Yoko Wing Chow Ding—who knows?" John quipped, losing patience.

"Wait a second. It's on the tip of my tongue. Now I remember seeing it on her backpack." Maria grabbed a pencil and a scrap of paper and wrote out the name to help her get it right. Showing John, she said,

"Her name is Kyong Suk Song. Her middle name is pronounced like Sue, and Koreans use the first two names together. She is Kyong Suk. I heard the kids pronounce it Kiong Sue." Then Maria smiled mischievously and said, "You know who Franco is!"

"Yes, believe me, I know who Franco Russo is. Doesn't his little sister have a strange name? Crisco. Who would have named her that? Crisco shortening is white, and her complexion is dark. That's strange, isn't it?"

Maria studied the names, "Crisco Russo…Franco Russo…Franco and Crisco Russo. Whoever handed out those names was into rhyme. That's for sure."

John smiled and asked, "The noble fellow who turned down the music, what was his name?"

"Terence?"

"No. Now I remember. It was Daniel."

Maria nodded. "Oh, Daniel was the kid who said his parents put down his friends and pry into his business. Who was the nice African-American guy who didn't say anything?"

"That was Terence. I know him. He's one of the most popular students on campus."

"He's the one Ray said didn't have enough credits to move up to his senior year," Maria remembered.

"Right…That's everyone. We remembered them all. We're a good team."

John leaned back, put his arm around Maria, picked up the remote, and pressed the power button to the TV.

The local news blared on.

…almost lost his life today to a sniper's bullet. The bullet missed his head by inches as he got into his car to leave the Women's Clinic. According to the executive director of the clinic, one of his physicians, Dr. Weldon Knight, had filed an earlier report with police saying that he was being stalked by a man armed with a high-powered rifle. Police are now taking his report seriously and have stepped up security measures.
On the international front, the war in…

Zap. Maria turned off the TV by placing her hand on John's and pushing his finger down on the power button. She explained, "We don't need to hear any more bad news tonight."

Then she cuddled close and kissed him passionately on the lips.

John dropped the remote and gathered Maria into his arms. "I love you so much. I'm glad you were at my side tonight."

They kissed again. Maria made her way to his ear, nibbling affectionately. But a chilling thought hit her. She stopped cold. She whispered, "I wonder if that pervert is messing with Candace right now."

John leaned back and made eye contact with his wife. "Was what Ray said true? How much of what he said can we believe?"

"I don't know."

"Good grief, I hope none of it's true!" John dropped his forehead onto Maria's shoulder. "Candace seems so sweet," he groaned. "I hope she's not being molested."

They were silent for a few moments, in deep thought, holding each other.

"Maria, these kids need a coach," John said. "More than a football coach. A coach for living life!" Then slamming his fist down on the arm of the couch, he exclaimed, "Someone's got to help them sort this stuff out! I don't think most adults have a clue to what teenagers are facing today!"

"John, they have the best kind of coach," Maria observed as she combed her husband's blond hair with her fingers. "His name is Coach John Bright." She kissed him tenderly. "May I be your assistant coach?"

"Me, the best kind of coach? I'm just a dumb phys ed teacher, according to Mr. Rumley," John teased. The pain of Rumley's bawling out had come back to his mind.

"Not true!" Maria shot back. "I know you, and you won't stop until you see these kids get the help they need. And I'm just as determined as you are."

Maria and John went to bed without making love. They could not get their minds off their new teenage friends.

As they fell asleep, John sighed and mentioned once more, "These kids need a coach for the game of life."

Maria gave him a slight squeeze of agreement, and they drifted in and out of sleep throughout the night.

(Note: For remembering who's who, see character reference page in the back of this book.)

SCENE 4

*Rumley
labels
Coach
John*

FOUR

THE NOTE began…

> Big Rump's mad as heck, and he's
> gonna be calling you to his office
> again. Leilani thinks we need to
> name him Rumpley Grumpley.

"Oh, great!" John muttered to himself. "What a way to start a new week."

Kaprice Gibson had walked by John on her way to class and stuffed the note in the front pocket of his coach-style T-shirt.

Stress piled higher and higher as he read the rest of it:

> I had lunch with my mother today. I
> was so unthrilled and so embarrassed…
> Anyway, she told me that Ray's
> father had called Rumpley about our
> tailgate party Friday night. He's plenty
> mad. You'd better get your game plan
> together because you've got to appear
> before the horse's rump again.
> Good luck!   —Kaprice FAFF ☺

The smiley face drawn beside her name seemed out of step with the theme of her note. John wondered what FAFF could mean. *Does it stand for something I'm supposed to know?* he asked himself.

John ripped up the note as he stared into space and wondered what was coming at him. He thought, *I can do anything I want on my own time. Rumley can't control that.* But he knew he was in deep trouble. He was frightened. His heart was pounding with dread.

As John called roll for his last class of the day, the public address system crackled on. A woman's voice echoed throughout the gym, "Coach John Bright, please report to Mr. Rumley's office."

The students teased him, "Big Rump's gonna chew on your butt now!"

John asked another coach to watch his class.

In the principal's office, the scene was the same as before, Rumley behind his big desk, peering over his skinny black reading glasses, Ms. Gibson poised to take notes, John feeling like a deer caught in headlights.

Rumley began, "Mr. Ray Beavers, Senior, called me. He said that you had his son, Ray Beavers, Junior, out all night Friday night, and Junior was plastered! Is that true?"

"I was with Ray from about eight to nine. I saw him leave with Brady and Leilani. I don't know what happened after that."

"Brady and who?"

"The cheerleader. Leilani something."

"Leilani Summers," Ms. Gibson volunteered.

"I guess," John said. "She's the girl the kids call Princess Leilani from Hawaii."

"Ms. Gibson, send a runner for Leilani Summers."

During the wait, Rumley returned to questioning John. "Where were you and the students?"

"They weren't students. They were teenagers. It was after school hours. We were in the mall parking lot."

"Why?"

"I just wanted to get to know them better."

"Why?"

"Because I care."

Obnoxiously, Rumley talked down to him. "Coach John Bright, I learned a long time ago that you can't get emotionally involved with your students!"

"I already am!"

"That's unprofessional, Mr. Bright!" Rumley exclaimed impatiently in his booming bass voice.

Ms. Gibson returned to the room before the conversation got completely out of hand. Things quieted down.

Rumley took on his I'm-superior-to-you posture, saying, "Franco Russo was there, wasn't he?"

"Yes."

"You talked to him about his family problems, didn't you?"

"Not really."

Rumley rearranged a stack of file folders on his desk, then

suddenly demanded, "Did you have a beer that night?"

John was caught off guard, but recovered. "Yes, at home with my wife."

"Did you see alcohol among the kids in the mall parking lot?"

John dodged the question. "I plead the Fifth."

Leilani Summers walked in.

Rumley gestured in her direction, keeping eye contact with the coach, "Is this the right student?"

"Yes."

The principal focused his attention on the cheerleader. "Leilani, have a chair. You were at a beer party in the mall parking lot Friday night. Ray Beavers didn't go home. His parents and the police looked for him all night long. He got home at nine the next morning, smelling like a brewery. He told his parents he was with Coach John Bright all night. Do you know anything about that?"

"Brady and I were driving around, and we saw Ray in his driveway at about 9:30 or so. That was the last we saw of him. Coach John wasn't with him. He was with his wife. Have you met her? She's really nice."

Rumley tilted his head down to see over his reading glasses, raised one eyebrow, and said to the cheerleader in his deepest voice, "That's all you can tell me, young lady? If I find out you're holding back information or lying to me, you know I won't be putting your name up for any scholarships."

She replied, "*I know* that Coach John didn't do anything wrong. We just sat around and talked. That's about it. Ray did whatever he did. He's his own person."

Obviously irritated that Leilani took up for the coach, Rumley dismissed her. "You may be excused, Ms. Summers." He motioned for her to leave.

Wanting to have the last say, she snapped back, "And it wasn't a beer party!"

After she shut the door, Rumley leaned toward John and said, "Look. We are two weeks into the new school year, and you've had two disasters with two sets of parents. This is strike two. Strike three, and you'll be out! You can relate to that, can't you, Coach?"

Instead of replying, John asked, "Are you aware of how many problems these students have and how serious their problems are?"

Rumley answered John's question with a question, "Are you aware...are you aware, Coach John Bright, that I received the leadership award for having the best programs in the state for preventing juvenile delinquency? I'm proud to inform you that I have the reputation for maintaining the cleanest campus anywhere!"

"I'm not talking about juvenile delinquency. I'm talking about family problems, social problems—problems that are overloading these kids' mental circuits!"

"I've not been advised of any such tidal wave of social problems."

"No, because the kids won't talk to you. They know you won't listen, and you don't give a dam—darn, excuse me."

That slip of the tongue burned Rumley bad and turned up the heat on his temper. His voice became a thunder boomer. "Coach John Bright, from this moment forward, my agenda is to fire you! One more serious complaint in your file, and I will have met state regulations for firing an employee, and you'll be out of here!"

Then he calmed down and said, feeling superior, as if he was proud of himself for being a step ahead of John, "That's why Ms. Gibson is taking notes."

"Are we finished?" John asked, seeking permission to leave.

"One more thing," Rumley snarled as he pushed his chair back from his desk and removed his glasses, "if you're ever foolish enough to put me on a job application as a reference, I promise you that I will bury you!" Then pointing his skinny black reading glasses at John like a finger, "You will never coach again in this state if I can help it."

"I'm sure that's true," John said, firmly believing the threat.

With that, the conversation ended.

Meanwhile, Leilani told Brady about Ray.

Brady told Dale.

Dale and Brady found Ray after school, and they shoved him up against a brick wall behind the gym.

Brady grabbed him by the collar and got in his face, saying, "Coach John just took heat from Rump Face because of you. Why did you lie to your dad about Coach John?"

"Dad was beatin' me half to death with his belt, that's why! What was I supposed to do? He doesn't know when to quit!"

Brady pressed, "Where did you go after we took you home?"

"Nowhere! I fell asleep on the seat of my truck. If they had checked my truck, they wouldn't have had to look for me all night. The fact is, they lied. They didn't look for me at all. They just waited for me to come in, and Dad nailed me."

Dale said, "Let go of him, Brady. I know his dad. The man's crazy as a cockroach!"

Ray looked around. Seeing no one, he dropped his pants and underwear and showed Dale and Brady his backside. Ugly long bruises and welts ran across him from the middle of his back to his calves... and it was two days after the beating.

Brady and Dale were speechless.

Tugging at his underwear and pants, Ray said, "I wasn't even drunk that night. I only had one beer. I acted the way I did to try to get Candace some help. I wanted Coach John to find out what's been happening to her. Someone's got to stop it!...I thought it would embarrass her less if I told everyone else's problems, too." Ray confessed, "Okay, I handled it wrong and made everyone mad at me. I blew it! I admit that. I just didn't know what else to do. I was feeling desperate. Where's the how-to book on helping a friend who's being molested?"

Brady felt like a jerk, remembering how cruel he'd been to Ray that night. He told Dale, "We've got to arrange another meeting with Coach John."

That evening, Leilani called John's apartment for Brady. The coach was still at football practice, so Leilani gave a message for Maria to relay to him.

The phone rang again. This time it was Kaprice Gibson, the secretary's daughter, calling for John. Maria took her message, too.

SCENE 5

Forced underground

FIVE

JOHN CAME home after practice later than usual. He was extra tired and deeply stressed. Maria met him at the door with a long hug and a warm kiss.

John enjoyed the affection and said, "Nice appetizer, what's for dinner?"

"I came home at lunch and put a roast on. I'll heat it up again."

John and Maria sat down at the table. Maria said, "A couple of the kids phoned you. I took their messages. Here's a short one from Brady. Leilani called it in."

> Don't blame Ray. There's been a big misunderstanding. We need to meet again.

John crumpled the message and tossed it at the trash can, hitting it. "It's impossible for that little drunk not to be as guilty as Satan himself!" he said with disgust, still angry.

Maria handed him the other message. "This one's from Kaprice."

> Kaprice said her mom told her that after you left Big Rump's office, he called the school board members. He's narcing on you so the board will be on his side when he fires you. Kaprice said not to tell anyone she told you. If you do, it will cost her mom her job and Kaprice her neck. P.S. She said they love you even though they are hazardous to your health at LHS.

John laid the message on the table and told Maria what happened in Rumley's office.

Maria handed John the cordless phone, saying, "You need to return Brady's call."

Brady answered the phone. Brady told John about his and Dale's encounter with Ray. John said, "Well, that improves my attitude toward Ray. He tried to do the right thing, although it was a clumsy way to go about it. Hold on a moment."

John moved the phone away from his mouth and spoke to his wife. "Maria, I've got to start playing a smarter game. The other side is winning. Do you mind if we have a meeting here this Friday? There's no football game."

"Not here at the apartments, John. There's no parking. We can't even park our pop-up camper here. Every space is assigned. Besides, this needs to be a secret meeting. You guys have got to go underground!"

Back to the phone, John told Brady, "We shouldn't meet here."

"I heard."

"Where then?"

Brady answered, "There's a place five minutes from town. It looks like a thick forest from the road, but after you go through some trees and underbrush, it opens into a meadow. Just our group knows about it. It's our special and secret party place. We can go there. The entrance is hidden, but you can ride with me. I promise you, no adults know about this place." Then taking on an Australian accent, Brady mimicked Ray, "You can bring your mate!"

John was too stressed out for humor. He said, "Make it at 7:30. Tell your friends. Let me know how many can come. Talk to you later. Oh, Brady, are you still there?"

"I'm here."

"Be sure to tell everyone that this is a top-secret meeting. My job depends on us keeping this quiet. Okay?"

"We've got you covered, Coach. Remember, we're teenagers, and teenagers are good at doing stuff behind adults' backs. Don't worry about it."

"Don't worry about it? I am definitely worried about it! Report to me when everything's worked out, okay?"

Brady said, "Leilani or Kaprice will stuff a note in your pocket. Talk to you later."

Placing the phone handset on the table, John reached for support from Maria. "Sweetheart, I may lose my job over this."

She responded in a flirting way, "Babe, I'm attracted to strength, and you look very strong to me right now."

"But what if I lose my job?"

"We're both used to doing without nice things. I didn't have much growing up; neither did you. I'm by your side, John. I married you for richer or for poorer, for better or for worse. You've gotta do what your conscience tells you to do! You can't do *nothing*. Silence is acceptance."

After rubbing his eyes, John said, "Things may get a lot worse before they get better. But losing my job is better than losing what we believe in, right?"

"Right."

John told Maria about Ray. Maria appreciated Ray's effort to be a hero for Candace and agreed that it was horrible that his dad beat him whenever he got mad.

John said, "I'll have to admit, Maria, I don't understand this. Why am I having to fight the principal because I care about these kids? He's acting like I'm some kind of criminal from whom he's gotta protect his school."

Maria stepped behind John and began to massage the knots out of his shoulder muscles. He hung his head and asked, "What have I done wrong? I alerted Franco's mom to his depression and told her I'd be praying for them. Is that so wrong? I met with some kids at the mall parking lot after school. Is that so wrong? This is crazy! I'm not believing this! Is this happening in our country?"

SCENE 6

*Ms. Gibson,
cool
or
what?*

SIX

THE NOTE was written so lightly in pencil on the back of a little card that John could hardly read it. He flipped the card over to see the front. There it was, big and bold: **Alfredo H. Rumley, Principal, Lincoln High School.**

Ms. Gibson had written a note to John on the back of Rumley's business card and handed it to him as he waited in her office. She didn't give the coach a chance to ask her anything. Her eyes were glued to her monitor and her fingers tap-danced rapidly on her keyboard.

John was having second thoughts about the secret meeting with the students. He knew he was teetering on the edge of a cliff and unemployment was written on the rocks below. He simply couldn't believe that he and the students had to resort to hiding. He wanted to try to reason with Rumley one more time, when Rumley wasn't already mad. That's why he had requested this meeting with him. He was hoping he could appeal to him to arrange free professional therapy for the kids. His mind wondered in frustration: *Hadn't Mr. Rumley heard that the Berlin Wall had come down, and that Russia was no longer communistic? Didn't he know our country should also be free of oppression? Is he a total control freak, or what?*

He noticed a picture frame on Ms. Gibson's desk between a bouquet of flowers and a small fish bowl filled with pastel M & M's. On one side of the golden frame was a picture of Kaprice, her mom, and Kaprice's little brother. The boy looked to be about eleven or twelve. On the other side was a portrait of Kaprice in her cheerleading uniform. A small snapshot of her brother in his soccer uniform was tucked into the left bottom corner of the frame, with the loose edge curling. John assumed Ms. Gibson was a single mother. The warmth of her office felt good to him as he shivered and rubbed chill bumps, dreading another close encounter with Rumley.

Ms. Gibson turned her computer screen toward John so he could see a message for his eyes only. She had enlarged the letters to make them readable from where he sat. He read the screen to himself:

I will be giving out business cards in
the meeting. Let the sight of them
remind you of the message on the
back of yours. Hide yours!

John looked back to Ms. Gibson. Their eyes met for a brief
moment. Her eyes seemed to say: You are in big trouble, and I care.
John's tension increased as he saw how worried Ms. Gibson seemed to
be. He began to kick himself for asking for an appointment with Rumley.

Ms. Gibson's phone beeped. As she answered, she pressed the
delete key on her computer. The screen blanked.

Picking up her notepad, she said, "Coach Bright, they're ready
for you now."

"They! Who's they?" he whispered in alarm.

She couldn't answer. Rumley was turning the doorknob to open
the door. The door opened wide. John looked in. A stranger stood up.

"Coach," Rumley said, "I have someone I want you to meet.
Ms. Gibson, you certainly have your hands full. I don't think you'll be
needing your purse."

She replied, "I have some student aides coming in to work in my
office. I'd like my purse with me." She put it on the floor beside her
chair.

"Very smart," Rumley said, standing behind her chair like a true
gentleman, showing off in front of the stranger. "Some of our students
can't be trusted."

She handed a card to each of the three men. "This is Mr. Rumley's
new business card. I printed it a few moments ago on the new printer the
school board purchased for me. It does a great job, and it's saving print-
ing costs for the school district."

Rumley seated her and turned toward the men. Acting ever so
proper, he said, "Mr. John Bright, I'd like you to meet Mr. Robert Means.
He's president of our school board, and he's also president of Carlton
and Means Investments downtown."

Shooting pains of emotional stress raced through John. Rumley
had brought in a higher authority to make his point with him. John's
mind raced. *Why has Rumley whipped out a nuclear weapon in the form
of the board president when I am trying to make peace? Why is Rumley
making this big power play?*

The introduction continued. "Mr. Means, meet Mr. John Bright," Rumley said. "He's new. He's the one I've been telling you about."

The men sat down. Rumley was behind his big desk. Across from the principal, John Bright and Robert Means faced each other a bit but mostly faced Rumley. Ms. Gibson was off to the side, leaning over, reaching into her purse to find something to write with.

Rumley appeared meaner than usual as he rubbed his hands together, grandstanding, acting stereotypically professional, his face glowing as if he couldn't wait for the kill. He had stuffed John into a pressure cooker, and he was getting his kicks off watching him squirm.

He directed his first comments to John. "I invited Mr. Means to join us because things have gotten tense between us. I felt it would be good for both of us to have a witness to this meeting."

Rumley leaned back in his chair, laced his fingers behind his gray hair, elbows out, and confidently said, "Well, Coach, you requested this appointment. What would you like to talk about?"

John felt like smarting off and saying, "Now, aren't you feeling just a little too special!" But he was too intimidated. He began, "I...I was thinking that I...uh...would like to talk to you when we weren't angry with one another. We might get more done."

"You were the one who got mad. I wasn't. I've always acted in a professional manner toward you," Rumley lied. He didn't give John a chance for rebuttal but raised his right eyebrow and ordered, "Go ahead. The floor is yours. Tell us why you wanted this meeting."

John licked his lips and said carefully and timidly, "It seems...it seems that we've gotten off to a bad start together. I'm not the rebellious person you seem to think I am."

"And?"

"I...I'm not trying to go against you. I'm just trying to make myself available to some students who are...uh...dealing with some very...some really serious matters."

John hated that he was pausing so much and was so unsure of his words, but he knew his neck was on the line, the guillotine's blade was razor sharp and positioned over his neck. He was very, very nervous.

"And?" Rumley prodded.

"Well, I feel like you're making me out to be something I'm not. I mean, well, uh..."

"What are you trying to say?" Rumley pressed.

John didn't know how to say what he wanted to say. But he tried again. "Look, can we just put our differences aside and help the students?"

Rumley said, "No. Not *we!*" Jetting forward in his chair, he exclaimed, "You are not qualified as a professional counselor! You are merely a PE teacher! That's all you are!"

Catching himself, Rumley sat back with a cautious glance at the board president. He changed his voice to sound like a top-gun administrator. "We have a counselor on campus. We have professional clinics in our network. We have treatment centers. No one needs a PE teacher to do counseling!"

Rumley's insult stung John. John looked around the room. He saw that Ms. Gibson was holding one of Rumley's business cards between two fingers, like a cigarette, as an obvious reminder of her warning: *WHAT YOU SAY CAN AND WILL BE USED AGAINST YOU!* Her support helped the coach keep his cool.

Means held Rumley's business card between his thumb and index finger, making it bend one way and then the other. He spoke up, "Mr. Bright, your principal is tired of your ego trip. We of the school board feel that he has been very patient with you, perhaps more patient than any of us would have been."

Rumley leaned back again and smiled, fingers laced behind his head, elbows out. John observed him and thought: *You are such a weasel!*

Means went on, "I think it's fair to warn you that your job is on the line. We hired you to teach PE and coach sports. If you don't want to do that, then you should resign before you get fired. Furthermore, the school district's law firm has advised us that your Lone Ranger tactics are leaving the district open to lawsuits."

Rumley caught John's eye, and Rumley tilted his head toward Means as if to say: *You'd better listen to him, boy!*

Rumley's pressure cooker was spewing steam, and John's competitive blood was boiling. John realized Rumley had set him up, and he could see that Rumley was pathetically proud of himself.

With aqua-blue eyes aflame, John looked at Ms. Gibson again. Rumley and Means looked at her, too. Without reacting, she dropped her eyes to Rumley's card. Once again, John understood her silent warning. The other men didn't catch on.

Somehow John found the courage to trust his ally, Ms. Gibson. Instead of telling them to take his job and shove it, he simply answered, "Well, I guess I don't have anything more to say."

"Are we finished?" Means asked.

Rumley took his victory march by saying, "It's your meeting, Coach. Are we finished?"

"Yes, we're fin...finished," John said, feeling outnumbered, tricked, insulted, defeated, deflated, and frustrated.

Means stood up, "I need to excuse myself then. I'm running late for an investors' meeting. See you at six, Alfredo. Oh, call Bundik. He said if we're only going to be at the driving range for an hour or so, he wants to come along."

"Mr. Bundik is secretary of the school board," Rumley informed John as he got up to escort Means to the door.

Then with Means gone, Rumley let his temper flare. He bent down and began poking his business card in John's face, saying, "Let me give you a little coaching, Coach! I am an administrator who has forgotten more about education than you will ever know, and you'd do well to listen to me! The kids you're losing your job for aren't worth it! Kids like them have peed on me time and time again! And they will pee on you, too!"

He paused momentarily. "Pardon my language, Ms. Gibson."

He returned to John. "I'll ask you about it in twenty years, Coach. If you know what's good for you, you'll get off your savior kick!"

Rumley's breath smelled like he had eaten anchovy pizza for breakfast as he asked, "Do you know why Means was here? Because I'm getting everything lined up to fire your butt! All the members of the school board are always on my side because I know how to work them! I've got them in my back pocket."

Rumley proudly continued, "In a few hours, Means and I will be at the driving range with Bundik, and we'll brief him on this meeting. Bill Wycoff and I are in Lions Club together. Estelle Rutherford is on a Chamber of Commerce committee with me. Elaine Simmons and I are going to a seminar together next Monday. Viola Jeffries attends the same church that I do, and I'm taking flying lessons from her. So if you're stupid enough to try to talk to board members behind my back, you'll be terribly sorry you did. They are turned off by people who go over their supervisor's head! At Lincoln High School, we do everything strictly by the book. I make no exceptions, and I stay out of trouble."

Still pumping his foul breath into John's face, Rumley got louder. "Your coaching career is just about over! I've got friends all over the state! You'll wish you had never taken me on before this is finished!"

That was it. John had all he could take. He jumped up so fast that Rumley had to back away quickly or get knocked down.

Ms. Gibson dodged behind Rumley where only John could see her. She held up Rumley's business card high above Rumley's head as if she was the Statue of Liberty.

John was about to have a total meltdown, but the sight of Ms. Gibson, trying so hard and taking such a great risk to help him keep his cool, caused him to get a grip. He stopped and stared at Rumley for a couple of moments. Then still breathing fast from anger, John said with valor, "No. I won't give you strike three. You can't strike me out. I'm walking." He walked out of Rumley's office without waiting to be dismissed by his superior.

Rumley yelled after him in his deep obnoxious voice, "Grow up!"

Rumley was not a happy supervisor. He barked to Ms. Gibson, "I want to read those notes after you get them typed. That brat is not going to act like an immature and rebellious teenager and get by with it. Ms. Gibson, your notes will not include my private comments to that, that, that embarrassment to the evolutionary process!"

"I understand." She picked up her purse and headed to her office.

"Ms. Gibson?"

Rumley stopped her with a gruff voice. She became fear struck. She thought he was mad at her, too. Nervously, she turned around.

He instructed, "I may need to call on you to tell the school board that you saw Mr. Bright lose his temper and almost knock me down."

Her fear waned, and Ms. Gibson assured him, "I saw everything, and I hope you do include me in any board meeting of that nature."

Rumley smiled at her show of support. "Loyalty like that will certainly mean a nice raise for you," he said. He felt very close to his secretary.

John rushed to his office and called Maria. Without saying hello, he began shouting. "Big Rump couldn't be the principal of a zoo! He's lower than the animals! Do you hear me, Maria? He's lower than the apes!

I hate his filthy guts! He is the south end of a north-bound mule! His name fits him perfectly! I've never met a bigger manipulator. Oh, the man makes me so mad!"

John stopped to catch his breath. Maria could hear his labored breathing over the phone.

"Feel better?" Maria cautiously asked in the eye of the storm.

"I had to say it to somebody," John groaned. "I couldn't say it to him. I was about to burst."

"I don't think I need to ask if the meeting went well," Maria said, offering to listen.

"I'll tell you more when I get home, but I didn't do very well. I stuttered like a first grader, and I didn't say the right things...The creep ran the president of the school board in on me! I am so-o-o sick of him! Pardon me, Maria, but I'm going to go beat up the punching bag in the gym. Thanks for listening. Gotta go. Bye."

Muttering with every punch, John worked the bag over for ten minutes, imagining it was his boss. He heard the bell ring to signal class changes. Hot and sweaty, he grabbed a towel and headed toward class.

John was weaving his way through the student body when Kaprice stuffed a note in his shirt pocket. John caught her hand and whispered in a stressed voice, "If anyone finds out about our top-secret meeting Friday, I'm dead meat! Your mom must know about it. Is she on my side, for real?"

"Don't worry. She hates the man! But he's so controlling that she's afraid to ask for a transfer. He might take it personally, as an insult or something, and fire her."

Too angry to be careful, John did something out of order. He put down a staff member to a student. "He's a total slob, Kaprice!"

"You speak the truth," Kaprice said, squeezing his hand and letting go.

"Who, Coach?" a passing student asked.

Fear struck John as he searched for a name, "Uh, Saddam!"

"Bush should've kicked butt in Baghdad," the student agreed and disappeared into the crowd.

That was a close call. John always hated being in a one-more-strike-and-you're-out situation.

In the classroom, he read Kaprice's note while students pulled books out of backpacks. It said:

We're all set for 7:30 p.m., Friday. Those
who have jobs and were scheduled
to work have traded schedules with
others. Everyone can come except
Terence. Terence can't come because
he won't lie to his parents about
where he's going. No problem. Terence
is no snitch. See you there.
                                    -Kaprice FAFF ☺

There's that FAFF again, John thought as he opened the textbook. "Students, I'm substituting for your regular teacher today, and I've been told that we are to begin studying the chapter titled 'Your Source and Resources.' It is about the theory of evolution, your origin as a human being."

A student with bright red hair, who had won district at the science fair last year, raised his hand. John called on him. The student announced, "My dad told me how to think of the theory of evolution when it leaves God out: It's from the gasses through the masses to the atheistic jackasses."

John smiled in amusement, his bad mood easing a bit.

The student went on, "My dad told me that I was created by God. God has a reason for me being here and loves me so much that He even keeps up with how many hairs are on my red head. That makes me feel real good."

A wave of laughter spread across the room.

John responded, "Red, you can believe whatever means the most to you. As for me, I have to punt. We teachers have been told that we are to discuss only the theory of evolution, without including God as its designer. I plan to proceed as ordered and stay out of trouble."

I'm in enough trouble already, John thought to himself.

He told the class, "Open your books to page 157, and let's check out the introduction."

SCENE 7

Girl talk and more

SEVEN

FRIDAY EVENING had finally come. John and Maria rode with Brady and Leilani. Brady's sound system was awesome. There was so much bass bouncing around in the truck that they not only heard it, they felt it vibrating their insides.

John noticed that Leilani was holding a white greeting-sized envelope with *To John* neatly written on it. A cheerful smiley face had been drawn beside his name, and the initials FAFF were written within a heart beneath it. John was plenty curious but not bold enough to ask what was in it. He figured she would give it to him at some point in the evening.

Brady yelled over the music to John and Maria. "You guys are privileged! No adult has ever been to our party spot before!"

Then he began acting official, like a bailiff in a courtroom. He assumed the bailiff role because he was nervous about asking adults to take a vow. Brady shouted with determination, "Raise your right hands and repeat after me!"

He looked around his girlfriend to see if John and Maria had raised their hands. Satisfied, he continued, "I do hereby promise that I will never tell anyone about the place I am about to see." Brady looked again to be sure both were promising. He couldn't hear them over the music.

Maria had said it once, but repeated louder, "I promise!"

"Coach?" Brady pressed.

"Sure! I promise! No problem!" he yelled. "Who am I going to tell, Mr. Rumley?"

"Can't take any chances, Coach! You are about to see where we party!"

Brady pulled off the country road onto the shoulder. Rock and fallen pine needles went all the way to the edge of the woods. No tire marks leading to the entrance to their secret party place would show and give away its location.

"C'mon, Coach, we've got work to do." Brady slid out of the truck and slammed the door. John joined Brady. They crossed a shallow ditch and began moving the huge potted plants that hid the secret entrance.

The kids had planted wild bushes and small trees in pots. No one could see the pots from the road since they were hidden behind a little ridge they had formed from small rocks and brown pine needles.

Maria and Leilani watched their men work. Maria turned down the radio as she said, "Brady reminds me of someone who would ride bulls in a rodeo. He fits the part well—boots, plaid shirt, cowboy hat, red hair, thin, has sexy freckles."

"Rough, tough, and bowlegged," Leilani added, smiling with affection. "He used to dip Skoal. He quit 'cause I told him I wasn't going to French with him anymore if he didn't. My kisses were more important," she said with pride. "So, he quit, and that's that."

"You love him, don't you?" Maria said, smiling.

"More than anything," Leilani replied in a dreamy way. "I love him so-o-o much. Oh, I know he's not the cutest guy on campus, but you can't beat his heart. He's got a great heart."

Leilani scooted under the steering wheel and drove the truck past the **NO TRESPASSING** sign into the edge of the forest. Brady and John began "closing the gate" by replacing the plants. It took longer because two of the bushes fell over and had to be repotted.

Leilani told Maria, "I'm glad I'm not on my period this week. The great outdoors turns Brady on. Making love with him is the best! It's like going back in time to the Wild West. He's so romantic."

Amazed at how open she was, Maria responded, "I hope you and Brady use protection."

"Of course, we practice safe sex. We practice it a lot!" Leilani exclaimed bursting out in laughter, amusing herself. "We keep our condoms right here in the purse Brady gave me for my birthday." Leilani held up a blue denim bag. "The school nurse furnishes them for us. I told him to order me some in our school colors. He's checking. Can you believe that? Condoms in purple, white, or gold?"

"The school nurse is a he?" Maria questioned.

"Why not? Discrimination is a thing of the past. One thing you gotta get used to about Lincoln High School is that it's definitely on the cutting edge, liberal as hel—uh, heck. The attitude is: If it's new, it's gotta be better, and we wanna be there first."

Maria said, "Having a male school nurse would be new to me."

"Oh, he's okay, I guess. His name is Cris Platt. He wants us to call him Crissy, but we won't. That's just a little too weird. We call him

Platypus instead, 'cause his name is Platt and his puss, uh, face, is kinda squished flat. He's old, old—like in his forties, maybe. He's not as old as my grandfather, for sure. I think Grandypa—that's my pet name for him—I think he helped build the pyramids or something. He's in his seventies."

Maria chuckled.

Leilani said, "Grandypa's pretty neat, though. He's tall and looks like…uh, you know that guy on KFC boxes, that Colonel Sanders guy. Grandypa looks better than him. He's beautiful, I mean, handsome for his age. Gray hair, gray beard, ice blue eyes, wears John Lennon glasses, and walks with a black cane. I bought him the cane for his birthday. He wanted a thick one. One that he could use to defend himself from a dog when he goes for walks.

"Grandypa dresses in suits most of the time. And smart! Whoa, he's really smart! He reads every news magazine on the market and spends a lot of time in front of CNN and C-SPAN. He'd, like, ace current events tests at my school. He'd teach the teachers!"

Maria couldn't get over what Leilani said earlier. She asked, "You have to ask a man for condoms?"

"And tampons, pads, and panty shields if we forget ours," Leilani answered matter-of-factly. "Well, what difference does it make? If the nurse was a she, the guys'd have to ask a woman for condoms. Anyway, it's no big deal. He's gay!"

"He's gay?"

"Gay as gay can get. I could take off my shirt and bra right in front of him, and he wouldn't even get turned on. He grosses the guys out, though. He makes weird sounds at them as if he's wanting their bodies. He whistles at them when he walks through the gym. Some homosexuals don't act that way, and I don't think they would approve of how he acts."

"I don't think the most basic issue is gay or straight," Maria commented. "Heterosexuals, as a group, have an awful reputation. I studied in college history about U.S. soldiers leaving 35,000 babies behind in Vietnam. Isn't the issue being moral or immoral, no matter how people label themselves? Aren't we equally responsible before God to live right before Him, to keep His laws?"

"You can't be serious!" Leilani exclaimed, laughing. "Nobody goes by that anymore! Where were we, anyway?…Oh, yeah, Platypus.

He teaches sex education classes. Boring! Like we don't already know all about that subject!"

Leilani laughed, then added, "His big thing is celebrate diversity. Platypus says it all the time...All he taught me that I didn't know was that Vaseline weakens condoms, and you can get HIV from oral sex and maybe even from French kissing...but not with Brady 'cause he'd never fool around behind my back...Oh, and that spermicidal foam can make it easier to get HIV because it sometimes makes tender skin raw...and guess who he said could catch HIV easiest of all. Virgins. Virgins having sex for the first time. That's 'cause their tissues tear, and HIV in semen can get right into their bloodstreams. Platypus told us that the HIV virus villains are so small, millions of 'em could have a big orgy in the pore of a condom...He cracked me up 'cause he thought he needed to teach us that birth control pills don't prevent disease. Who wouldn't know that? Duh!"

Leilani asked through her laugh, "What were we talking about before I got off on sex ed?"

"Girls asking a man for condoms," Maria said weakly.

Leilani remembered, "Oh, yeah. I guess they could divide it up to where the guys would get their condoms from Platypus, and the girls would get theirs from Chester. Oh, if you don't know who Chester is, she's the school counselor, Ms. Evelyn Rouse. I call her Chester 'cause *her* ain't got no *chest*. I have nicknames for everyone. It's my thing. Chester's straight."

Leilani kept talking. "Anyway, Platypus, being gay, may get turned on by a guy who goes to him for condoms. Heterosexual teachers have been known to get a crush on a student of the opposite sex, you know; so why wouldn't a homosexual get a crush on someone of the same sex? Whatever. I just think it's better for girls to ask Platypus for condoms. Who knows what's best? Trust me, Maria, things are a lot different than when you were a teenager."

"Hey! I'm not that much older than you!" Maria protested. She was ready to change the subject. "You and Brady are so different. He's a cowboy, and you wear cute short sets. I like to wear them, too. My favorite is a red-and-white sailor set I have. Leilani, your clothes look like they came right out of a teen fashion magazine."

"Our group is made up of all kinds. There's cowboys, preps, kids who follow the fads—everyone. We found each other because of the corruption—well, that's what our group has learned to call it—the corruption that some of us are dealing with from our parents and other adults. Finding each other just sort of happened if you know what I mean. We're a pretty weird crowd."

Brady and John returned to the truck. Both had worked up a sweat. John asked, "Why do you guys go through all this work?"

"The big parties that are arranged on the Internet are too dangerous. Cops see the announcements, and they bust the parties. Out here, we don't get busted. The parties are small, but we can party as hard as we want. No one can find our secret place."

Brady hit the gas and zigzagged through the woods. Small bushes slapped the bottom of the truck. Tree branches raked the sides, making screeching noises, sending chills through the girls.

"Oh, I hate that!" Maria exclaimed.

"Ooooo! I dread this part every time," Leilani complained. "That noise is so-o-o totally annoying."

John asked Brady, "How is it that Dale lives in the inner city and drives such a sharp new truck?"

Brady talked slowly because driving demanded a lot of attention. The truck bucked and jerked as Brady dodged trees and drove over uneven ground. "Dale's mom was a street prostitute, and it killed her. She got AIDS and died last year. Dale helped take care of her. He saw her waste away to nothing. It was very traumatic for him."

"Tell them about his little brother," Leilani reminded.

Brady hit the brakes and drove around a mud hole. "Yeah, his little brother got his head blown off in a turf war a couple of years ago. He joined a gang when he was twelve. Dale did everything he could to talk him out of it. The kid didn't last three months. I guess Dale had to be about fifteen then."

"And don't forget to tell how he got the truck," Leilani urged.

"There was this rich pimp, a fat cat who dealt drugs and girls, that felt sorry for Dale."

Brady fought the steering wheel as he continued, "That son of a gun stuck a wad of money in his pocket and took Dale to a car dealer. Like a big spender, he told them to give Dale anything he wanted. 'Nothing's too good for my friend!' he told them. Strutting around like a cocky rooster, he let Dale pick out that cool machine he drives. The guy paid cash for it. Can you believe that? Cash!"

Leilani took over. "Dale is seventeen. He is a tough-looking junior with a magnetic smile, dark hair and bright eyes. You've both seen him. You know he could play a tough guy in the movies. He's 175 pounds of pure muscle, and I'll bet he's every inch of six feet tall. Nobody wants to get on his bad side. I guarantee you that."

What Leilani said agreed with the rumors. John had heard that Rumley talked to Dale with respect. It was funny. Rumley would ask Dale's permission before he would get onto him about something.

"Dale's handsome, and he's really a cool guy," Leilani noted.

Brady added, "But parents won't let their daughters go out with him."

John knew why. Dale dressed like someone from the streets. He probably didn't have the money to buy better clothes. And word must have gotten around about his mother and brother.

Brady said, "I think Dale is deeply hurt by the way adults seem prejudiced against him and also by the hand life has dealt him. Seems like his only goals are to survive and punch people's lights out if they cross him."

John pictured a wounded wolf, angry and dangerous, one that could burst into violence, one that could kill.

"Are we about there?" Maria asked, her anxiety showing, feeling swallowed up in the dense forest. "If anything happens to us in here, no one would ever find us!"

SCENE 8

Stupid cheerleader tricks

EIGHT

MOMENTS LATER, a smooth, grassy green meadow, sprinkled with late-blooming yellow wildflowers, opened majestically before them. It was about the size of half a football field, and the circle was surrounded by tall pine trees that seemed like a huge wall. The trees stood taller than the light poles at the high school's stadium.

Everyone's tailgate was already in place, except Brady's. He wheeled around, slammed his pickup into reverse, and claimed his space.

Maria stepped out and looked up. The tall trees framed a brilliant orange sky, where clouds trailed lazily along without a care in the world. She felt like she was standing in the bottom of a beautiful tunnel, standing on its end, extending all the way to heaven. From up there, Maria imagined the trucks must look like the petals of a giant daisy and the kids pollen in the center of the flower.

Kyong Suk's motor scooter was peeking in the circle, between two trucks. Maria thought of it as a tiny honeybee, seeking nectar from the daisy. A few cars were parked off to the side, under trees.

Everyone was happy to be there. John and Maria settled in together on Brady's tailgate.

Like an announcer at the Academy Awards, Kaprice dramatically announced, "The envelope, please!"

Leilani handed the envelope to John. The kids had naughty looks on their faces. They were all in on it, and they were feeling extra proud of themselves.

"What might this be?" John asked as he opened it.

Inside John found a sympathy card that one of the kids had made on a computer at school. On the front was a picture of a fuming horse's behind sticking up over a large office desk. A jock was facing it. COACH was printed on the back of his shirt.

"Read it out loud!" someone yelled. John obeyed by reading the print beneath the picture…

> **You have our sincerest sympathy for the time you've served in Big Rump's gas chamber. We've heard he's causing you a major stink.**

John cracked a smile, and the whole meadow erupted in hilarious laughter.

"Look inside!" Ray urged.

John did and read aloud:

WE DO HEREBY PROMISE
NOT TO PISS ON YOU!

Below that, the kids had all signed their names:

Truly yours,
Leilani, Kaprice, Kyong Suk, *Brady*,
Ray, Terence, Damiel, Fred,
Candace, Hope, DALE, Franco.

FaFF

The kids loved seeing John's shocked look when he discovered that they knew about Rumley's insane comment. John glanced at all the kids in the circle, sensing their love, and he began shaking his head yes. He broke out in laughter, too.

Again, the meadow echoed with sidesplitting laughter. The kids knew they were good.

Kaprice popped out into the middle of the circle and said, "Coach John, I've made up another cheer for you." Little Crisco jumped in beside her.

Kaprice objected, "No, no, sweetheart. You can't help me with this one. You go sit by your brother...Franco, cover your sister's ears. My cheer is rated PG-13."

Crisco objected, "I didn't get to write my name on the card either. I'm always too young."

Being a good sport, John urged Kaprice, "Go for it."

With one knee in the grass and wildflowers of the meadow, she began performing:

Coach John Bright, we are so proud,
We're glad that you're in our crowd!

Bongo Buns has never been so out of his tree,
As when he said we will not be true to thee.

Don't be sad, Coach. Don't be blue,
We will never ever piss on you!

Yea! Yea!

She jumped and touched her toes again and again. "Yea!"

The kids and their coach exploded in another round of laughter. A couple of the kids rolled around in the backs of the trucks, laughing themselves to death.

Maria thought the whole scene was a little crude and immature, but she was glad to see John enjoying things for a change.

Leilani jumped into the circle and yelled for attention. "I made up a cheer, too!" She bumped Kaprice out of the spotlight with her rear end. The kids started laughing with anticipation. Crisco tried again.

"Stop laughing, you guys," Leilani said as she directed Crisco back to Franco. "You gotta be able to hear my cheer. I've worked hard on this."

Having gained her audience's attention, she began her cheer.

Ready…one…two…hit it!
We're the students of LHS,
What we'll do, no one can guess!

Leilani started giggling and couldn't finish. The kids urged her on. She started over.

We're the students of LHS.
What we'll do, no one can guess!

We're drinking a lot of beer,
Holding our pee,
Saving it for old man Rumpley.

Leilani jumped, kicked, and spun. "Yea!"

Her cheer sent everyone into more fits of wild laughter. The fact that it was so junior-high-like and a varsity cheerleader was doing it made it the comedy it was. All were having fun at the principal's expense.

But someone heard something in the underbrush and nudged the next person. Soon all had noticed the strange noise, and the circle became ghost-town quiet.

Rustling sounds grew louder!

"What was that?" someone whispered.

"There it goes again. Something's out there!"

"Shhh...," someone urged.

Darkness had set in, and black shadows hung in the background. The rustling noises became accented by low grunts.

Crisco jumped on Franco's lap and began hugging him like a scared baby monkey.

Dale stepped to the cab of his truck and pulled out a huge pistol. He aimed it in the direction of the noise and cocked the hammer back.

At the sight of the gun, Crisco buried her face in Franco's neck.

Maria shouted nervously, "Dale, wait! It may be a person!"

Dale yelled, "If you're a person, speak up now! There's a loaded .357 Magnum pointing in your direction!"

The rustling and the grunting stopped. Then a shaky voice came from the darkness. "It's me, Terence! I was trying to scare you guys!"

Dale, lowering his gun, commanded, "Get out here, Terence!"

Terence turned on his flashlight and emerged from the darkness, pushing his bicycle.

"Come on over here and give Maria a big kiss," Dale said, flashing his magnetic smile. "She is responsible for saving your life!"

Candace teased Dale, "Shame on you, Dale! You nearly wasted one of the most popular guys on campus!"

As Terence sat down on the tailgate beside Maria, Kaprice said, "I thought you weren't going to lie to your parents."

"I didn't. They went out to eat, and I told them I was going for a bike ride."

John was super glad to see him. His appearance meant perfect attendance.

To Maria's relief, Dale put his gun back where he kept it, a cardboard box he had padded with foam. He pushed it under his truck seat.

SCENE 9

Teens tell painful secrets

NINE

EVERYONE SETTLED down after the scare. To add a special flare, the truckers had brought Tiki torches atop cane poles, and they placed the torches around the circle.

The scene was awesome—all their best friends, their secret place, their trucks, torches licking the night with flames, crickets making weird noises, an owl hooting in the distance, and Dale waxing the ivory handle of his switchblade. Everyone was on a natural high from just being there together. They were ready to talk.

Ray went first, "I'd..." He stopped and cleared his throat. "I'd like to explain why I acted the way I did last weekend."

Candace responded quickly. "Ray, give it a rest, okay?"

Brady followed her. "Ray, you don't have to explain anything. We've already spread it around."

"Okay, but Coach John, I want to apologize to you. I let you down big time."

John responded, "You don't have to, Ray. Brady told me how it happened."

"I should've been stronger. My dad just doesn't know when to quit hitting me." Turning to Terence, Ray said, "I've found out how the slaves felt when they were beaten. I'm glad we live in a better time for you. I wish we lived in a better time for me."

Maria changed the subject to take the pressure off Ray. Speaking to the whole circle of kids, she said, "Tell Coach John and me about yourselves. What are your families like?"

Maria turned to Kaprice. "Your mom is Mr. Rumley's secretary and my husband's secret friend. What does your dad do?"

"My dad? Who knows? Who cares? He sure doesn't care about me. He may call me once a year, but that's about it. He walked out on us when I was only five."

"I'm sorry," Maria said.

Kaprice continued, "But my mom, she's great! She's a very wise woman. I'm not letting her know I feel that way, though. I don't want her to be able to throw it up to me when we're arguing. I hate it that she's a single mother, and Dad won't pay any child support, and she can't up and tell Mr. Rumpley what an old slime ball he is and walk out on him."

"Leilani, what's your story?" questioned Maria.

"I live with my grandparents. My dad's an alcoholic, and my mom's into coke. They met when my dad was a sailor stationed in Hawaii. My grandparents went to court and spent a lot of money and fought for me. Grandypa showed his lawyer how to outsmart my dad's lawyer, and he and Grandestmother were awarded custody of me when I was about seven. Grandypa is the greatest! He's the one that started that Princess-Leilani-from-Hawaii thing. He calls me his princess, but he has to share me with Brady." She glanced at Brady and said in a movielike voice, "Right, darling?"

Maria turned to Terence. She remembered Ray saying in the mall parking lot that Terence hadn't been able to move up with his senior class. She wanted to know more. "Terence, tell me about yourself."

"My family is still together. My parents are okay people I guess, but they're way too strict. I think they're too worried about what God thinks about how they parent. They don't want to let Him down. Like, they track me all the time. Most of these kids here can go and do what they want as long as they keep their curfews. But not me. I have to call and tell my parents everywhere I am or I'll get in trouble, if you know what I'm sayin'."

"I don't know how you stand them," Hope said. "I told my parents where they could go—and it wasn't to heaven, either!"

Brady spoke up, "I just tell my parents to get off my case when they get freaked out. They're good country folk—go to church and all— but they definitely get on my nerves, big time. I have to straighten 'em out now and again."

The teenagers laughed. They liked the thought of straightening out parents.

Brady finished his comment. "My parents are not all that bad, I guess, just a little stupid, that's all. I can put anything over on them."

"And he does!" someone yelled. Everyone laughed.

Franco went next. "Everyone knows my story. My mom offers stud service. I never know which sleazy creep I'm going to see in our home when I wake up every morning. Her present lowlifer has put her in the hospital twice.

"I try to tell her that these guys are taking advantage of her, but she sides with them against me. She screams at me and says that I don't have a right to judge her significant others, and she screams that they're better than I am. So I leave the house as soon as I get up and don't go home till after midnight. Except on weekends when Crisco flies in."

"I wish we were her significurt...significult...," Crisco said, looking up at Franco.

"Significant others," Franco said, supplying the right words for her.

"That's what I wish I could be to Mom," Crisco said, dropping her eyes.

Crisco was sitting on Franco's lap, leaning back against his chest, with her legs dangling on each side of his legs. His arms were around her waist. Franco continued, "Crisco here lives with her dad in another city. I stay around the house more when she's in town to keep Mom's sicko men away from her. I don't want her molested. Either I stay at the house with her, or she goes with me everywhere I go. She even hangs out with me at Donut World, which she loves."

Changing his attitude to one of disgust, Franco added, "The only reason Mom takes her on weekends is so her dad'll have to spend money on airplane tickets. She warned him not to move away. Besides, she doesn't want people to think she's an unfit mother."

John wasn't sure it was a good idea for Franco to say so much in front of his eight-year-old sister. He tried to change the subject. Addressing the little girl, he said, "Crisco is a pretty name. How did you get that name?"

Crisco answered, "My mother gave it to me." She twisted in Franco's lap to face him. "Is it all right to tell?"

"If you want to."

"My mother was really mad when she got pregnant with me. She didn't want to be pregnant, and she got big and fat, and no men would pay attention to her...what did Mr. John ask me, Franco?"

"Coach John asked you why Mom named you Crisco."

"Oh, yeah. Mom's face got oily and greasy always when she was pregnant with me. So she came up with the name Crisco. You know, like Crisco oil? I'm just glad she didn't name me Mazola."

"I like your name," John said, "and I like you, too."

Crisco followed, "I like my name okay, but I hate it when kids at school tell me that I've got oil on my brain or call me fat head when I don't know the right answers. Just because I got some learning problems from my mom's drinking during our pregnancy together..." She paused and put her finger to her head and drilled one way and then the other, saying, "That doesn't mean I'm a total moron or anything."

"How can you explain it so well?" John quizzed.

"A lady at school, not Mrs. Tucker, my teacher, her helper told me that my brain doesn't work as good as other kids' brains. That's because Mom didn't stop drinking alcohol when I was growing in her tummy. She said that's why I need more help than other kids. She told me not to worry about the teasing. Kids act mean and make fun of my name only 'cause they don't understand my problems. That's what she told me. And I felt better after she told me that."

"Why don't you go by Cris or Crissy?" John asked.

Franco answered for her. "Because I won't let her. Cris or Crissy reminds me of someone at school who pushes things way too far."

The boys made kissy noises, making fun of Platypus.

John wished he hadn't asked Crisco about her name in front of everyone. Maria put her left arm around John's neck and inched herself behind him. She didn't want anyone to notice the tears forming in her brown eyes or the way she was nervously biting her bottom lip. The home reports were getting her down. She didn't realize life could be so bad for kids.

Fred took his turn without really wanting to. He began, "My dad and Ray's mom are having sex. That's why I was so mad at Ray in the mall parking lot the other night. I thought he was gonna tell. But I've decided it's no big deal if you know. Most people know. So what? It's him! Not me."

The volume on Fred's voice steadily increased as he said, "My parents are worse off than I am. Man, like, I counsel my parents! A lot of kids are trying to be a parent to their parents these days. It's like, well, we've traded places, and we have more morals than they do. I like sex as much as the next guy—"

"More!" the kids shouted together, laughing.

"Okay, more. But I'd never cheat on my wife...especially not with the mother of one of my son's best friends."

Kyong Suk was next. "My home is a major disaster right now. My parents are getting a divorce. Mom told me why she hates Dad. Dad told me why he hates Mom. But, you know, it's hard for me to listen to how much they hate each other when I love them both. I feel like I'm partly to blame for their divorce. I mean if I could have been a better daughter, maybe my parents would still be together. I've gone to Hope's dad for counseling."

"Fat chance he'll help you! He's not a professional therapist! He doesn't know what he's doin'!" Hope snapped. "Give me a break! I wish Dad would just stay away from my friends and butt out of my life!"

"He has helped me!" Kyong Suk objected. "He taught me what to say to my parents when one of them tries to win me over by criticizing the other parent, or when they try to make a counselor out of me by telling me stuff that I'm too young to deal with. He said I could say, 'Please stop. I can't emotionally handle that, and I just want to love you both.' That's a good thing to say because it puts how I feel into words."

She thought a second and continued, "I said *please stop* when my mother started to tell me how bad their sex life was. Mom stopped and went to another subject. I was so-o-o glad. No kid wants to hear about her parents' sex life. Gross!...Oh, and I'm going to say it if they start telling me how much they hate each other again. I'll just say: Please stop. I can't emotionally handle that. I just want to love you—"

"Okay! Okay! We get the point!" Hope interrupted, unimpressed. "You don't have to go on and on!"

Kyong Suk stood up and lit two cigarettes from a Tiki torch. She put one in her mouth and offered the other around the circle. Dale accepted it. Everyone had been wondering what Dale would say when it was his turn.

John inquired, "Dale, I'd like to know more about your life."

Dale didn't smoke the cigarette. He only held it up and watched the smoke curl one way, then another, and vanish in midair.

Crisco watched Dale, wishing she could play with that cigarette.

Dale said, "I don't know which john my father was. My mom died of pneumonia and brain cancer caused by AIDS when I was sixteen. My brother was blown away in a turf war when he was twelve. For the last several days, I've stayed with this older guy who does maintenance work for one of the missions. He hires me so I can pay my way. I do his heavy lifting and stuff."

Kyong Suk asked, "How did you keep from walking in on your mother having sex? I walked in on my parents a couple of times."

"Mom taught me," Dale replied, "that anytime she played 'Strangers in the Night' on the stereo, she was working, and her bedroom was off limits to me and my little brother."

Dale seemed uncomfortable telling his facts of life, so John took the attention off him by asking someone else to take over. "The youth home. What's it like, Hope?"

But Dale wasn't finished. Barging ahead of Hope, he said force-fully, "Coach John, my goal in life is to repair my limb on my family tree. I will raise my children right. They will raise my grandchildren right. Then they will raise my great-grandchildren right. And none of us will ever live on the streets again. No one has to stay a victim! We each can control our destinies with the choices we make. Our choices are our tools. Choice by choice, we can rise above our problems. Our futures depend on our choices *today*, not on our parents or our pasts."

Looks of surprise traveled around the circle. Dale had more going for him mentally than they had thought.

John commended him. "Well said, Dale."

Maria followed with, "Would you put that in writing? Your speech was perfecto."

Dale agreed to do so. John called on Hope again.

"The youth home's better than being at home, but it bites, too. My house parents think they're so great. They said I could come tonight because I had earned enough points to go out. Woo! Woo! I woulda come anyway. No one tells me what I can and can't do!"

"May I ask why you are living there?" John probed cautiously.

"I kept running away from home, skipping school, cussing my parents, coming home drunk, and doing neat stuff like that. My parents said I was out of control. Maybe I was, but they asked for it! They kept poking their fat noses into my business! They always invaded my privacy, read my personal notes, and all! My parents are so disgusting!"

"Did your family try family counseling?"

"Yeah, because I reported them to Children's Protective Services and told them everything. The CPS worker and I became close, and he took me away from them and placed me in the youth home. And he told my parents that they were too radical and that they were way off base when they invaded my privacy.

"The CPS worker assigned me a child advocate and made us go to family counseling. And get this—the therapist took my side right in front of my parents! He told them that they were way too controlling, and he told them they should trust me more. Smart man! My child advo-cate said the same thing, and she said that my parents haven't showed her a single thing that makes her believe that they are trying to improve their parenting skills."

Ray said sarcastically, "You need a probation officer, not a child advocate! What's a *child advocate* going to do, side with the parents? Hardly!"

"Mom says," Kaprice contributed, "that a few of the child advocates she has seen at school have the attitude that parents are guilty until proven innocent. She believes they ought to be called family advocates instead, and they should be equally concerned about the health of all family members. She says balance is the key."

Catching John's eye, Ray snapped, "Hope's dad is pastor of the huge True Life Church downtown, but can't control his daughter! Does that make sense?"

"Who cares what makes sense to you, Ray? You always have diarrhea of the mouth!" Hope exclaimed, making a vulgar sign at him with her left hand.

Crisco laughed at the wrong time.

"I hate being a preacher's daughter," Hope told John with enough venom in her voice to prove it. "Friends back away from me. They hide things. They stop talking when I walk up. All because I'm a preacher's kid. They treat me differently than they do other people. I don't want to stick out. I don't want to be a goody-goody. I want to be my own person."

"Is he a hypocrite like most ministers?" John asked.

Maria was shocked. She whispered sternly, "Don't ask a question like that in front of all these kids!"

"Most ministers are not hypocrites!" Hope almost shouted. "I've been around preachers all my life, and most of them are not hypocrites. People are prejudiced against them, that's all. And another thing that bothers me is when people act like Ray and judge my dad by what I do. Why can't people just back off and let him be him and me be me? I'm my own person."

Hope saw the offended look on John's face, and she realized she had been too obnoxious. "Sorry, Coach. I'm PMSing, and I'm not in the best of moods. Maria, do you happen to have a Midol?"

"This is confusing," John said. "You reported your dad to CPS for mistreating you. Now you defend your dad. What's the deal? Is he a hypocrite or not?"

"Reporting him to CPS was my ticket to freedom. Dad's not an immoral person. Neither is Mom. They just don't want me to have a life."

Dale chimed in, "Hope is right. Her dad is not a hypocrite. Most of the hypocrites around here passed through Mom's bedroom. Hope's dad has a good reputation on the streets. He's one of the people we believe truly cares."

Hope ran her hand through her brunette hair. She was tired of telling her preacher's kid story. "My parents are okay people. They're just boring—BORING! And they want me to stay bored along with them. They don't want me to have fun. They don't want me to have a life! They want me to be virtuous! Give me a break! That's not me. Too bad for them! No big loss, though. I have a Goody Two-shoes sister who gives them the daughter they want.

"At the youth home, they at least accept us for who we are." Hope's mood brightened a little. "We get to smoke cigarettes, and they don't snoop in our rooms for drugs or anything. I think they suspect they're there, but they seem to believe that kids will get over it if they don't make a big issue out of it. They let us watch MTV and take us to R-rated movies, and we can read any kind of books we want and date whoever we want.

"They trust us. And to tell you the truth, I'd rather be in the youth home than in the religious prison my parents call home...Oh, and let me tell you what an old bi—uh, biddy from my dad's church did. This grosses me out completely. She saw me in the mall and told me that she had been praying for my family. She said that God gave her a dream and in that dream my dad and I had our arms around each other, and we were standing up together for truth and justice. She said it was in a public place. Yeah, right! Like I'm going to be seen in public with my arm around my dad. Hell will have to freeze over first!" Hope laughed in a scoffing way.

She continued, "That old bag of bones said that it was going to happen very soon. I told her she needed to give up sleeping so she wouldn't have any more pathetic nightmares. I said that right to her face. And I don't care if I hurt her feelings, and I don't care if she tells my parents. It was her fault for making me mad. Like she knows the future! Give me a break."

Dale said, "Hope—"

Hope interrupted Dale to add, "But don't get the idea that I'm not spiritual. I'm New Age. A house parent at the youth home loans me her books and teaches me about it. She gave me this crystal I'm wearing."

"Hope," Dale tried again. He spoke slowly as if he was reaching deep for his thoughts. "You're known as an intellectual on campus, but you're acting like a robot that's been programmed by rebellious attitudes. All you're doing is letting your carnal appetites and your friends decide your direction in life. You are not being your own person."

"And what's that supposed to mean?" Hope asked, ready for a fight.

"Well, think it through, Hope. If you're going to go through a stage of teenage rebellion against your parents, how are you gonna do it? Are you gonna rebel by becoming better than your parents? No. The word *rebellion* means *'opposite of.'* You'll do stuff that's opposite your parents. What's opposite your parents? Drinking, doing drugs, having sex, partying, getting into New Age—the junk you're doing!"

"I happen to like to have sex!" Hope exclaimed, trying to get a laugh, trying to discount what Dale was saying, trying to escape the impact of his words.

"I happen to like to eat ice cream," Dale answered, "but that doesn't mean I'm going to eat it off the bathroom floor at the bus station. Hope, you can't get happy by getting guilty."

Hope sizzled.

Dale thoughtfully and slowly continued as if he were thinking out loud, "New Age, yeah, that'll do the trick. It has astrology and communicating with the dead in it. That's about as opposite your dad as you can get...unless you go into satanism."

Hope was mad. She tried to slam-dunk Dale, "If you're the counselor on call, I didn't call!"

Dale tried to calm her. "Hope, I'm rebelling, too! My mom was a whore, so I'm going the other way. I'm trying to be a decent person. People just need to let me. That's all I need. I just need a chance."

Hope didn't know how to get rid of Dale. She asked for help. "Coach John, do I have to listen to Dale run his mouth? Would you get him off my case?"

Before the coach could say anything, Dale leaned on her hard, "Hope, your rebellion is betraying you. You are destroying everything I've ever wanted! You don't get it, do you? You are saying how bad your home is in front of a homeless person. I'd give anything to get out of the ghetto and live in a nice home and be a part of a respected family, if I didn't have to move away and give up you guys. I'd...I'd trade my truck for that!! Honest to God, I would! What would I have to do to take your place in the home you left, Hope? Not smoke dope, or drink, or sneak out, or skip school, or cuss your parents. I'd have to keep curfew and do a few chores. I can handle that. May I call your parents and volunteer to take your place? What's their phone number?"

"How about 1-800-GETLOST!" Hope said in a snotty way, giving him a drop-dead look and the same nasty hand sign she had used to insult Ray. But she wanted more revenge. "Move in with my parents? What's the point? My dad's already supporting you. His church has a ministry to the homeless, and I've seen you in his soup line more than once."

A stunned silence descended on the group.

Dale looked at Hope, not believing that she had said that in front of everybody. Insulted and angry, Dale chose his words carefully and spoke them slowly. "You...are...homeless...too, don't...forget." Then faster, "But you are homeless by choice! You are homeless because you want to be a party girl! Trust me, Hope, I've already seen where you are headed, and it ain't pretty. Girls get used and trashed."

With piercing eyes, he continued, "You think you are so good at being bad, but you've already had a narrow escape. You went out with Bo Langley. He slipped you a date-rape drug. But you were lucky. Someone had sold him a dud, and you didn't go under. Maranda Donnell went under, and he phoned three friends to come over. They raped her in every hole in her body for two hours. She was in the hospital three days. They got by with it because the drug Bo used blocks memory. She couldn't remember anyone but Bo, and she only remembered him before she blacked out. But her vagina was torn! She was bleeding out her butt! Her mouth was bruised! Her throat was sore!

"Get a grip, Hope. Their filthy body fluids and Maranda's torn flesh were at the same place at the same time. That means—hello!— if any of those losers had HIV or herpes or genital warts, Maranda is now infected, too! Hope, that's the kind of wickedness that your parents have tried to protect you from. You've pulled trains, and you've been in on at least one gang bang. Don't think I'm announcing anything that's not already known. Everybody knows. Guys brag.

"Your reputation is in the toilet. No decent guy wants to date you. Decent guys who want to respect their girlfriends and be proud of them won't date girls whose sexuality has been community property.

"You've locked yourself into dating takers and tail chasers. You can't make a decent husband and father out of one of them. That's the kind of trap your parents were trying to protect you from. Always remember this: At some point in your life, you're gonna have to stop and live with what you've become and think about the way you've treated your family. Your parents aren't disposables."

"I'll trade my mom for your parents any day," Franco interrupted.

"For real?" Crisco sat up and asked her brother. "I don't want to lose Mom!"

Franco squeezed her and whispered, "Don't worry. It's not gonna happen."

"I'll trade dads with you," Ray joined in. "And I will never get another beating."

"See, Hope. Good parents aren't disposables," Dale repeated. "Why don't you just give a little and be fair with your parents?...Invading your privacy, that's what proves they are bad parents, right? Wrong! Privacy is not something you get awarded to you just because you're breathing. It's *the reward* you receive for expressing maturity and earning trust. No trust, no privacy. If you compromise your maturity, you compromise your privacy. Teach reasonable parents that they don't need to check up on you, and they won't. Your parents are only responding to what you have taught them about yourself. I'm saying that in most cases, kids are teachers and parents are responders. *You* control how much privacy you have or don't have. Teach your parents to trust you, and they will respond by giving you more privacy and more freedom, and they will check up on you less. I promise."

Dale's magnetic smile opened across his face. "Besides, your parents are going to be the grandparents of your children one day. If you lose them, who's going to keep your kids while you and your husband go on great vacations?" Dale asked, trying to reduce the stress.

He got serious again. "Anyway, Hope, you gotta stop letting your rebellion betray you. Ask yourself: 'What price have I already paid? What price will I pay?'"

Hope was rude in return, "I don't have a problem! I'm not changing! No one is going to get to brag about straightening me out! Not you! Not my dad! Not the people at True Life Church! Not anyone! And get one thing clear, a social worker took me away from my parents and put me in the youth home. If my parents were right, and I was wrong, he wouldn't have moved me...and my therapist wouldn't have tried to straighten them out."

Hope propped her hands on her hips and gave everyone a hard look. No one said anything. She took a couple of steps as if to leave and said, "I didn't know I was coming out here to get a lecture. I could have gone to see my parents to get that. I'm ready to go back to the youth home. Anyone with wheels ready to leave?"

No one volunteered.

SCENE 10

Confessions of a sexually abused girl

TEN

CANDACE BEGAN to cry softly. "I wish I was in Hope's home."

Kyong Suk was sitting next to Candace. Kyong Suk reached over and pulled Candace close. "It's okay. You can talk. Everyone here already knows."

Dale handed Candace a paper towel torn off the roll he kept in his truck. Candace pulled away from Kyong Suk to blot her tears and runny makeup. With her head down and long blond hair shielding her face, she said, "It's true, Coach John. My stepdad's dad makes me do stuff with him. Everything's so weirded out. He's...he's even jealous of my boyfriends! Can you believe that? Gramps is jealous of sixteen-year-olds. He's afraid I'll let them do it with me. He's afraid he'll get a disease from them or something. He's so gross!"

There was silence in the meadow. It was as if even the crickets chose not to disturb Candace's painful words.

Maria was crying, too. She asked Candace, "Does your mom know?"

"No!"

"Why not?"

"It would kill her."

Maria slipped from the tailgate and knelt at Candace's knees, placing a hand on her leg, showing support.

"Kill her?" Maria repeated.

"My mom has been married three times, and now, for the first time in her life, she is happy. Nothing could make me take that away from her." Candace began to cry again. She spoke slowly between sobs, "I...love...her...so...much,...and...she's...had...it...so...hard."

Maria tore off a piece of Candace's paper towel and blotted tears and makeup from her own eyes, "There are authorities that you can report this to. They'll know how to handle it."

"I know. I called the police. I didn't tell them who I was, but I told them my story."

Candace leaned close to Maria's ear and said, "They asked me if I had ever had sex before. I said I had done it with two guys. They said I didn't have a good case. I'd be made to look like a slut in court, and it'd probably be thrown out. They said the burden of proof would be on me.

I don't have any proof! I asked the police, 'Why wouldn't I have sex with guys? Gramps taught me how to do it! Sex wasn't anything new or mysterious to me!' They said that didn't matter. They wouldn't get a conviction, Maria! Gramps would be on me even worse! I'm scared to death of him!"

Candace shuddered with chills of fear. She said, "Gramps warned me that if I ever told, and he went to prison, I'd go to the graveyard! He said strangers would throw dirt on top of my body!"

Some of the guys overheard what Candace told Maria.

Candace dropped her head onto Maria's shoulder and sobbed. Maria embraced her and rubbed her back while she cried. The other teens and John remained quiet and respectful in the presence of Candace's pain.

Trying to regain her composure, Candace sat up, blotted her face with her paper towel, and spoke to the group again. "I don't want to drag my mom through court. She doesn't deserve that!"

Maria stood up and placed a hand on Candace's shoulder. She turned to John and asked, "What are we going to do?"

Candace began screaming, "You can't do anything! Promise me! Please promise me that you won't tell anyone!"

Sliding off the tailgate and dropping to her knees, Candace began hugging Maria's legs. Becoming a beggar, she pleaded with Maria, "Pleeease! I've trusted you! This is what I was afraid of!"

Suddenly, Candace let go of Maria, took a couple of deep breaths, and insisted, "I was lying! No one's molesting me! I wouldn't let anyone do that! I'd kick and scream and fight, and someone would hear me and come. Please, please don't tell!"

Candace collapsed onto the grass. She lay on her left side, in a bed of trampled yellow flowers, her body jerking in sobs. The blossoms, like Candace, had been crushed by someone walking on them.

Franco tightened his grip on Crisco and whispered in her ear, "This is what I've been trying to protect you from."

Every person in the meadow stared at the scene. John knew that they would never forget it, that it would remain in their memories to be played and replayed many times during their lifetimes.

Ray muttered helplessly, "Welcome to the world of teenagers."

John and Maria knelt beside Candace, and John pulled Candace to her knees. They enveloped her in a loving embrace.

John gave in to Candace's plea. He whispered, "I promise you. We won't tell."

Startled, Maria studied her husband's face. "John!"

He repeated, "We won't tell, Candace. We won't!"

Ray protested, "Someone's got to tell! I love Candace, and someone's got to stop it!"

Unbelievable though it sounds, at that moment, an owl hooted twice as if asking, "Who? Who?"

No one as much as uttered a word. It was just too eerie. The timing, too awesome. Moments passed.

Kaprice walked up and took Candace away from John and Maria and seated her beside her on the tailgate. Holding Candace's hand in both her own, Kaprice announced, "If no one is going to tell, then Candace is going to stay with my mom and me till somebody figures out what to do."

Candace appeared doubtful, but Kaprice said, "Your mom will let you. She knows how close we are."

Ray moved to Candace's other side and began to gently massage her neck. Candace seemed not to mind Ray's attention now—now that she understood how much he cared.

Dale spit in disgust. "No one has to tell. I have friends that will," he held up his switchblade and pushed the button, swish, clunk, "take him out! And flush him down the sewer where he belongs, piece by piece. Aah! Sounds like fun!"

Crisco could be heard asking her brother, "Is Dale a bad guy?"

Franco whispered back, "No. Dale's just a mad guy."

Kaprice said quickly, "No, Dale. Candace doesn't need to hear that. Don't upset her any more than she already is. Promise to wait until we've tried everything else, okay?"

"Whatever," he said, slapping the shiny blade against his palm.

"Dale can't ever cut Gramps up," Candace said weakly.

"Okay. Okay," Kaprice comforted, squeezing her hand.

Maria suggested, "It's getting late. I think we should be going."

"Please don't leave," Candace cried. "Talk awhile more. I don't want to have ruined the party for everyone."

John agreed with Maria that the party was already over, but he wanted to be sensitive to Candace. "Daniel, you haven't told us about your family."

"My parents are too strict. They don't like my friends. They think I'm running with the wrong crowd. Coach, do these people look like the wrong crowd to you?"

John didn't hesitate although he was concerned about some of the things into which the kids were drifting. "These people are my friends."

"Well, they're the wrong crowd in my parents' eyes. But I've got news for them. I don't like their friends, either! I'd never run around with the creeps they run around with!"

A smile sneaked across Daniel's face. He chuckled. "Mom has this friend that's so huge that her fat rolls over when she sits down. It takes her three tries to get back up. All she does is watch soaps, pig out, pick her nose, and gossip."

The kids began to smile.

"She has this other friend who can't drive. I kid you not, the woman can't drive! She has a fender bender at least once a month. Last week, she was following her husband home in his new car, and he stopped and she didn't! The crazy woman wrecked both their cars!"

A chuckle raced through the teens. John and Maria laughed a little, too.

Daniel went on, "My dad plays golf with this man that eats like a stupid crawdad that never learned any manners." Daniel was beginning to act out his words, and everyone began to laugh loudly. Even Candace smiled a little.

He poured it on more. "The guy is so gross! He eats like this. He pokes it in with both pincers and holds onto his food while he eats it. Gah, he's nastier than nasty!"

Daniel was on a roll, "And you ought to see him eat boiled okra. It looks like he's eating veggies in snot sauce! I can't even stay at the table with him!"

The fact that Daniel was usually so quiet only added to everyone's amusement. Franco laughed so hard he bucked Crisco off his lap. The whole meadow was roaring with laughter.

"Wait! Listen!" Daniel shouted, trying to regain their attention. "He strings it from his plate to his mouth. One time, he got it on his nose, and there it was, hanging from his nose to his plate. It looked like he was supplying his own snot sauce!"

Now Candace was shaking with laughter, too.

Daniel finished his comedy act by spreading his arms wide and confronting John. "Now tell me, Coach, which friends would you choose: my parents' friends, or my friends here in the meadow?"

John had a hard time keeping a straight face. "I really don't know your parents' friends," he responded, trying to be discreet, "but I do know the people on these tailgates, and I want all of you to know that I really care about you."

The kids got quiet in respect of what the coach was beginning to say.

"I've been through a lot these last two weeks," John said. "Each of you knows that. Yet, tonight…well, tonight has made everything worth it. Your trust and friendship have made me feel as tall as one of these pine trees right now, and I can tell you one thing for sure—I'm not backing down. I will continue to stand by you." He aimlessly kicked the grass with his tennis shoe. Then a smile etched its way onto his face as he added, "Now that you've promised not to pee on me."

The kids laughed a little.

Ray piped up and said, "Since I'm not going to piss on you, I've got to find me a tree."

"No way, man!" Dale scolded.

"Yes, way!" Ray groaned.

John said, "Cross your legs and be quiet, Ray. We're about to leave…Look guys, all of you are dealing with a lot, and Maria and I would like to volunteer to be your adult friends throughout this school year. We'll not try to be professional counselors, but we can be adult friends to you. You can lean on us, and we can wade through everything together. We don't exactly know how to solve your problems, but we can be good listeners."

Then as an afterthought, he added, "We can certainly do more for you than is being done now by your school counselor or by the community."

Maria whispered, "Careful, honey."

"Fix our parents," Fred suggested, "and everything'll be cool!"

"More than parents need fixing here," John responded.

Brady slid off his tailgate, saying, "You're on, Coach, and we gotta go. There's curfews in this here meadow. Terence, throw your bike into Ray's truck. Kyong Suk, get your scooter and bring it over here. We'll put it in Daniel's truck, and he'll take you home. Okay, Daniel?…

Come on, guys, we've got some weight to lift. Stand the scooter straight up in the truck and use those ropes to hold it in place. It's not good for it to lay on its side."

John eased over to Kaprice and whispered, "If Candace's mom won't let her spend the night with you, call me."

"I promise."

John surprised himself. He held two of his fingers together, kissed them, touched them to Kaprice's cheek, and said, "This is for your mom. I really appreciate what she has done for me. I agree with you, she is a wise woman."

Dale grabbed their attention. "Coach, you and Maria are gonna ride back with me." John assumed Brady had asked Dale to take them home for him.

All done. Everyone jumped into the vehicles. Someone hollered out of the back of one of the trucks, "We'll move the potted plants on our way out! Last one out, close the gate!"

Ray yelled back, "Me and Terence'll put the plants back."

John had Dale pull up beside Ray and Terence. John teased Ray, "Don't get home late. Okay, Ray?"

"Trust me, Coach. I'm going straight home."

Daniel started his truck. Playfully, Kyong Suk jumped on her scooter. While Daniel fought the steering wheel to miss bushes and trees, she acted as if she was driving the scooter in the back of the truck. That didn't last long. A leafy limb slapped her across the face. She slid off, crawled underneath a rope to the cab of the truck, and crouched down.

Leilani and Brady were at the end of the parade, except they dropped out. John hoped Brady had a condom with him.

Later that night, Dale showed up at Kaprice's home and left an envelope for Candace. A note and an article was inside. Candace read the note:

WHEN YOUR WORLD SEEMS
IMPOSSIBLE, IT ISN'T UNUSUAL
TO THINK THOUGHTS OF SUICIDE.
THAT'S WHY I WANT YOU TO
READ A COLUMN MY UNCLE
WROTE FOR THE NEWSPAPER
WHERE HE LIVES.

ALSO, DO YOU REMEMBER WHAT
MRS. BURLESON SAID IN BIOLOGY?
SHE SAID THAT YOUR BODY
REPLACES ALL ITS OLD CELLS
WITH NEW CELLS EVERY 45
DAYS. THAT MEANS THAT IF WE
CAN FIGURE OUT HOW TO STOP
THE SICKO GEEZER FROM
MOLESTING YOU, AFTER 45 DAYS
ALL YOUR CELLS WILL BE NEW!
AND HE WILL NEVER HAVE
TOUCHED YOUR NEW BODY!
YOU'LL BE CLEAN AGAIN!

                              DALE

Lying down on the couch, Candace asked to be alone to read the article:

REASONS NOT TO COMMIT SUICIDE

TEENS FIGHT ADULT CORRUPTION (the novel) by R. A. "Buddy" Scott © 1998 • Allon Publishing

Here are the top fourteen reasons for someone not to commit suicide:

14. Murdering yourself to get out of a bad situation would not be fair to you. Why let someone who has already made things difficult for you cost you your life? Fight like a gladiator! Make wise decisions that will improve your situation, and act on them!

13. Killing yourself to show someone how deeply you've been hurt by him or how mad you are at her is too fat a price to pay. If you are 21, you may live to be 80. That means you have 21,549 days to solve your problems, and to laugh again, and to have fun again—to LIVE! Who wins if you give up all your days and the "jerk" who did you wrong gets to keep all his or her days? The "jerk" wins! You don't want that! No way! That would merely leave things unjust forever.

12. Suicide would stamp THE END on your life on earth, and your life story would always be a tragedy. Your story could never have a happy ending. But if you hang in here and keep trying, God promises that you can live happily ever after. Healing comes naturally to those

who try within the will of God. That's a fact you can trust even when you can't see how it can possibly happen.

11. Suicide won't work if your goal is to make people feel sorry for you. It's a little weird, but the fact is: They mostly get mad! They say: "If he would have just told us, we could have helped him!" "What right did she have to do that to us?!" They get mad, or it may make them think they were right in hurting you. For example, if it was a marriage separation, the one remaining alive often says: "I got away from him just in time." Or, "She was worse off than I thought."

10. Suicide would put a black mark on your family tree that every family member would always have to live with. Twenty-five years from now, someone would be saying, "Your Aunt Gerty took her own life, rest her poor soul. Just pray that it's not genetic."

9. Suicide would prove to some folks that you had mental problems. People would say, "That guy/girl turned out to be totally bananas." You wouldn't want that to be what people think when they remember you, right?

8. Killing yourself would not be fair to people with terminal diseases who are pleading to live. You don't want to needlessly destroy your life while they're begging for their lives.

7. Killing yourself would not be fair to people with diseased eyes, hearts, kidneys, and livers who are waiting for transplants to save their lives or their sight. It's unjust for you to kill yourself and waste your perfectly good organs. (By the time bodies are found, organs have been without blood flow too long to be transplantable.)

6. Killing yourself after you weren't aborted before birth seems like a slap in the face of fate. Since millions of people are aborted before they are born, don't you think there was a reason why you made it through the womb? Does it make sense to abort yourself now?

5. Suicide would leave your friends and family members helpless. All they'd be able to do is cry, go to the funeral and cry, visit you in the graveyard and cry, sit alone by the Christmas tree and cry. You're too much of a caring person to do that to them.

4. Suicide short-circuits the years God has designed in His "flight" plan for your life. Read this intriguing Scripture: *"For you created my inmost being; you knit me together in my mother's womb...All the days ordained for me were written in your book before one of them came to be"* (Psalm 139:13, 16b, New International Version). The last sentence

of that verse says that God has a long-range plan for your life. Warning: Interfering with God's long-range plan for you may be hazardous to your eternal health.

3. Suicide ushers you into the presence of God right after you've sinned a great sin. You don't want to go before the final Judgment when the last thing you did was break one of the Ten Commandments: *THOU SHALT NOT KILL.*

2. Your sudden appearance before God would show Him that you hadn't trusted Him to answer your prayers to make your life better on earth. You definitely want to make a better appearance than that at His throne.

1. You shouldn't kill yourself because you must make a difference on this planet before you exit it. God created you on purpose, and He has a unique purpose for your life. Find that mission, and you'll be so excited, so busy, and so fulfilled that suicide will be the last thing on earth you'd consider. Then, God will use everything that happens to you— good or evil—to achieve His plan for your life. The Bible says: *"All things work together for good to them that love God, to them who are the called according to His purpose"* (Romans 8:28, King James Version).

Candace stared at the ceiling and tears trickled down her cheeks. She drifted to sleep praying in her thoughts: *God, I won't kill myself, but I have no answers. I couldn't be in a bigger mess. Please help me. Please make Gramps stop molesting me. Please don't let Mother get hurt. Thanks for sending John and Maria to me. Thanks for all my friends. Through them, I feel Your love. Amen.*

Candace, exhausted from stress, soon fell asleep. Kaprice slipped in and covered her with a blanket.

SCENE 11

Haunted by the past

ELEVEN

"**MARIA!** I'M outta here! I'm going over to Candace's house, and I'm gonna tell her stepgrandfather what a good-for-nothing pervert he is!" John yelled at his wife through the bathroom door while she was preparing for bed.

Shocked, Maria, in her underwear, flung open the door to see what was going on.

"Have you been drinking?" she asked, being careful not to seem accusing.

"Not really. I've only had a couple of beers... Where are my keys?"

Maria thought about objecting, but she was afraid he'd get more upset. Instead, she said, "Hold on. I'll help you look for your keys."

She found them before he did. She picked up her keys, too. She went back into the bathroom, locked the door, lifted off the top of the toilet tank, eased both sets of keys into the water, and put the top back on with a quiet hollow clank. She hoped John didn't hear it.

Maria went out and saw John standing beside the kitchen cabinet where his keys had been. He was downing another beer and didn't see her. She eased back into the bedroom and sat down on the bed.

The trip home from the meadow with Dale seemed to have taken forever. Maria had been in a hurry to get to the apartment. She was emotionally exhausted and anxious to talk to John about what happened in the meadow. But Maria also wanted to be fresh and clean for her husband before they talked. She showered, washed and dried her hair, and brushed her teeth. By the time she was ready, John had guzzled several beers. Now, Maria sat alone in the bedroom, disappointed.

"Maria! Where are you, Maria? Did you find my stupid keys?"

Maria tried not to lie. "Sit down and try to remember where you left them," she urged.

"No! I've looked up Candace Thornton's phone number in the directory. I'm going to call that perverted stepgrandfather of hers and tell him how rotten he is."

John started toward their cordless phone. Maria sideswiped him and beat him to it. She picked it up and held it to her chest with both hands.

"Please, John, you've been drinking! Don't do it!"

John kept walking toward her. He backed her up against the kitchen sink. His breath smelled like beer. John lunged for the phone and bent the antenna.

Maria leaned backward over the sink, crying, "No!...John!... Please!!"

"Give me the phone, Maria! Give me the stupid phone!"

She saw he was not going to give up. She turned around and jammed the phone into the disposal, mouthpiece first. John lunged again. Totally desperate, she hit the switch with her knee, hoping it would look like an accident. The blades made whirling, scraping, and crunching sounds. The phone jumped up and down and began to spin around.

John jerked it out. The mouthpiece was damaged. Thinking it was an accident, he didn't get madder, except that he was rude about it. "Now, look what you've done!" Examining it closer, he said, "Maybe the thing still works."

He punched in Candace's number. Maria leaned on the cabinet and prayed silently, "Oh, God, let it be broken."

"Hello." The voice was that of an older man. "Hello. Hello. Candace, is that you, honey? I wish you'd come home. I'm lonesome."

Gramps thought it was Candace because when she called home and he answered the phone, she often hesitated, wishing her mother or stepfather had answered.

Furious, John screamed, "You filthy pervert! You've got one foot in jail and the other in hell! You're not getting by with..."

A click sounded. "What! You hung up on me, you sorry creep!" John snorted. "Fine! I'll deal with you tomorrow in person. Then let's see you hang up!"

Maria watched him rip through the pages of the school directory. He punched in seven more numbers. Maria was weak with fear. "Who are you calling?"

"Rumley!"

Maria tried to wrestle the phone from John, whispering in sheer fear, "No!"

John turned his back to her as Rumley answered.

"Hello. Alfredo Rumley here."

John lit into his principal. "This is John Bright! You can take your job and shove it! You don't have to fire me! I quit!!"

Rumley didn't respond.

"Cat got your tongue, Rump Face? And one more thing, if you ever fire Ms. Gibson, you'll answer to me personally. She's a nice lady, and you're not going to walk all over her like you have me! If you hurt her, I'll take one of my ball bats to your head! That's a promise, butthead!"

Another click. The phone went dead.

"He hung up on me, too!" John exclaimed. "Who do they think they are, hangin' up on me? Where are my dern keys? They're gonna be sorry for hangin' up on me."

Maria hadn't dealt with drunks before, but she had heard that you shouldn't try to reason with them. Not knowing what else to do, she began to act mad, too.

She exclaimed, "They hung up on you? Both of them? That's terrible! You shouldn't let them get by with that. Let's talk about what all you're going to do to them. Come over to the table and have another beer."

Maria was hoping to buy time and get him so drunk that he couldn't do anything else stupid.

John drank and threatened...and threatened and drank.

Some minutes later, he became sad. He began to cry. "Maria," he slurred, "you don't know what it's like. You've lived a sheltered life. Your parents are still together. They've been married forever, and they're happy."

He shoved the empty beer cans out of the way. They banged into each other. One rolled off and clanked onto the floor. John slumped over the table, placing his cheek on his arm.

"I see myself in those kids, Maria. My dad was too busy tomcattin' around to be with me. Do you know what it's like to hate your daddy's girlfriends? They got to spend time with him...and laugh with him...and they got to be touched by him.

"Mom was good, but I rebelled against her. She had no choice but to be on me about the crowd I was running with, about church, about curfew, about chores...She was right, and she was loving, but I fought her and the rules she made to guide me. I wish I had been as good to her as she was to me. I hurt her. I chose the wrong parent. I chose the permissive parent."

Tears rolled down the side of John's face, dripping onto the table. "I went to live with my free-wheeling father. He didn't have any rules. I got into pot and dropped acid a few times. I didn't do cocaine, though, 'cause my dad was so ugly when he did it. He had hair growing out his nose, Maria, and when he stuck a straw up his nose to snort coke, he looked like a walrus with one tusk—a walrus that worshiped little rows of powder. I never wanted to look like that."

John groaned. "I want to be like your father...I know I crushed my mom. I didn't mean to, I just wanted...I just wanted to do my own thing, to have my own way. That's all. My mom talked my dad into putting me into a treatment program. It helped some."

After a long silence, John sat up and put his face in his hands. His thick tongue muffled the words. "Maria, promise me that you won't tell your dad about tonight. He thinks you married a guy from the wrong crowd. I don't want him to know he was right...I'm such a sorry person...You don't deserve me...I am a zero...I'm serious as sin, Maria, you don't deserve me! You are so wonderful...You are so beautiful."

John's words were coming more slowly now. He was winding down. "Maria, no kidding, you are...you are, without a single doubt, definitely the finest female God ever constructed, uh, built, uh, made."

Maria whispered, "Let's go to bed, John."

Yawning, he said, "That, my lo...love, is a very good ide...idea."

Maria helped him stagger into the bedroom. She tucked him into bed. He was in the same clothes that he had worn to the meadow. She left him that way since she was afraid that changing his clothes might rouse him.

"Aren't you comin'?" he mumbled.

"Sure, I'm coming, but I've got to use the bathroom first. You just lie there and close your eyes and think about what we're going to do together. I'll be back in a minute."

Maria sneaked the phone into the bathroom, shut the door, sat down on the commode lid, punched zero, and waited.

The operator said, "Hello."

"Hello, operator," Maria whispered as loud as she dared.

"Hello, this is the operator."

Maria shook the phone. "Operator!" she whispered again. "Can you hear me?"

"Hello. This is the operator. Hello."

Maria shouted into the phone, "John, I'll be there in a minute!"

The operator said, "If there is anyone there, I can't hear you. Please hang up and try your call again."

"The phone is broken," Maria sighed in relief. "Thank You, Lord!"

She sat on the commode and quietly sobbed for several minutes. She had never felt more lonely. After wiping away her tears with toilet paper, Maria slipped into her pink nightgown.

John had fallen asleep by the time she joined him.

SCENE 12

*After
the
disaster*

TWELVE

"**OH, YUCK!!** What now?" Maria sputtered. Something wet had awakened her Saturday morning.

Everything was soaked! Everything stank! John had wet the bed during the night. Maria was furious and terribly turned off at him.

She remembered John telling her about his bed-wetting problem during his childhood. He took medication back then to prevent him from sleeping too soundly to wake up when he needed to go to the bathroom. The alcohol caused him to sleep too soundly again.

Maria removed her nightgown and dropped it on a corner at the foot of the stinking bed. She took a long shower.

When she finished, John was still asleep. She walked back into the bedroom. The odor nearly knocked her down. Irritated and disgusted, she just wanted to get away for a while.

Maria dressed in her red-and-white sailor short set, put on her makeup, fished her keys out of the toilet tank, and wrote John a note. Putting the top down on the maroon Mustang, she left to go shopping for the day.

When John woke up, it was nearly noon. His head was exploding. He had a mean hangover. But something else felt wrong. He sat up in bed and felt all around. "Everything's wet!" he exclaimed.

Realizing that he had urinated all over himself during the night, he thought in fear, *Oh, I hope I didn't get any on Maria.* "Maria! Are you here?"

He saw her nightclothes on the corner of the bed. He picked up Maria's lacy pink nightie. It was soaked. He brought it to his nose and sniffed. There could be no doubt.

He sat there a few moments in the soggy bed, holding Maria's nightie in his lap, head bowed, wishing, by some miracle, it wasn't true. Maria was attracted to strength, and getting drunk and wetting the bed were so lame.

"God," he prayed, "please let this be merely a nightmare. Let me wake up and none of this be real." Even as he prayed, he could smell reality. He suddenly remembered the phone calls. *Was that a dream, or did I do that?* Fear shot through him like a lightning bolt. *Oh, God! I pray that I didn't screw up everything last night!*

John got out of bed and looked for Maria. He found her note:

> John:
>   You were a slob last night.
> I'm not going to live with a drunk.
> Do it again, and it's over between
> us. I've seen women on TV talk
> shows who stayed with drunks,
> and I don't plan to be one of them.
>   I've gone shopping, and I'll
> be back around 5. Wash the bed-
> clothes—I left some quarters on
> the counter. Do something about the
> mattress and phone. I love you, John.
> Get your act together, okay?
>
>   Maria
>
> P.S. Good news! The pervert and
> Rumley couldn't hear you last night.
> The mouthpiece was broken. You could
> hear them, but they couldn't hear you.
> I still can't believe you did that!

John stood there, rereading the note with the smell of urine in his clothing polluting his nostrils. Although greatly relieved about the phone calls, he felt horribly humiliated about the mistakes he had made. Waves, breakers of guilt crashed throughout his emotions. He pulled his wallet out of his back pocket. Everything in it was wet and nasty, including his favorite picture of him and Maria.

He swallowed a couple of aspirins, made his way to the bathroom, turned on the shower, lay down in the tub, and let the warm water rain down on him for about twenty minutes…while he hated himself and dreaded facing Maria again.

Later, John went to the washateria at the apartments and put the laundry through the wash cycle. While feeding quarters into the dryer, he thought about the mattress. *What am I going to do about the stupid mattress? There's no way to clean it,* he thought. *I'll just have to get rid of it. I can't have it around as a reminder to Maria.*

It was queen size, and John figured it would be difficult to handle by himself. *Maybe I can wrestle it out to the Dumpsters, and maybe no one will know which apartment it came from.*

As if on cue, a cocky-looking teenage jock walked by the door and glanced in. John had never seen him in the apartment complex. "Hi, guy," John said.

"Right," he returned.

"Do you go to Lincoln High?" John quizzed, hoping he didn't.

"Nope! I, like, wouldn't go to a school that has a sports program as dumb as theirs. I'm just here every other weekend to visit my old man. It's not my idea. He wants to spend quality time with me. Fun! Fun!"

John needed him too badly to object to his rude comments. He asked, "Would you like to make an easy five bucks by helping me move a mattress?"

"Guess so."

A *guess so* was good enough for a desperate man. They went up to John's apartment and tried to get a grip on the mattress.

The mouthy jock said, "Gross! This thing stinks. It's, like, obscene! Did someone use it for a urinal?"

John dreamed up an answer, "Uh, you might say that. We let a drunk sober up in our apartment last night, and he wet all over himself."

The jock passed judgment. "What an idiot! Like, what an immature fool!" Coughing as if he was choking, he rattled on, "Puu wee, dude! This is, like, unsafe and unsanitary working conditions. I, like, may have to sue you."

I'm beginning to hate this grunt, John thought angrily. John took the urine-soaked side to keep the teenager away from it.

They were tugging and heaving and coming off the bottom stairs when one of John's teacher friends, Winston Gambino, walked by. He saw the huge wet spot, and being a big tease, he said, "Airing your mattress out, Coach? You should've outgrown that when you were a kid."

Embarrassed, John dodged the truth. "Very funny," he said. "Maria was cleaning, and she spilled a big bucket of dirty water on it."

The cocky jock gave John an I'm-not-believing-this look.

Moments later, after the teacher had left, John said, "I lied to him because I hate nosy neighbors."

"Oh, I don't care if you lie," the jock mused, giving him some slack. "I lie to get myself out of trouble all the time. It's no big deal."

John wasn't impressed. He didn't like being classed with the rude and crude teenager.

They were almost to the Dumpsters when a swarm of children came running up. "Can we play on it? Can we use it for a trampoline?"

The jock answered before John could. "No, not unless you want to work for Roto-Rooter when you grow up!" He alone laughed at his pun.

They finally got the mattress securely situated between two Dumpsters. Suddenly, the apartment manager yelled and waved them over to where he was. As they walked toward him, he asked, "Why are you throwing away that mattress? It doesn't look bad."

John searched for an answer. "Uh, Maria and I hate the large puke-green flowers in the floral pattern. Nobody would want a mattress that ugly in their apartment."

The manager said, "I know a family who would. Their apartment caught fire, and they lost everything."

"Well," John gulped, "there's another problem. It's saggy and uncomfortable."

"Soggy, you mean," the smart-aleck jock grunted privately to John.

John gave him a shut-up-or-you're-dead look.

The manager said, "A saggy mattress beats the heck out of no mattress at all."

John tried again. "To tell you the truth, a drunken slob stayed at our apartment last night, and he didn't make it to the bathroom. He drenched the thing. That mattress is ugly, saggy, soggy—nasty!"

Turning away, the manager said, "Well, you can't leave it there. The city garbage trucks don't remove junk, only trash. You'll have to haul it to the dump."

"I don't have a truck!" John yelled after him, protesting.

"Neither do I," the manager yelled back, walking away. "Put it back in your apartment until you can arrange transportation!" he ordered. "I don't want my apartment complex to start looking junky like so many others do."

"That's just great!" John said, becoming totally frustrated.

The jock popped off, "Five dollars is for a one-way trip."

John shot back, "Okay, ten."

The jock made fun of John's crisis as they returned to the mattress between the Dumpsters. "Man, like, if I had known how funny this was going to be, I could've sold tickets and made some bucks. This is a comedy show. People would, like, pay to watch this! Scalpers would probably buy a bunch of tickets and resell them at higher prices."

John was angry. The kid had pushed him a bit too far. Still, he couldn't say anything, or the kid might think that he took it too personally, and that he was the one who had wet the bed. Besides, he still needed help.

So John said, "Just get hold of the mattress, and let's go." He tried to give the jock the wet side of the mattress on purpose.

"Stop," the jock said. "Change sides. This piss is from your apartment, from your slob. I do dry sides only."

They swapped places as John concluded that the kid was a complete disgrace to his parents.

Again, they tugged and heaved as they carried it back across the parking lot. Suddenly, a gust of wind pushed the soaked part of the mattress into John's face. John lost his balance and fell down. The mattress fell on top of him. He was trapped under the stench.

The jock laughed and laughed. He walked round and round the mattress, bending over in laughter. He laughed so hard, he was too weak to get the mattress off John! Between fits, he said things like, "Are we having fun yet? Yo, boss! I bet you hate your pee-peeing friend now! What's it like under there?"

Under there, John felt totally insulted by his own behavior the night before. He had made a fool of himself. Consequences were literally rubbing his nose in his shameful mistake. He didn't have the self-esteem necessary to fight what the kid was dishing out. But he had to keep fighting to get rid of the mattress before Maria returned. He kicked and pushed until he got the stinking thing off him.

With much huffing, puffing, and grunting, they finally got the nasty thing halfway back upstairs.

As Murphy's Law would have it, John's teacher friend was again at the wrong place at the wrong time. Winston hollered up, "Aired out already?" And then he joined them on the stairs. "That smells like urine, John," Winston observed.

"Maria had been cleaning the commode, and she spilled—"

The jock interrupted, "Wanna buy a ticket? Act two's about over, but act three will be starting soon!"

On the edge of losing his temper, John impatiently asked, "Winston, would you do me a favor? Would you just come back at another time?"

"Oops, I frustrated a fellow teacher," Winston said. "Okay, I don't know why on earth you would want that thing back in your apartment, but I'll give you a hand. Let's do it."

A few seconds later, the mattress was in the living room, standing on its edge, leaning against the men.

John explained further, "I couldn't leave it out by the Dumpsters since the city won't haul it off. The manager says I have to keep it in my apartment until I can find a truck."

"I have a truck, John," Winston volunteered. "Here, let's take it back downstairs, and we'll load 'er up."

The jock said, "My meter's running."

"Your mouth is running, too! It never stops, does it?" John went to his wallet in another room and got a ten-dollar bill. He handed it to the jock and said, "You're fired."

The jock held it up by the tip of a corner as if it were a dirty diaper and asked, "Like, why's it wet?"

"Like, it accidentally went through the washer," John answered tartly, mimicking the way the kid talked.

"Are you, like, lying to me, dude?"

"Like, take it or leave it, dude!" John said with a drop-dead stare.

"I'll take it. Stop and Shop will never know," he said as he lazily went down the stairs, still waving the bill by the corner as if to dry it.

John and Winston carried the mattress to the truck. John leaned against the tailgate, totally worn out. His aspirins had worn off, and his headache felt like it was trying to destroy his brain.

John opened the passenger's side of the truck to get in, but Winston stopped him. "There's no need for you to go. I'm just going to take it over to a friend's house and push it over onto his junk pile. Next weekend, he and I are going to make a trip to the dump. We'll haul off everything then."

Winston added a footnote. "John, if I teased you too hard, I apologize. This whole thing just struck me as kind of funny, that's all."

"No problem. Thanks for your help," John replied.

"John!" A woman's voice grabbed his attention. "Where is he going with our mattress?"

John whirled around. Sure enough, it was Maria! She had come home early. John had a stress attack.

"He's...he's taking it to the dump."

"Why?"

"Because of all that bathroom stuff that got on it!"

"It'll dry out if we leave it in the sun!" Maria exclaimed. "We can't throw it away! What will we sleep on? The box springs?"

Winston stood by his open truck door with a what-now look on his face. John pulled Maria out of his hearing distance.

"He thinks you spilled commode water on it when you were unstopping our commode or something," John explained. "Don't let him find out the truth, Maria. Just let him haul the nasty thing away. I don't ever want to see it again. I don't want you to ever see it again. I want it out of our lives, Maria! Don't push this! I've had a very bad day."

"Do you think I haven't?!" Maria snapped.

"I know you have, and I know I caused it...but we've got to get through it. Sweetheart, the mattress has to go!"

Maria cooled down and agreed.

John shaped an okay sign with his fingers and flashed it to Winston. Winston slammed his door and started his truck. The truck was leaving. The mattress was leaving, too—finally. John watched as the mattress got farther and farther away...and became smaller and smaller. "Thank God," he murmured.

Feeling a bit of compassion for her husband, Maria asked, "Is there anything I can do?"

"Yes, there is, Maria. If you can find it in your heart, you can forgive me. I apologize to you from the bottom of my sorry soul. Please forgive me for insulting you, for acting like a total fool. I'll never do it again. I will never let sin embarrass and humiliate me again like that...and I will never let it insult you again."

Maria responded, "I forgive you, John. But consider that note I left a contract. I meant what I wrote."

"Don't worry, Maria. Today I've learned that the author of evil is two-faced. He suckered me in, promising me relief and pleasure, but buried me beneath shame. A mistake like mine definitely subtracts from a person's dignity."

Maria supported John's conclusion. "A visiting priest once said: 'Sin is like a honeybee. It has honey in its mouth and a stinger in its tail.'"

"Truer words were never spoken, Maria. I never want anything like this to happen again."

"I believe you, John."

They held hands and began walking up the stairs. Maria carefully approached a tender subject. "Last night, you mentioned how badly you have treated your mother. Have you made things right with her?"

"You know I haven't, Maria. Not to the extent that I should. I'm just now beginning to come to terms with what really happened."

"But you will do everything necessary to make it up to her, won't you? She gave her best for you, John, and then lost you to someone who had ignored you in favor of drugs and a selfish lifestyle."

"I will. I definitely will, Maria. I know it was miserably unfair to her, and I will definitely go to Mom and undo the injustice. She deserves for us to be close again."

"John, I will support you in that. I love your mother, and I respect her. Let me know if there's anything I can do to help."

At the top of the stairs, John remembered the bedclothes in the washateria. Maria volunteered to go get them.

John was grateful because he had stale urine on him from his struggle with the mattress and wanted to shower before Maria smelled it.

He passed by the kitchen, popped two more aspirins in his mouth, and headed to the bathroom, spraying air freshener along the way.

Facing Maria again had been hard. No doubt, that day had been the worst day of his life.

John and Maria slept on a blanket on the floor that night. That, too, was humiliating.

SCENE 13

Hypocrites and life in the fast lane

THIRTEEN

"**HELP! HELP!** H-e-l-p!" John heard himself scream as he bolted upright, still half asleep.

Maria shook him. "Wake up, honey! You're having a nightmare!"

John fell back, exhausted.

"What were you dreaming? What could have scared you so badly?" Maria asked.

John wasn't about to tell her. He was dreaming that the mattress had sprouted arms and legs and was chasing him like Wile E. Coyote chases Road Runner. The thing had been after him all night.

"Could we just go back to sleep?" John responded.

"John, it's time to get ready for early Mass. Would you like to go to church with me?"

"No thanks, Maria. You know how I feel about organized religion. Churches are full of hypocrites," John said, out of habit. "Besides, I'm a Protestant, and that Mary thing, I don't go for that at all."

His careless words angered Maria. She spat out her reply in Spanish. "Fui nombrada con el nombre de la Madre de Jesús, y te reto a que le quites la santidad. ¡Un borracho loco no tiene el derecho de decir nada contra la santísima Virgen María! Tú me arrastraste por la mugre el viernes por la noche, ¿y tú has llamado hipócritas a otros? ¿Cuántos de ellos habrán orinado en el colchón y en su esposa? ¡Me das asco, John Bright!"

"Fine, Maria, you're mad. You always speak in Spanish when you're mad because you can talk faster."

Speaking in Spanish was like counting to ten for Maria. It gave her time to calm down. She felt like defending her church and the mother of Jesus by telling her husband to go look in the mirror. She tried not to. Instead, she said, "My back hurts. This hard floor is really uncomfortable. I'll pray for a new mattress at church."

John answered her volley, "That was a cheap shot, Maria!"

Maria got up off the floor and walked toward the bathroom door, leaving John on the blanket, propped on an elbow. She leaned back against a bedroom wall, looked up, and took a deep breath. Releasing her breath in a big sigh, she said, "Cheap shot? How can you judge others so harshly? What about you yesterday? You lied to Winston about what happened to our mattress. Wasn't that being a hypocrite? What if Rumley had seen you while you were drunk? Would he have thought you were a hypocrite? What about the kids? You were offering to help them, and then you get sloppy drunk forty-five minutes after you were the grand marshal of their meadow."

Holding the crucifix on her necklace between her thumb and forefinger, she asked, "What if this Catholic hadn't taken care of the Protestant Friday night?"

"Maria, throwing all that up to me is not fair!"

"Sure, it's fair! It's the truth! John, I'm just not in the mood for you to cut down my faith and my new friends at church."

Pointing to the bed, she got louder. "There's no mattress on those springs, and I've just spent the night on the floor. I have a backache. We don't have a phone. What about Candace and Kaprice? What if they had called for help? What was I supposed to do? I guess I should've put a message on our recorder that said: Sorry our phone is out of order, and John and I are out of order, too. This has been insane! Believe me, John, I'm in no mood to hear you judge others."

Maria caught her breath and tore into him again. "There are more hypocrites that don't go to church than do! Every man or woman who is having an affair, every person who is smoking pot behind people's backs, every person who is stealing from his company, every man or woman who takes money needed by his or her family to buy beer, every person who lies to get food stamps or unemployment checks, every person who takes something back to a store and lies about why they are returning it, they're all big, fat hypocrites! And most of them don't go to church!"

Maria continued, "Besides, the hypocrites who go to church don't show that Jesus Christ is a fake or that the church is a waste by their hypocrisy. All they show is that they don't have enough class not to be hypocrites. That's it! Nothing more!"

John decided to try to retreat from the battle. He said, "Okay, Maria, but you don't have to be so sore about everything. You know I think there's a god somewhere out there, and I pray to him. I prayed for Franco's family, and it got me in trouble with Mr. Rumley. You know that. You know I pray. Organized religion is where I have a problem."

"I'm not sore about everything."

"Maria, stop! Please. I don't want to fight. I thought you forgave me."

"I did forgive you, but you can't be judging others like that." Maria began to cry. "I'm hurt, and I'm angry."

She walked to the dresser and pulled a tissue from the box. Drying her eyes, she calmed herself. Turning around, she said warmly, "I really do wish you'd go to church with me, John. We've got kids to pray for."

"I'm not up to it, Maria. I need to find a quiet place to think. I've got a lot of things to sort out."

"Okay, but the Mustang will be with me at church. Don't forget, I'll be helping with the kids during the second Mass, and I'm staying for the church dinner. I won't be home until about three."

Maria stepped into the bathroom. John lay back down and put his left arm over his eyes. He was wishing he hadn't said anything against anyone. He was having to admit to himself that he, too, had been a hypocrite.

Maria dressed and left. John went to the kitchen in his underwear. He poured a bowl of the first cereal he found. As he began eating, he noticed the kids' card. He opened it and read it again. **WE DO HEREBY PROMISE NOT TO PISS ON YOU!** He smiled a little, remembering how much fun they had been.

"I wish I had promised not to pee on me," he groaned. *I wish I had promised not to let the devil pee on me,* he thought.

With that, John put down his spoon, bowed his head over his cereal bowl, and began to pray aloud. "God, it's not like I know You very well, but I pray that You will help me to never embarrass and humiliate myself like that again. And I pray that You will help me win Maria's confidence back. Oh, and God, if You have any extra mattresses on planet Earth, just leave one at my door. Amen."

His eyes returned to the card:

Truly yours,
Leilani, Kaprice, Kyong Suk, Brady,
Ray, Terence, Damiel, Fred,
Candace, Hope, DALE, Franco.

I wish I could remember to ask what FAFF means, he thought. Probably some secret code from the meadow.

"God, I love those kids," he said aloud, half praying. Somehow, someway, John knew he wanted to help them survive and heal from their hurts. He knew he wanted to heal from his own hurts, too. He hadn't realized he was carrying around so much old baggage from the past until this fateful weekend.

Rumley was right, he thought, *I don't know how to help anyone. I really am just a PE teacher...a phys ed major who's made a major mess of things this weekend.*

John showered and dressed. As he finished putting on his coach-style knit shirt, shorts, and tennis shoes, someone knocked loudly on his apartment door.

He opened the door, and all he could see was large puke-green flowers.

The mattress was back! It was pushed up against the door like a giant plug.

John's heart sank to his stomach. A manly voice sang fresh words to an old tune...

> **Amazing grace!**
> **How sweet the sound!**
> **That saved a poor mattress like me!**
> **I once was gross,**
> **But now am clean;**
> **Was dumped,**
> **But now I'm free.**

The mattress tipped backward, and a head suddenly appeared over the top of it.

"Winston!" John shrieked. "What on earth are you doing?!"

"Surprise!" Winston exclaimed with a wall-to-wall grin. "My friend with the junk pile decided this mattress was too good to junk. He has a carpet cleaning business, and he steam cleaned it with his machines. We put electric heaters on it all night, and it's like new. We hurried 'cause I figured you and your pretty wife were sleeping on the floor, right?"

"Right."

"Look here, there's no stain! Not even a trace! It's saved! Feel it. It's clean and dry, and it has that showroom sheen back. Slap your sheets on this baby, and you'll never know it was messed up."

"I'm totally speechless," John admitted.

"You don't have to say a thing, just heave ho, and let's get it on your bed."

Winston balanced the mattress on its edge to stabilize it and worked his way to the other end. While his back was turned, John looked up to God and screamed in his thoughts: *When I prayed for a mattress, You know I didn't want this mattress! I don't find Your sense of humor amusing!*

They plopped it down on top of the box springs, and John walked Winston to the front door. "I can't tell you how much I appreciate all the trouble you've gone to," John said, lying.

"You owe me a favor. I won't forget to collect. By the way, where's Maria, John?"

"At church."

Winston responded, "I should've known. Me, I don't go to church. Churches are full of hypocrites."

Instantly, John was on a guilt trip. *Maria's at church, and we're not,* he thought. *I think that makes us the hypocrites.*

"Earth to John," Winston said, jolting him out of his trance.

John thoughtfully said, "You know, Winston, I've been thinking about the hypocrite thing. The fact is that there are more hypocrites out in the world than there are inside churches. Perhaps both of us should be in church like Maria this morning."

John couldn't believe he'd said that. But neither could he believe the mattress had made its way back into his apartment, and Winston was standing at his front door talking about the subject that he and Maria had fought over that morning.

Winston didn't want to pursue a religious conversation. "Gotta be going, my friend. I've got a busy morning."

Winston left. John went back to the bedroom. He spoke to the mattress as if it were a human. "Why can't you just get outta my life? You're not staying! Do you hear me? You are not staying!!"

John went to the fridge and grabbed a beer. He sat down at the table and began drinking. His eyes fell on Maria's note where she had written: *I'm not going to live with a drunk.*

"Just one," he said, taking another big swig.

He saw the kids' card on the table. His eyes slowly scanned their names again: Leilani, Kaprice, Kyong Suk, Brady, Ray, Terence, Daniel, Fre—

"Okay, just none!" His conscience had won the battle. "Good grief! Has the whole world ganged up against me?" he asked aloud.

He walked over to the sink and poured the beer down the drain. He gazed at the trail of foam it left behind. "This has had a bigger grip on me than I thought," he said aloud to himself. "I can't be turning to alcohol every time I get depressed."

John went next door and called a department store. He asked to speak to a salesperson.

"This is Sandra, may I help you?"

"I hope so. I'm in a bind. I want to arrange a surprise for my wife before she gets home from a church dinner. I'd like to buy a new mattress…uh…and a new phone, and I need them delivered."

"I'm sorry, sir, we don't have Sunday deliveries."

"Look, this is really, really important, and I don't have a way to haul a mattress. Is there any possible way you could make an exception?"

"I'll try. I sure could use the sale. Hold on." The phone went silent. Then, "Sir, a delivery man is here cleaning up the warehouse. He said he'd run the items over to you, but you'll have to pay him instead of the store."

"How much?"

"Hold on. I'll ask." There was a short pause. "It'll be twenty-five dollars."

"Okay, will he haul my old mattress away?"

"For ten more dollars, I'm sure he will," Sandra answered.

Encouraged, John said, "I'll be there in fifteen minutes."

John had no idea of how he would get to the store. Maria had the Mustang. Then he remembered the family that lived below them and down a few doors. They had been friendly toward him and Maria when they were moving into the apartments.

John knocked. The woman answered the door.

Without saying hello, John asked, "Is there any possible way you could give me a ride to the mall? A salesperson is waiting for me there."

"I can't. I've got lunch on the stove. My husband's not here."

"Can you turn your burners down? It's very important."

She thought a moment and said, "My sixteen-year-old son, Bruce, can take you if you're brave enough to ride on the back of his motorcycle."

"Get Bruce!" John exclaimed.

Bruce came to the door and recognized the coach from his high school. He told John he couldn't take him 'cause he didn't have an extra helmet.

John's mind raced. "No problem, Bruce, I've got my own helmet. I'll meet you at your bike."

John ran upstairs and grabbed an old football helmet out of his closet. He pulled it on as he jogged down the stairs. Bruce was standing beside his cycle with the motor running.

"Dude!" Bruce exclaimed when he laid eyes on him. He laughed louder than the noise of the engine. "Where's your pads, Coach?" Bruce teased.

John felt ridiculous behind the face mask, mouthpiece hanging, bulldog stickers on the sides of his helmet, and a big 33 painted on the back of it.

Bruce mounted his rebuilt red-and-white 750cc Ninja ZX-7R and yelled over the engine, "Get on, number 33, and hold on tight. We're going for a touchdown!"

Bruce hit the gas. The front wheel left the ground! John was barely able to hang on! He thought he was a goner! Bruce drove like he was racing, since he didn't want other bikers to see him and think he rode with dorks.

The mall never looked so good to John. He felt lucky to be alive. He resolved in his thoughts, *I'll give this idiot an F if he ever shows up in one of my classes.*

Within a couple of minutes, John handed Sandra his credit card. She started the paperwork. He shoved his hand toward the sky, made a fist, jerked it back, and whispered loudly, "Yes!"

He celebrated too soon. Sandra's computer reported bad news. "Sir, I'm sorry, but your card is almost at its limit. I can put the phone on it, but not the mattress."

Thoroughly disappointed, John signed for the phone. He caught a ride home with a student who had been shopping.

Hurrying to get everything done before Maria got home, John sprinted up the stairs, unboxed the phone, plugged it in, ran the broken one to the Dumpster, shot back upstairs, and stopped to confront the mattress.

Out of breath from running, John breathed heavily as he said, "Okay! Big stubborn mattress with ugly puke-green flowers, you win! But I'm going to have the last say. I'm going to cover your butt up, and you had better not put up a stink, or you're outta here forever. Is that clear?"

John startled himself. He sounded like Rumley! He hated it and decided to try again. "Okay, Mr. Mattress, you win. And I guess that if I'm a fair-minded man, I should thank you for saving me a few hundred bucks and teaching me a lot of lessons. So, thanks!" John slapped the end of the mattress as if he were giving it a high five.

Becoming amused by how goofy the whole scene was, he said, "By the way, since we're making up and are going to buddy around together every night, may I call you Mat?"

John knew he was so tired, he was acting silly. He spun around and said "Timber!" as he fell stiff as a tree onto the now-clean mattress. He said in a weary voice, "After all you've done to me, Mat, at least you can hold me while I sleep. Oh, by the way, I apologize for how grossly I treated you." John eased into a deep sleep...but not too deep.

SCENE 14

More painful secrets are told

FOURTEEN

"IT'S WORSE than you think, Coach John." Kaprice lowered her voice and looked around to make sure no one else could hear. "Dale may have HIV. His mom made him do a threesome with her and a customer. The guy would pay more if a child was involved. Dale won't get an HIV test 'cause he doesn't want to know. He says that if he's going to die, he'd rather die without having to worry about it so long."

It was lunchtime on Monday. Kaprice had dropped by John's office in the gym while she was selling ribbons for their first football game. The ribbons were white with gold and purple letters that spelled out: *Tame the Wildcats*! Beside the words, there was a cartoonlike football player cracking a whip and holding a chair.

John was sitting in his small office trying to recover from the horrible weekend. His chair had a rip in the left side with white stuffing hanging out about an inch. He munched on an energy bar that one of his students had tossed him during a PE class. Kaprice in her purple, gold, and white cheerleading uniform sat on a basketball. She had a McDonald's coffee-stirring paddle sticking out of her mouth like a sucker. She moved it from side to side with her tongue, clicking it against her teeth.

"Speaking of threesomes," Kaprice said, "Hope really has pulled trains. That's one thing her parents found out about when they read her notes."

"Dale mentioned that in the meadow," John remembered. "I wondered about that."

"Pulling trains is when a girl lets several guys, well, uh, stand in line by her bed and take turns with her," Kaprice explained shyly. "If there's more than one girl there, and, like, they're all doing it at the same time, it's called a gang bang. Hope was in on those, too."

"I know the vocabulary, but why did Hope get involved in that?"

"Everybody's involved in stuff. The teachers do it, too. I don't mean pull trains, but some of them are having affairs with each other. We students aren't blind and stupid. We know who's doing what with whom. Give me a break!"

Trusting John with more secrets, Kaprice continued, "Mom thinks Bongo Buns and this board member named Viola Jeffries get it on in his office. Every time she comes to see him for an appointment, he gets all nervous and happy, and she's the only one he sees with his door locked. One day they thought Mom was gone to borrow photocopy paper from another school, and Ms. Jeffries came out wearing a different outfit. She had changed clothes in there with Rumpley! You'd have to think they're pretty cozy together, know what I'm sayin'?" Kaprice said, raising her eyebrows.

"It's looned out!" she continued. "I mean they have sex education programs, and they tell us that abstinence is safer than condoms—but they do it! They tell us not to drink—but they do it! They tell us not to do drugs—but they do it! We know several teachers who do drugs! It's all such a big joke. How do they expect us to do better than they're doing? They're teachers!"

John wanted to get off the subject. "Hope is a bright girl," John said. "I'm sorry she has allowed those things to happen to her."

"Hope can't hold her alcohol. The guys can get her polluted really fast. Then they have a free-for-all."

"Does she use protection?"

"Coach, she's polluted when it happens! When you're drinking, you are carefree and careless. When kids get loaded, sex education goes right out the window. That's why sex ed'll never work all that well. Nearly everyone drinks, and alcohol makes you do things that aren't smart."

"Yeah, I know," John replied, feeling guilt shoot through his emotions, remembering the weekend. "Mat taught me that getting drunk is a foolish thing to do."

"Who's Mat?"

"A very stubborn friend," John answered, amusing himself.

Kaprice returned to revealing all. "Hope's had two abortions. Leilani's had one. They took Kyong Suk for one, but the clinic ran a test, and she wasn't pregnant. Her period was late for some other reason."

"Who's they? Who took those girls for abortions?"

"The school nurse and counselor, Platypus and Chester."

"Did their parents know?"

"Heck no! The school's prejudiced against parents. Parents aren't professionals!"

"Oh, great. That again," John moaned as he remembered his first encounter with Rumley. Then something else clicked in John's mind. He had heard the same kind of talk when he was a teenager in the treatment center.

Kaprice kept explaining, "Platypus, Chester, and Rumpley, they think parents who might object to an abortion are all close-minded and don't know what's best for their children. Anyway, that's what my mom says they think, and she sees and hears everything that goes on in the office. She also types the minutes for the school board meetings. She misses nothing.

"Mom says that the three stooges—that's what she calls Rumpley, Platypus, and Chester when she's really mad—violate their own values. They put down people they label as close-minded and intolerant, yet no one could be more close-minded and intolerant than they are. They are totally close-minded and intolerant of what conservative people believe. In their private powwows in Big Rump's office, they make fun of conservative people, and they call them bigots and hypocrites. I'm not lying! It's true! They do that! Mom hears them! She says they are so-o-o arrogant."

"Wait a minute, Kaprice. Are you saying that the school can get a student an abortion without her parents' knowledge, when I know for a fact that it's against school policy to give out medication without parental consent?"

"It's true," Kaprice confirmed. "I needed a Tylenol for a headache once, and Platypus had to get written permission from my mom to give me one. Well, I guess they could give a girl medicine if it was connected to her abortion, but that's about it."

"Who makes up these rules?" John asked as if he were thinking out loud, not actually meaning to ask a teenager.

Kaprice replied anyway. "Our government, I guess." She followed it with, "Coach, you've got to get used to Lincoln High School. Like, baby, our administrators are *with the program!* They like to be on the cutting edge of social reform."

"That's for sure," John agreed.

Kaprice rocked from side to side on the basketball. "They've stopped inviting ministers to speak at assemblies. Now, they have psychologists or social workers. They wouldn't dare invite a minister to speak at a sex ed class. No way. And get this, they changed the name of Christmas holidays to winter holidays. Christmas, they say, is religious and saying the word in school violates the separation of church and state. Mom said they're interpreting the Constitution to guarantee freedom *from* religion instead of freedom *of* religion. Prayer's out—none during morning announcements, none in assemblies, none at football games, none at graduation."

Kaprice continued with her nonstop revelations. "I'm tellin' you, it's weird, Coach. They're always talking about values, and they're kicking faith out of school at the same time. Does that compute?"

She took the McDonald's stir stick out of her mouth and shook it at John. "No, it doesn't. That's demented, if you know what I'm sayin'."

She placed it back in her mouth with a click against her teeth. "I'm just a teenager, and I know better than that. Mom says that to hear them talk in the office, you'd think they are prejudiced against Christian leaders and are in love with professionals from the field of psychology. She doesn't understand it. The ministers used to work with the schools without charging, and the professional therapists charge the school thousands of dollars. I'm telling you, things are cuckoo!"

John moved to the edge of his chair, both elbows on his knees, hands clasped, looking down at the floor.

Kaprice raised her eyebrows. "Can you believe the therapy people would charge thousands of dollars for counseling kids on campus for a month? That's what they charged last year when a kid committed suicide in the bathroom. Mom saw the bill. It was for $10,000. Everything's so stupid now. The ministers are supposed to be the bad guys for some reason, but the professional therapists won't even let you talk to them unless you can stick money in their hands. They're like the video games at the game room. If you don't poke money in them, they don't do a thing. How do you figure?

"Mom says the ministers ought to take additional training, improve their counseling skills, and shut down the commercial counselors. She says that the psychologists are the ones who messed up families in the first place by being down on the Ten Commandments and all, and now they're charging ungodly amounts of money to counsel the dysfunctional families they helped make! No one seems to get it. Is the world crazy or what?"

John barely heard what Kaprice was saying. He was thinking of something she had said earlier. He said, "Wait a minute, Kaprice. Let me get this straight. Mr. Rumley gets all over my case for trying to help Franco Russo with his depression and the school counselor won't counsel Franco, yet they are taking girls to get abortions behind their parents' backs?"

Kaprice rolled slightly forward on the basketball. "They did it behind Brady's back, too! They told Leilani that it might be best not to tell Brady till it was over. Brady's still mad about it. He was the child's father, know what I'm sayin'?"

John leaned back in his chair and stared in silence. He was angry and sad.

"Are you okay, Coach?"

"Yes, I suppose, but we've got to change the subject. If anyone finds out that I was sitting in my office with a cute cheerleader talking about sex, I'll not only be fired, I'll be tarred and feathered."

"No one'll know," she assured as she slipped off the basketball with a thud. Laughing nervously, she flipped her skirt back down to hide her white bloomers. "I'm so coordinated—not! And so-o-o embarrassed!"

She balanced herself again on the ball. "Candace is at my house. Her mother said she could stay till Wednesday. What are you going to do to help Candace since you've promised not to tell? She can't go back to be drooled over by that old sleaze bag."

"I honestly don't know what to do, Kaprice," John admitted painfully. He wanted to avoid the subject for the moment. He fixed his attention on a calendar in his office that featured a picture of him and his football team, but he wasn't seeing it. Kaprice's revealing report on the kids' problems and the school administrators' attitudes was very discouraging and depressing. Candace's being a sex slave had been on his mind every moment of the day. John was feeling overwhelmed and insecure.

He was thinking about how Rumley was right: He wasn't qualified to help. He really didn't know what to do for Candace. His office was cluttered with balls, nets, gloves, bats, paddles, racquets, and wads of paper that had missed the trash can. There were no books in his office about how to counsel kids and their families. *You are merely a PE teacher! That's all you are!...You are merely a PE teacher! That's all you are!...You are merely a PE teacher! That's all you are!* Rumley's words were doing reruns in John's mind. But he thought, *The professionals who are supposed to be qualified aren't doing any better. These kids are going without help.*

John was a weakened man. He felt as if he was drowning in personal failure. He was failing in his career because his boss had him in a headlock. Alcohol had made him look weak and immature to his wife.

A mattress had hassled him for thirty-six hours. A smart-aleck jock had poked fun at him while he was down. To make matters worse, the kids had dumped problems on him that were too big for him to handle.

John knew state law required that child abuse had to be reported. If an adult knew about child abuse and failed to report it, he or she was committing a crime and could be arrested and jailed. John knew Ray and Candace were being abused, and he wasn't reporting either case. Not only was his job in jeopardy, his life was in jeopardy.

Kaprice waved both her palms in front of John's face as if she were cheerleading. "Come back," she said.

Startled, John responded, "Oh, pardon me, Kaprice. I was day-dreaming."

"Penny for your thoughts!" Kaprice said cheerfully, rocking on the basketball, acting as if his private thoughts might be very interesting.

"My thoughts are not for sale," John chuckled, hiding his pain. "What's Terence like?"

"He's wonderful. He's a great Christian guy. He's a member of the student council. He doesn't make good grades—not because he doesn't try. He has, like, a special problem. It's called dyslex, uh…"

"Dyslexia."

"Yeah, that's it. That's the one where numbers and words get jumbled up on their way into your brain or something."

"How about you, Kaprice? How are things with you?"

"I've made my share of mistakes, but basically, I'm okay except for my father." Tears welled up in her eyes. "Gotta go, Coach, or I won't get any of these ribbons sold." Kaprice bolted out of his office. The basketball rolled to John's feet.

He thought about the new information Kaprice had dropped on him. He threw his half-eaten energy bar at the trash can and missed, hitting the wall. Oats and nuts splattered all over the floor.

He picked up the basketball. He put it on his desk, placed his forehead on it, and prayed.

His mind drifted to his own family. Maria had come home from church the day before in a better mood. She was glad they had a mattress again…sad the credit card was maxed…glad they had a working phone again…sad she and John had experienced such an awful weekend…and glad they could make love and make up. John promised Maria that he would repair the damage he had caused to their relationship. Maria promised John that she would try not to hold grudges. John knew he'd have a hard time forgiving himself.

More than ever, John wanted to find time to be alone and think. No time was available. He had classes to teach, football practice to coach, and a booster club meeting to attend that night.

His thoughts were interrupted by a runner who handed him a note and asked, "Hey, Coach! Whatcha got goin' with that basketball?"

"Dam it up, dude!" John said in fun, remembering what Dale had screamed at Ray in the mall parking lot.

John read the note. It was a summons, ordering him to report immediately to the principal's office. Fear swept through John like a heat wave.

John's steps dragged toward Rumley's office. He felt weak and in danger of getting hurt. His weekend had been an emotional disaster, and he knew he wasn't strong enough for another battle with his boss.

Ms. Gibson handed him typed copies of the notes she had written in the meetings with him and Rumley. She said, "Mr. Rumley is requiring that you sign these before they are placed in your file. I typed them as per his orders. Signing your name will mean that you agree with the content."

After reading a few paragraphs, John threw them on her desk and exclaimed, "These are obscene! I'm not about to sign 'em! They make Mr. Rumpley look like Mr. Perfect, and they make me look like an idiot."

Ms. Gibson cut her eyes to Rumley's office door. It was not completely closed. Rumley had heard John call him Rumpley.

John grabbed the pages off her desk and stormed into Rumley's office without permission. He slammed them onto the big desk and stated, "There's no way I'm signing these!"

Rumley said, "Suit yourself, Bright. Your refusal will go into your file as will the fact that you called me Rumpley to my secretary. Do you enjoy committing slow suicide? You've started your swing for strike three!"

Disgusted, John limited his answer to, "I have a class to teach," and he left.

That night, John roboted his way through the booster club meeting. Other members talked about how to build attendance for home games. John couldn't keep his mind off Rumley's attitude problem and how unfair he was. John was kicking himself for calling him Rumpley in Ms. Gibson's office.

John felt that he was trapped on death row, and he couldn't do a thing about it. Building attendance for home games wasn't important to him at the moment. He was preoccupied with the bigger issues of life.

Besides, his heart was in the meadow. The teens were in an emergency meeting there, guys only. They were talking about Candace's problem.

SCENE 15

A molester is challenged

FIFTEEN

SWISH! CLUNK! The blade from Dale's switchblade almost hit Gramps in his left eye as it flew open. Dale ordered, "Don't move a muscle, macho man! You're one twitch away from wearing an eye patch the rest of your life!"

Having laid down a basic ground rule, Dale took on a witch's voice and cackled, "Hi ya, pervert! Ain't your name Lester?"

Dale had Gramps by the neck of his shirt so he couldn't get his eye away from the point of the knife. Two nineteen-year-old dropouts, street people, held the senior citizen by his shoulders from behind. Another stood guard, keeping an eye out for anyone who might interrupt their adventure.

"We'd like to introduce ourselves," Dale told Gramps. "I'm Dale. Brady's on my right. Ray's on my left. The two hoodlums layin' on you from behind have street names. The one on your right is Rat, not as in rodent, but as in rattlesnake! Too bad you don't have time to view his art gallery. He rewards himself with a new tattoo every time he cuts somebody. The other dude's Copperhead. Our lookout is Python. They're from a street gang known as the Reptiles. So, greetings, dirty old man! We're Candace's friends!"

Dale tightened his grip. "We don't care if you know our names and see our faces 'cause, buddy boy, you ain't gonna wanna tell a soul that we came callin'!"

Brady, Dale, and Ray had skipped school for a couple of hours to pay Candace's stepgrandfather a visit when no one else was home. The posse of six found him sitting at a picnic table on the unfinished patio. He was unshaven, wearing an old white T-shirt and old-timey-looking blue jeans. The bottom half of his brown-rimmed glasses were bifocals. His thick unclipped toenails poked out of floppy sandals.

The T-shirt and jeans had tiny burn holes in them from his welding machine and cutting torch. It was the wrong T-shirt at the wrong time—the sight of it added fuel to the boys' fire. The thing was terribly pornographic. On the front of it, there was a cartoon character under a hood welding in such a posture that his welding rod seemed to be coming from between his legs. The caption below it read: *"WHEN WELDERS DO IT, SPARKS FLY!"*

Dale moved his blade from side to side in front of the guilty man's face as if trying to decide which eye to cut out.

The man was so scared that he could barely talk. "Wh... wha...what do you want?" he stuttered. "You can...can have my money and ma...my credit cards. Just...just don't cu...cut me!"

In a witch-sounding voice, Dale cackled, "We don't want your money! We want to cut you, you sleazy child molester! The Bible says, *'The wages of sin is death.'* Maybe we want to help the Bible come true for you! Hee! Hee!"

Gramps desperately tried to hide his sin. "I...I haven't molested any children! I would ne...never do any...anything like that."

Dale got madder. Yanking him closer and poising the knife point an inch from his right eye, Dale growled, "Do you want to wear two eye patches, pervert?! Candace has already told what you've been doin' to her! And that you threatened to kill her! Threaten her again! Mess with her again! And we'll dissect you like we do the frogs in the lab and strangers will throw dirt on top of your dead body!"

"I ha...haven't," he stammered.

Dale planted the point of his knife in the skin of the man's upper cheek. A blood droplet formed around the buried tip.

"I me...mean I won't!" he stuttered. "Ple...please don't cut me!" the man pleaded.

In the witch's voice again, the teen cackled, "I'm already cutting you, man! You bleed really well! I like it! I owe a pile of revenge to the likes of you!"

Brady lightly touched Dale's arm. He knew Dale could be trigger-happy, considering all he'd been through as a child.

Brady said, "Hold that pose, Dale, while I explain things to Gramps."

Then acting like a Wild West lawyer, Brady put a boot up on the bench of the picnic table and leaned his elbow on his leg. He summarized the problem. "You've been having sex with Candace. Candace hasn't told because she doesn't want to mess up her mother's happy marriage. Now, we're putting you in a bind. You're not going to tell anyone—not even Candace—that we came for a visit. And you're going to move out of this house before Candace comes home because you don't want these Reptiles to prune the bottom of your torso! Understand?"

"Y…yes. Yes." He cried, "I'll do as you say!"

"Of course, you will, you demented freak! You'll do what we say because you've got a big problem!" Then even louder, "We're not helpless like Candace!!"

Dale took over, saying, "You're not going to call the police, no matter what we do to you, are you? No, because you don't want the police to get involved, right?"

"R…right. I'll l…leave. L…let me go, and I'll p…pack right now."

Dale pulled the knife back. Drops of blood trickled down Gramps's cheek like tears. Then he pushed it back in the skin again, having another point he wanted to make. He cackled in his witch's voice, "Mess with another kid, Lester the molester, and I'll seriously kill you!"

Dale pulled the knife out again, saying, "You've got two holes now. They look like eyes crying blood over your sins against Candace."

The man was scared half to death. He was sure Dale was going to end up killing him.

Dale had other plans. "Now, Copperhead here is going to apply his skill. He's a tattooist."

Dale locked his arm around Gramps's big balding head, and Copperhead's tattoo needle began to buzz on his cheek, depositing black ink like a fang. Beneath the knife wounds, he tattooed a cartoonlike picture of a mole, wearing prison stripes. The nasty-looking thing was an inch tall.

With Copperhead stinging Gramps's face with his tattoo needle and Brady calling him every filthy name he could think of, Ray was right on cue: "Welcome to the teenage world where we're dealing with adult corruption!"

"Yuck!" Dale exclaimed. "Your breath smells like you've been eatin' cow crap! Poor Candace!"

"All done!" Copperhead snarled. "Oh, no! I forgot to use a clean needle! How unsanitary of me."

Dale let go of the old man's head and said, "Now, Lester the molester, you have a mole on your face. Every time you look in the mirror and see the black mole, remember that the word *molester* begins with m-o-l-e. There's a mole in every molester! Since you've taken the grand out of grandpa, maybe Candace should call you Grandmole. By the way, mole brain, how are you going to explain this tattoo?"

Brady pulled Dale back as if he was pulling a starving dog off a steak.

Ray said to Gramps, "We're going into the house with you now, and you're going to cough up all the phone numbers and addresses of your grown children, just in case we decide to tell the whole world about you. One of the faculty members at our school already knows."

Fear struck Gramps like an electric shock. He knew that faculty members were required by law to report child abuse.

The posse escorted Gramps up the stairs to his room. He nervously fumbled at his pocket-sized spiral notebook. Ray jerked it out of his hand. "Tell me the names! I'll check 'em off."

After they had finished, Ray kept the whole book.

Dale folded his knife, saying, "You've got some packin' to do."

Gramps tried to defend himself, "I guess I'm a sick man."

Dale objected. "No, you're a pathetically selfish man! You are a sinful man! You have taken advantage of a helpless girl in your own son's home. You're lower than the johns who killed my mother."

Then to the other four guys, "Let's get out of here. The very sight of mole brain makes me want to puke!"

As the others started out of the room, Dale spun around. Swish! Clunk! He held his blade up a few feet away from the pitiful-looking man with the bleeding tattoo on his upper right cheek. The startled man flinched. The others watched.

In a calm, but fierce voice, Dale said, "See that blood on the end of my knife. Go ahead, tilt your head back and take aim with your bifocals. It's yours, old man! And I'm sure there's more where this came from. Get your butt out of our town, or we'll be back, and I'll be bringin' *all* the Reptiles with me!"

Dale threw a parting shot. "Don't think I'm bluffing, either! My mom died of AIDS. She was a prostitute. My brother was killed by a gang. I'm holding a big grudge against lowlifes like you. So, perv, don't think I won't gut you like a fish!"

Dale folded his knife as he walked backward toward the door, his eyes fixed on Gramps.

Dale again took a step toward the man but forced himself to stop. "Don't tell Candace we were here. We'll tell her ourselves. We don't want her to get any bad feelings about having narced on you. Is that clear, pervert dude? Good. Now, get a life!"

Dale was surprised that his own hurt had poured out so freely. A morbid thought struck Dale. He walked back over and got nose-to-nose with the shameful man. He hissed in his witch's voice, "If you've been with any women of the streets, Lester the molester, half of them have HIV. Me and Candace are going for tests in six months. If she tests positive, I'll stalk you like a panther—a panther foaming at the mouth with rabies—and I'll get revenge before AIDS kills you. I promise you that, sucker! I'll get you before AIDS does!"

Dale turned and the boys stepped out of the room.

Gramps could hear them clomping down the stairs. He ran to the bathroom to look in the mirror. He didn't like what he saw. The kids had forced him out of denial. He was exposed—a child molester, a dirty old man who had been disciplined by teenagers. The tattoo on his guilty puss would remind him that he was a sleaze. He desperately tried to clean out the ink with soap and water, but the mole wouldn't go away. The kids had forced Gramps to be a fugitive.

He ran back to his room and started packing wildly. He couldn't allow anyone to see his tattoo. He didn't know how to explain it. He was also terrorized that the faculty member who knew about the molestation might report him to the authorities and get him arrested and thrown in jail before he could escape. In two hours, his welding truck was packed, and he was breaking the speed limit to get out of town.

Dale, Brady, and Ray wrote excuses for themselves to get back in class, and Brady and Ray forged their parents' names. Dale didn't have to. He didn't have anyone to sign slips for him. The attendance clerk didn't catch on to the forgeries. She routinely believed the boys.

Brady put Leilani up to giving Candace a note that contained the following message:

Brady, Dale, and Ray had a nice talk with your gramps. He was very ashamed of himself for his actions, and he wasn't mad at you for telling. He decided that the best thing for him to do would be to leave, give you your space, and not come back. Don't worry. He's not going to be telling your mom

anything. He promised. Relax, girl.
It's over.
                    Leilani
                    FAFE

At Kaprice's house that Tuesday evening Candace received a call from her mother for their nightly talk. Mom said, "Guess what? Gramps had to leave. He left a note saying that he was sorry he had to leave so suddenly, but his wife needed him to come home. His note said that it didn't look like he'd be able to get back anytime soon, so he said to hire someone to finish the patio, and I could send him the bill. Isn't he sweet?"

Candace controlled her emotions. She held back her tears because if she cried, she knew her mother would ask why.

She stayed at Kaprice's that night. She needed to regain her composure before returning home. Kaprice was there for Candace.

After giving John time to get home from practice, Brady, Dale, and Ray phoned him on a four-way conference call. They charged it to Rumley's home phone. Maria put her head with John's to listen in. With much bragging and pride, the boys told them about their wild adventure. They told them every little detail. They didn't want them to miss a thing.

Chills played chase up and down John's and Maria's spines as the boys went on and on. John said, "This is like something out of a movie, and you guys pulled it off!"

"Man! We sent the pervert packin'!" Ray announced, plenty proud of their posse. The high schoolers had taken the law into their own hands since the system was allowing Candace to fall through the cracks. Ray said, "Maybe it'll become a fad, and more gangs will begin to act like knights instead of pirates!"

Being against taking the law in one's own hands, John and Maria were extremely uncomfortable with what the guys had done, but were delighted that Candace had a safe place to live...and could go home...and they were off the hook...unless the police found out that John and Maria knew about child abuse and didn't report it.

SCENE 16

*Brady & Leilani
manipulate
John & Maria*

SIXTEEN

"**LET'S GET** our pop-up camper from the storage yard and take it out this weekend. We could go to the meadow," Maria suggested to John with a peck on his lips. "The kids probably wouldn't mind. You could ask Brady."

Maria was responding to a comment John made after they got off the phone with the boys. He said, "Maria, things have got to slow down. More has happened in the last couple of weeks than in my whole life put together. I need to get away and think. You and I need some time alone together."

Maria agreed. "Friday's game is a home game. We could go right after the game."

The next day, John checked with Brady about using the meadow and offered to grill hamburgers for the whole gang on Saturday night. Brady checked with the others. Everyone voted in favor.

Leilani slipped a note into John's mailbox—his shirt pocket.

> Of course, you and maria can spend a romantic weekend in our secret meadow. Brady used to camp out with his family in a pop-up camper. He can pull yours out and set it up after school Friday before the game. Okay? Let us know.
>
> Leilani
> FaFe

Brady hitched up the pop-up on Friday afternoon and pulled it to the mall parking lot. Leilani was waiting for him in her cheerleading uniform, and she climbed on board. She lit up a joint, and they passed it back and forth as they drove.

They met in the parking lot because Brady didn't want to pick her up at her grandparents' house. He didn't think it would be a good idea for them to see him pulling a camper trailer even if Grandypa attended a noncondemning church, felt Rev. Jimmy Falderal, the TV preacher, was too radical, and was not an old fuddy-duddy. Grandypa had heart disease and didn't have long to live. Brady didn't want to take a chance on upsetting the old-timer.

Soon, Brady had set up the camper under the trees at an edge of the meadow.

Leilani lit up another joint and said, "Now, let's warm it up for them."

She kissed Brady lustfully, pressing herself against him in a seductive way, blowing sweet-smelling smoke into his face.

"That was our plan from the beginning," Brady said as he rubbed his lips against hers and pulled up her short skirt.

"Get a condom out of my purse," Leilani urged. "Get one of the new purple ones."

Brady whispered, "No, no, no, Leilani. I don't want to have sex in a sock. I don't want anything between you and me."

Leilani pulled away. "Then, like, get away from me! I'm not having another abortion! I've never felt right about that. I lost some of me at that clinic. This cowgirl will never put her feet in those stirrups again. If you get me pregnant, you're marrying me, cowboy, and we're going to have a little wrangler."

Tearing open a condom package with his teeth, Brady mumbled, "Leilani, I'm not sure marriage is in our stars. After I graduate, I want to go to that party school in Texas—the one *Playnet* talks about—and I don't want to be tied down when I go."

Sex wasn't good for Leilani. She merely went through the motions. Brady had hurt her feelings by telling her that he was planning to ditch her after high school. As Leilani tried to smooth the wrinkles out of her uniform, she tried not to think about his comment. "I wish we could do this without having to be sneaky and without feeling guilty for tricking John and Maria," she said.

"Me, too," Brady agreed. "If we didn't have to be sneaky, we could take our time. I'll be sure we don't leave any evidence behind. I'll lose the condom. You watch for roaches and ashes. I'm sure Coach John and Maria would be ticked off if they found out what we've done."

Leilani had a gift she wanted to leave behind. She left three condoms on the bed—purple, white, and gold—with a note to Maria:

In school colors to celebrate John's big win tonight. But even if he doesn't score on the field, you can score here. Enjoy!

Brady didn't feel as badly as Leilani about having sex and smoking dope in John and Maria's camper. He walked bowlegged toward his truck, imitating a cowboy, as he said, "If we'as married and homesteadin', and John and Maria didn't have a place to have sex and wanted to do it in our covered wagon, we'd shore let 'em. We'd stock it with moonshine and say, 'Pull it out to the back forty and go for it.' Of course, we'd have to sneak up and see if it was rockin' and rollin'."

They both laughed as they stepped into Brady's pickup. In her heart, Leilani wasn't laughing. Brady had mentioned marriage again, and that reminded her of his earlier remark. *Had he really said that he planned to break up with me when he left for college? Surely he wasn't serious...not after what we've been through.*

Hours later, John and Maria arrived in the meadow. Maria saw the condoms and the note before John did. She quickly hid them in her purse. She didn't want John's weekend to be ruined by learning that Platypus was passing out condoms to the students in school colors.

John and Maria lay out on a blanket by a little lazy campfire. Small lanterns hung from the front corners of the camper. Clumps of wildflowers peeked in from the edge of the darkness.

Maria loved the smell of the campfire. She breathed deeply as she listened to the crickets playing their legs like fiddles, birds joining their impromptu concert, and a couple of owls exchanging hoots from time to time.

"Look, Maria, the moon is full," John said. "Do you think I'll turn into a werewolf at midnight?"

"Love nest monster would be more like it."

John didn't respond. His mind had quickly drifted back to the football field. With a sigh, he said, "I needed that win tonight, Maria."

"Congratulations! You've won your first game! The guys did really well. I was proud of them. I was proudest of their coach."

"Thanks. Your support means everything to me...But I'm sure the big win didn't gain me any new ground with Rumley. Did you see him sitting with Mr. Means in the stands?"

"I don't know what Mr. Means looks like. But I didn't even see Mr. Rumley for that matter. I guess I was trying to avoid eye contact with him. Did you notice that Leilani was late for the game?"

"No."

"She didn't come until the end of the first quarter. Her grandparents appeared worried sick. Do you suppose she was out here helping Brady?"

"If she was, knowing them they probably had sex in our pop-up."

Maria didn't like that thought. "John, our teenage friends not only have serious problems at home. They are making big mistakes themselves. We can't just close our eyes to that because we like them so much."

"C'mon, Maria, I'm definitely not blind to the mistakes they make, but I've been trying to put out fires of every other kind. What can I do anyway? If I get on their case about their alcohol, drugs, sex, shoplifting, pornography, rebellion, and whatever else they're into, I'll lose them!"

"I know, John. Don't take me wrong. I'm not blaming you. It's just that these kids need a way to figure out what is good for them and what is self-destructive to them. They don't seem to know. How could they know? Most of them are from dysfunctional families."

"The TV and the movies sure aren't good substitutes for decent parents," John commented. "But even if the students change, they won't stick to their commitments without solid support. Where are they going to find solid support on an ongoing basis?"

There was a moment of silence while both thought of John's question. John offered his thoughts, "Maria, they have corrupt adults in front of them, and they reject the decent adults who try to parent them...like Hope and Terence and Daniel do...or like Leilani. She does things behind her grandparents' backs after they fought for her and took her into their home. You couldn't find a sweeter elderly couple than them. They are in their seventies, and they go to the football games to support her cheerleading."

"I saw them struggling tonight to get up the steps of the bleachers," Maria mentioned.

Then John suggested a change of subject. "Good grief, Maria, my mind needs a rest. Could we talk about the day we met?"

Remembering happy times was refreshing. John and Maria moved into the camper a little after midnight. Both immediately fell asleep.

SCENE 17

John and Maria make love of a divine kind

SEVENTEEN

THE NEXT morning, Maria placed a mint in her mouth and awakened John by slipping a mint into his mouth.

The scene was postcard quality. They could see the green grasses and the wildflowers through the camper's screens. The flowers were accented by shafts of light streaming through the tall trees. They glistened with morning dew. A touch of pine scent freshened the cool, still air. Butterflies flitted, adding every color of the rainbow to the scene.

Birds flew through the serene meadow singing romantic songs to John and Maria while they made love. Husband and wife tenderly expressed their deepest feelings of affection toward each other. They held each other for several minutes in warm embrace.

Maria placed her pillow under her chest and surveyed the beauty of the meadow, framed by the camper window. John did the same.

Maria said in a deep voice, trying to sound biblical, "God created the heaven and the earth, and behold it was very good!"

John smiled and said, "God has a cute accent. He sounds like a Mexican speaking English."

They laughed together.

"That reminds me of something that happened in a biology class I taught last week," John said. "I was starting the chapter on evolution when a redheaded kid popped off and said something like, 'My dad says that when the theory of evolution leaves God out: It's from the gasses through the masses to the atheistic jackasses!'"

John stopped talking to enjoy laughing with Maria. He continued, "The student said his dad told him that he was created by God, and that God loves him so much that He even keeps up with how many hairs are on his red head. 'That makes me feel real good,' the kid said."

"What did you do?" Maria inquired with a searching smile.

"I punted. I'm in a one-more-strike-and-you're-out situation, don't forget. I told the student he could believe whatever meant most to him, but I have orders to teach evolution and nothing but evolution."

Maria became intense. She asked, "What if all the biology teachers succeeded? I mean, really succeeded, and all the high school students suddenly believed in the theory of evolution. Completely believed it, I mean. What then?"

"Then some scientists would be happy."

"Not really, John. There'd be too many suicides."

"Suicides?" John repeated with a puzzled look on his face.

"Yes, suicides! If kids suddenly believed that they came from nowhere, have no decent destiny, and have no noble purpose for being here on earth—other than letting a luckier civilization build a better life on their skeletons someday—there'd be deep depression among kids everywhere. They'd have no great reasons to live and few reasons not to die. No God! No final justice! No heaven!…Suicide rates would go up like crazy!"

Maria paused to think and watch a redbird fly by. She then summed up her feelings. "To me, John, evolutionists—I mean, those who don't believe God had anything to do with creation—are like dogs chasing buses. If a dog catches a bus, what will he do with it? If evolutionists succeed, what will they do with the depressed kids? Or their bodies? It wouldn't be a happy victory!"

John thought a moment and responded, "Maria, the title of the chapter on evolution was so godlike—'Your Source and Resources.' I thought, even while I was in front of my class, that God is our Source, and we have all His resources. Why is that being locked out of the classrooms? What's so bad about that?"

Maria turned on her side to face John, leaned on an elbow, placed a hand on his side, and said, "Promise me you won't get mad if I ask you a question?"

"Okay."

"Why is it being locked out of your life?" Maria asked as sweetly as possible. She added, "I heard a guy who once was an atheist speak at my church, and he said that merely ignoring God turns out the same way as atheism. If a person ends up without God, it really won't matter if it was from atheism or neglect. And you know," she giggled, "you don't want to end up with the atheistic jackasses."

John laughed a little to be courteous, but didn't say anything in response. He just stared out the window at the meadow.

Maria felt inspired to say with passion, "John, God loves you, and God is trusting you!"

"Maria, it's hard for me. The hypocrites really, really get in my way."

"What is it with you and this hypocrite thing?"

John answered, "When my parents had me in the treatment center, the therapists seemed to not respect Christian people. Oh, they didn't often come right out and say that—except sometimes—but you could always tell that they thought that a lot of the kids' problems were a direct result of their parents' faith. Parents and Christian faith—to them that was the root of our problems. I didn't comprehend that fully until Kaprice came by my office this past Monday and explained what Rumley, Platypus, and Chester think of committed Christians. They crucify them by mocking them. Kaprice said the administrators violate their own values. She said they put down people whom they label as close-minded and intolerant, yet no one could be more narrow-minded and intolerant than they are. They are totally close-minded and intolerant of what people with traditional values believe.

"When Kaprice explained that to me, I suddenly realized that her description of their attitude perfectly matched the attitudes of the therapists I had in treatment. I guess since treatment, I've found it hard to want to be identified as a Christian. The people I respected at the treatment center saw Christians as bigots and hypocrites. As a vulnerable teenager, I adopted their attitude toward church people."

Maria asked with a chuckle, "You mean the therapists didn't think being a Christian was professional?"

John replied, "Now that you put it that way, Maria, that is precisely what they thought. Maria, I just realized something. When I was at that particular treatment center, I was receiving therapy from the wrong crowd. I wonder how many therapists are that way...Maybe in one way it's good that most students can't afford professional counselors. They might get one like the ones I got."

Maria returned to the subject, "God loves you, and God is trusting you, John."

"Trusting me? Yeah, right. Trusting someone who has labeled His people as hypocrites? Trusting a drunk? If He's trusting me, He's in big trouble. I'm falling way short."

Maria kept quiet. She wasn't sure what to say next.

John thought about what he had just said and followed it with, "Well, Mat taught me that anything can have a great comeback." John knew Maria had no idea who Mat was. She didn't ask.

He returned to what Maria had said to him. "God is trusting me? I thought trust was my part. Are you saying it goes both ways? Almighty

God, the Creator of the whole universe, is trusting me? My principal doesn't even trust me! Maria, what on earth are you talking about?"

A redbird lit on a twig only ten feet from the camper, tilting its head one way and then another, looking toward John and Maria as if it was listening. Was this a heavenly spectator?

Almost whispering, Maria said, "The Creator of the whole universe is trusting you." Maria began rubbing his back. "You always hear about how you should trust God. Well, John, God is trusting you, too."

"Trusting me for what? I'm just a phys ed major, remember?"

"No problem. The person God trusted to give birth to His only begotten Son was a teenage girl. I'm sure He can trust a good coach."

"Trust me for what?"

"He is trusting you to heal from your past. He is trusting you to get right with Him. He is trusting you to be a good example. He is trusting you to help the students. He is trusting you to pass His love along to others."

John was thirsty for approval. A show of confidence from heaven would be just divine after all he'd been through. He whispered, "Maria, that's a whole new way to think about things."

John didn't say anything for a while. He surveyed the lovely meadow. Maria gave him time to think. Moments passed.

Without prompting, John bowed his head and prayed aloud, "God, I used to know You when I was a child, but I wandered away. So much happened. But You've blessed me anyway, and now I want to do right by You as well. Please forgive me for ignoring You. Please forgive me for all my sins. I promise to be more worthy of Your trust. Amen."

The redbird tilted its head as if it had heard John's prayer.

Maria leaned over and kissed John on the cheek and whispered, "Welcome home!"

John whispered back, "Thanks. I believe I can begin to heal from the pain of my past now. Mat taught me that if I turn to other things besides God, like alcohol or something, to escape past pain, there can be stubborn consequences."

"Who's Mat?"

"No one, really...Maria, when I got drunk, the worst thing was that I became weak in front of you. I know you're attracted to strength, and I wanted to be so strong for you."

Maria replied thoughtfully, "John, no man is strong alone. It's his connection that counts. Now you are networking with Christ, and you'll be strong. I'm sure of that."

"God is my Source, and I have all His resources," John recited, agreeing with her, feeling a bit stronger.

Maria gave it a new twist, "God is our Source, and we are His resources—His resources for helping the students."

"Oh, God, let that be true," John prayed. After a brief silence, he said, "I don't want to offend you, Maria, but I want to go to my own church. You know I'm not Catholic. How about if we worship at our own churches and go to special events at each other's church?"

"That's fine," Maria agreed.

Maria and John lay together for a few more minutes. They silently watched the redbird, each treasuring their happy feelings: Everything is okay at the moment in the meadows of their lives.

SCENE 18

New ideas are born in the meadow

EIGHTEEN

COOKING BREAKFAST was wonderful in the great outdoors. Maria tended the pancakes while John stood guard over the strips of bacon, flipping them too often. They ate at a fold-out picnic table that was made for four people, but more comfortable for two.

After breakfast, John grabbed a clipboard out of the Mustang and removed his whistle from it. He tossed the whistle back into the car. "Maria, we've got to come up with some guidelines for the game of life that will keep our teenage friends from fouling out. Let's think of them now, and we can begin to teach the ideas to the teens here in the meadow."

"We could call our times with them Meadow Meetings," Maria suggested.

"That's perfect."

Maria accepted the clipboard from John, and she wrote at the top of the page: Principles for Meadow Meetings. "Where shall we begin, John?"

He thought a moment and replied, "Write…uh…write…uh… I don't know what to have you write. I just know these kids have to survive in spite of the mistakes of the adults around them and in spite of their own mistakes. They just have to make it, that's all."

"I don't know where to begin, either," Maria confessed.

Both of them were silent. Maria doodled aimlessly on the paper and finally said, "It'll just have to come from the teens. We'll ask them tonight at the cookout."

"I like that. Let's you and I come up with the way the group should be organized."

Maria turned to a clean page. John and Maria joined hands and asked God to help them think and to bless their thoughts.

John said, "I don't want it to look like the group is only for kids who need to recover from terrible situations. I want it to be also for good kids who need support."

Maria understood what he was getting at. "You don't want joining our group to label a kid bad and in need of help."

"Exactly," John confirmed. "I want being seen as a member of our group to be special and good."

"How about naming the group…uh…Survivors Unlimited?"

"No. That title says they've had something awful happen to them or to their families."

"How about...Teenagers for Independence?"

"That sounds political. The name should say that the members are solid thinkers, that they want to have their acts together, that they want to be trusted and respected."

"That they're reasonable people," Maria summarized.

"Yes."

"How about...how about...Teenagers Within Reason?"

"The Teenagers Within Reason Club," John tried the name slowly, enjoying the sound of the words. "But I like the word *wisdom*. Wisdom sounds like God's thoughts. I memorized a Bible verse when I was a child that went this way: 'For the Lord giveth wisdom: out of his mouth cometh knowledge and understanding.' We must use wisdom in the name."

Maria exclaimed, "The Teenagers With Wisdom Club! That's the name, John. You could call it TWW for short."

"That'll work," John agreed.

Maria wrote at the top of the page: Design Concepts for the TWW Club. Beneath it, she wrote: The Purpose of the TWW Club.

John said, "Okay, let me think...Here goes: Our Teenagers With Wisdom Club is a fellowship of teenagers who have formed an oasis of friendship and support in a stressed-out and confused culture. Our purpose is to help each other muscle up and rise above his or her problems, frustrations, or mistakes, and build an invincible life. How's that?"

"Can we add something about Christ?" Maria encouraged. "After all, God is our Source and Resource."

"Write...uh...write this: Our common goal is to be truly independent—to live quality-controlled lives based..."

Maria finished it excitedly, "...based on the wisdom of Christ!"

John had reservations, "Maria, on second thought, that's a little much, isn't it? Adding Christ might make some teenagers not want to join the group. We need to say it in a less obvious way."

"John, I have faith in teenagers. I think they can handle it just fine. They are a lot more open than people suppose. Besides, I think being up front with Christ will help keep the group from drifting away from its purpose. If Christ isn't included as central, where will the kids go for purpose? Where will they find faith, hope, and life after life? Where will teenagers go for wisdom? With so much stuff coming off the Internet now that fogs true truth, I think we need to be clear."

"I want to be clear, Maria, but still I'm not so sure the kids will want to include Christ. I don't think we should press the point."

SCENE 19

The teens
prepare
to help
themselves

NINETEEN

THE COOKOUT that night overflowed with food.

The kids had raided their parents' refrigerators and cabinets and arrived in the meadow loaded down with boxes and bags of chips, dips, candy, cookies, and pretzels. There were hamburgers and steaks, plus hot dogs and all the fixings. A couple of ice chests held soft drinks, and one was filled with beer.

They had come to party!

They had a lot to celebrate. Candace was no longer the target of a pervert, LHS had won its first football game, and their favorite coach and his wife were camping in their secret meadow. Everyone was on a natural high.

Brady strung up a volleyball net between two trees at the edge of the meadow. As he tied the last knot, he hollered at John, "We stole this from the school gym! Hope you don't mind! You can return it for us Monday!"

Hope yelled from where she and Candace were busy putting together the poles of a badminton set. "This came from the gym, too, Coach!" She dropped to one knee and pleaded dramatically, "Please don't turn us in!"

John dodged a Frisbee that barely missed his face. Crisco looked guilty. John retrieved it and turned it over. Sure enough, lettered on the back was: *Property of the athletic department of LHS.*

"Why didn't you guys just bring the whole doggone school?" John snapped, but in a friendly way.

"You wanted Big Rump out here?!" Kaprice shrieked, knowing better.

"On second thought, confine your raids to the athletic department!" John shot back.

Everyone was there except Kyong Suk. Hope got to come because she had earned enough points at the youth home to spend the night with Candace, now that Gramps was gone and Candace could have a girlfriend over again. Terence got permission to spend the night with Daniel.

John and Maria ended up on opposite volleyball teams when captains chose team members. That was great fun.

John was pleased that the kids had set up their ice chest of beer a good distance from his and Maria's pop-up. He saw a few of them drift over to soak up suds. He wished they hadn't brought beer. Maria was also disappointed. She thought, *The kids are risking John's job with that alcohol.* The kids themselves seemed uncomfortable about it, and they didn't drink much.

"Circle 'em up," Brady yelled as if he were the boss of a wagon train. "It's getting dark."

Starters cranked and engines roared to life as drivers turned their trucks around and backed them into a semicircle. The tailgates formed an arc in front of the camper, much like an audience facing a stage. They set out two Tiki torches on each side of John and Maria's pop-up. Fred lit a small campfire in the middle of the circle.

John and Maria's campsite was center stage. The two of them sat in lawn chairs, and the eleven teenagers, plus Crisco, sat on tailgates. From left to right around the small crackling campfire, there were Maria, Kaprice, Leilani and Brady, Dale, Ray and Candace, Terence, Daniel, Fred, Hope, Crisco, Franco, and John. It was a ready-made situation for John and Maria to bring up their idea.

John started the conversation. "You have included Maria and me in your inner circle of friendships. Because of this privilege, we have become very near to you—near enough to know that you are dealing with serious problems and those problems are very real."

Maria joined in. "That means you haven't had to pretend in front of us. You have been yourselves."

"I see you on campus," John said, "and you walk around acting as if everything's cool in your lives in front of other faculty members, but I know better. I know you're struggling with many problems. You've shared them with me."

"John and I want to help you. But as you've already figured out, we don't have the answers you need."

"Maria and I have been talking here in your meadow, and we've both agreed that you are intelligent individuals, and that you can come up with the right answers yourselves."

Ray couldn't hold back his smart remark. "I'm glad some people finally recognize geniuses when they see them!"

Maria spoke through the cheers. "What John and I are leading up to is this. We would like to offer you a challenge. We challenge you to develop a system of helpful principles for surviving problems and avoiding mistakes. These principles will be there for you; but not only you, but also for young people in other schools and communities."

John said, "I once heard of a teenager who left a suicide note that read: 'Being a teenager is harder than being dead.' Kids are hurting everywhere. Maria and I know this. And we've prayed about it. It's clear to us that you need coaching for the game of life."

"But you must learn how to coach yourselves," Maria said earnestly. "You've tried to go to professional therapists for help, but you've not been successful. Their fees are so high that you can't go to them, and most other teenagers can't afford to go to them, either. Besides, more often than not, I fear, their values are outside the foul line anyway. So you young people must counsel yourselves. How will you do that?"

"Maria and I would like to recommend that you organize this group into a club that's based on the principles you design. If this works for you, you can teach kids in other school districts how to organize a club like yours...and how to make it through their problems."

"We have a name!" Maria said excitedly.

"Wait, sweetheart!" John said. "The name we are about to suggest makes it clear that you guys can make sense out of the nonsense you live in or around. It's a name that means you can be smart when so much around you is corrupt...Okay, Maria, go for it."

Maria stood to emphasize the importance of what she was about to say. "How about the Teenagers With Wisdom Club? The TWW Club. We'll have TWW Club meetings here in the meadow! We can call them Meadow Meetings. What do you think?"

"Cool!" Candace said. "This group's already saved my life and exorcised my home."

Maria sat back down, somewhat deflated. She and John weren't trying to encourage gang behavior. *What Brady, Dale, Ray, and the Reptiles did to Candace's stepgrandfather can't necessarily qualify as wise,* she thought.

"I'm in a club," Crisco exclaimed. "I wore my tag to show every-body!"

Ray grabbed the conversation. Ray asked, "That's a good name, except that it sounds too juvenile. What about calling it the Teenagers With Wisdom Society?"

Excited about his idea, Ray asked, "Did you guys see *Dead Poets Society*? The movie, I mean. I didn't agree with all of it, but they were having secret meetings like us. This is great!"

"That works, Ray, if that's what everyone wants," Maria said. "You'll sound mature when you tell others that you are a member of the Teenagers With Wisdom Society. It'll put you above kids who are satisfied to be blown around like pieces of paper in the winds of every trend."

"Yeah," Fred said, "but the wisdom part will sound like you guys are on an ego trip. Like, you think you are already smarter than everyone else."

Dale had an answer for him. "Maybe it will to some at first, but think of the power of the name. Wisdom is having the mind of Christ. Saying teenagers with wisdom is really saying teenagers with the mind of Christ...make that teenagers who are trying to develop the mind of Christ. As far as outsiders are concerned, we'll be saying Teenagers With Wisdom Society. Insiders will know our secret. We are saying Teenagers With Christ Society."

Dale is a mystery to me, John thought. *How can he know Jesus Christ and wisdom are synonymous? Where did he get that kind of training, parented by a prostitute?*

"Whatever," Fred said. "But you ought to call it Students with Wisdom Society. The words *students* and *wisdom* go together better. Anyway, I don't even care. I'm not into what's going on here."

John instantly remembered that Fred was the librarian of the porno videos, and he didn't react to Fred's last comment. John felt the teenager had a lot of growing to do. He sincerely hoped Fred would soon come around. John knew all the kids would have to warm up to the idea of the society.

John supported Fred's contribution: "Students With Wisdom Society. Right! Way to go, Fred! What does everyone else think about it?"

All agreed on the new name...except Fred. He backed out of his own suggestion. "Hold on!" he said. "What about the kids who've dropped out of school but have decided they want to succeed anyway? It's not just people at school who want to make something of themselves. You can't leave out the dropouts who have the guts to keep trying. They're teenagers, but they're not students. They wouldn't feel like going to something for students. You guys had better stick with Teenagers With Wisdom. Except that most of us don't like to be called teenagers. We like the word *teens* better."

"That's sharp of you to see that, Fred," John said. "Teens With Wisdom Society, is that the name you want?"

Everyone decided it was the best name.

John continued, "Maria and I made up a description and purpose that we'd like you to discuss." He handed the clipboard to his wife. "Maria will read it to you."

Maria read with emphasis, "Our Teens With Wisdom Society is a fellowship of teens who have formed an oasis of friendship and support in a stressed-out and confused culture. Our purpose is to help each other muscle up and rise above his or her problems, frustrations, or mistakes, and build an invincible life."

Ray interrupted. "Build an invincible life? How about wording it: to design better lives? We can have designer lives like designer clothes!"

Maria read more, "Our common goal is to be truly independent— to live quality-controlled lives based on the wisdom of Christ."

"Based on the wisdom of Christ?" Fred objected. "Give me a break! Is this turning into a Sunday school class or what? This meadow is our party spot! You are getting carried away!"

"Sounds plenty cool to me," Dale said. "I'm in."

The other teenagers didn't object to including Christ since Dale supported it. But Dale sensed the need to say a few words, "We can't be shy about including Christ. Jesus said, 'Whosoever shall deny me before men, him will I also deny before my Father which is in heaven.' Leaving out Christ would be stupid and cowardly and most definitely shortsighted."

Signs of agreement came from around the circle. Maria slipped her hand into John's hand.

"What we should do this evening," John coached, "is come up with some principles for the TWW Society that would help kids survive anything they go through, any temptations they face."

Maria pitched in, "Some of you are trying to survive the terrible mistakes your parents or other adults have made in your lives. All of you are trying to outlive your own mistakes. Let's develop some principles that will help you make it no matter what's already gone wrong in your life."

"Last time we met here in the meadow," John reminded them, "some of you talked about the mistakes you feel your parents are making. How are you going to survive their mistakes?"

Maria surveyed the circle. "Kaprice, your father deserted you...Leilani, your parents are into drugs and alcohol and haven't been there for you...Fred, you said that your dad and Ray's mom are having an affair...Ray, you're a victim of abuse...Daniel, Terence, you guys have parents who have to know where you are, who you're with, and what you're doing...Brady, you say your parents get in the way...Dale, you don't know who your dad was, and your mom has passed away...Hope, you said your parents want you to be a goody-goody, but you find it too boring...Kyong Suk's not here, but she's in the middle of an angry divorce...Franco and Crisco, your mom puts you guys in awful situations...What is each of you going to do about your relationship with your parents?"

John listened to his wife, but his eyes were on Crisco. An airline tag hung from a large colorful pin pinned on her shirt: *Wings for Kids Club*. The tag was for shipping Crisco from her dad to her mom. *This eight-year-old child is being tossed about like a suitcase,* John thought.

Maria invited the teenagers to do something difficult. She said, "To reach beyond what you believe is wrong with your parents, you need to develop some practical principles that you can believe in...anchor to...live your lives by. Can you think of the right wording for them?"

John put it in coaching terms, "See it like this. We're in the field house at halftime. The game could go either way. Some players on the other team are roughing you up, and the refs aren't noticing. What are you going to do?"

He slipped out of the lawn chair onto one knee as if he were talking to his athletes. "We've got to win anyway! We can't give up! We're in this game to win! We didn't come out here to be losers! Okay?"

He paused to drive home his point. "To be winners, we've got to come up with a game plan, a path to victory in spite of everybody else's mistakes and in spite of your own errors." He looked around the circle, catching the eye of every kid there. "Your game plan will be the principles of life that you design here in your meadow."

Kaprice and Leilani began to chant as John slipped back into his chair. They made a game of it. They took turns making up verses and saying them.

>   We will win!
>   We will win!
>   We ain't givin' in to hell!

Crisco ran over and sat between them and tried to follow them in their chant.

>   We will win!
>   We will win!
>   We do not plan to fail!
>
>   We will win!
>   We will win!
>   Hey! Hey! Ain't that right, Dale?

Dale's magnetic smile spread across his face, and he blushed while everyone else laughed at the cheerleaders' spontaneous chant.

Maria held up the clipboard. "Let's make up some positive statements about surviving your parents' mistakes." She waved her pencil. "I will...what?"

"I will...uh...do right no matter what is wrong with my parents," Fred said, seeming impatient with what they were doing.

"That's good, Fred," Maria affirmed, surprised that he would keep participating.

The battle between good and evil is raging within Fred at this very moment, John thought. *He's going to come around.*

"But could we make a small adjustment?" Maria asked. "Maybe some of what you guys think is wrong with your parents isn't really wrong with them. Later in life, you'll see why they did some things they've done. We could add 'I think,' and it would read this way: I will do right no matter what I think is wrong with my parents. How's that?"

"Add 'or guardians,'" Dale suggested. Leilani and Hope agreed.

"Right," Maria responded. "I will do right no matter what I think is wrong with my parents or guardians."

"It's not a matter of *I think* my dad is wrong for getting it on with Ray's mom," Fred observed. "*I know* he's wrong. It'll never be right. I'll never decide that Dad was right about that."

"Neither will I," Ray agreed.

"But, guys," Maria explained, "there are others here who will change their minds, and saying, 'What I think is wrong with my parents,' includes them, without excluding you."

John said, "You know, as a coach, I tell people in training that they are not responsible for what others do. They are responsible only for what they do...I just don't want you guys to be so immature that you use your parents' mistakes or sins to excuse your own mistakes or sins. So, what about beginning the next principle with: I will be responsible..."

Dale fixed his eyes on the coach and said, "For myself and not try to use my parents' problems to excuse my own stupid sins."

Maria was thrilled by how perfect Dale's first try was. Her pencil sailed across the paper, recording it while it was fresh. "That's super, Dale! I'm adding 'or guardians.'"

John laid his hand on Franco's arm. "We need one for you— your mom has a lousy opinion of you." Then glancing across the circle, "This'll be for you, too, Ray. And maybe for you, Hope. How will we word it?"

Leilani said, "Why don't we just tell it like it is? I will do well even if my parents or guardians have a lousy opinion of me."

"Great," John said as he moved on. "If any of your parents have a favorite child, and you are not that child, you can't let that bench you and make you want to give up."

"Right. How about this?" Kaprice said. "I will succeed even if I'm not favored for success."

"That's wonderful!" Maria could hardly contain her excitement.

John was fascinated. *Earlier today,* he thought, *Maria and I couldn't get a thing on paper. Now it's coming together. This is exciting!*

"Can I say something?" Crisco asked.

"Sure," John answered the little girl.

"What if your mom doesn't care enough to have a favorite child?"

Maria felt her eyes begin to water.

"The saying still works," John explained. "Say it with me, Crisco: I will succeed even if I'm not favored for success. See? The saying can apply to both you and Franco since neither of you is your mom's favorite."

Maria had to work to keep her voice from quivering. She was about to cry over Crisco's lack of a mother-daughter relationship. Pulling herself together, she asked the group, "Who else is in your homes?

Can you think of a principle to help you deal with the animals known as brothers and sisters? Let's see, I will not give a brother or sister—"

"Or significant other's child," Franco interrupted. He explained, "A lot of parents have live-ins now, and we kids have to put up with their brats when it's not even their home. It's our home, and they shouldn't even be there!"

"Yeah!" Crisco said.

"Teenagers are facing so much now," Maria murmured as she made the addition. "I will not give my brothers or sisters or my parent's significant other's children...what?"

"The right to ruin my life or Crisco's life forever!" Franco shouted as he held up a clenched fist to represent power.

Maria exclaimed, "That's it! That's it exactly! Way to go, guys."

"Yea for us!" Crisco shouted.

Everyone was quiet for a while as if the ideas were running dry. John spoke up. "I've thought of another principle that you need. I need it, too: I will not let narrow-minded people—"

Hope interrupted, "Like Bongo Buns!" She burst into laughter.

"Very cute!" John said. He tried to get serious again. "Listen: I will not allow open-minded-but-narrow-minded professionals to judge me to be a wasteland and make me compromise my positive contribution in life."

"Bongo Buns!" Hope shouted once more.

John wanted the kids to see that it wasn't only for him. "How about Franco? Franco said his mom told him that her one-night stands were smarter than he is. Others of you get put down by other authorities. I know what's going on out there in the real world of your futures, and you guys have gotta make it in spite of selfish supervisors. You are going to run up against teachers, college professors, or bosses who are jerks. You can think of it this way: I will not let people in authority to judge me to be a wasteland and make me give up on making my positive contribution in life."

Kaprice's beeper went off. She looked at it and saw her home number on the display. "I've got to go pretty soon. Mom's wanting me to call home."

"You could use my cell phone if the thing hadn't stopped working a few days ago," John said, checking it again to be sure it was still broken. "I haven't had the money to get it fixed."

Maria handed John the clipboard. She crossed the circle and sat down between Ray and Candace. She put her arms around both of them and said, "The two of you need a principle to hold onto. You both have been abused." Then to the others, "Let's think of a way to word it."

John looked at the beautiful living portrait of his wife framed by teenagers. He watched her giving of herself to Ray and Candace. He knew that he had never been more in love with Maria than at that moment. He prayed a silent prayer, *God, I pray that Maria will truly see me as a strong person again. Please help me undo the damage that my sin has done.*

John's thoughts were interrupted by Dale, who was suggesting a principle for Candace and Ray. "I will leave the slime dogs' sins in the past where they belong."

Maria edited his words slightly. "What about substituting *offenders* for *slime dogs*? Is that okay, Dale? And let's add the word *finally* in there."

Maria pulled Ray and Candace closer to her and said, "I will finally leave the sins of offenders in the past where they belong. Good. Say it with me: I will finally leave the sins of offenders in the past where they belong."

Maria slipped off the tailgate, and Ray and Candace scooted back together. Maria took Ray's left hand and placed it in Candace's right hand.

The circle grew quiet until Hope observed thoughtfully, "Have you noticed that each of our principles begins with *I will*? Could we title them our STRONG WILLS? Everyone accuses us of being strong willed."

"Excellent idea!" John said, turning to Leilani. "You need to make up a cheer for this girl. She has made a *classic* suggestion."

Maria retrieved the clipboard and said, "Although Kyong Suk's not here, she's going through a divorce with her parents. She needs a principle to hold onto. Let's make up one as a gift for her."

Kaprice suggested the obvious, "I will make it through the divorce."

"Wait," Candace corrected her, "change that to: I will make it through the storms and disappointments of family life. That way it can include other things that happen to kids in families."

Suddenly, across the meadow came the sound of the whining motor of Kyong Suk's scooter and the beam of her headlamp bouncing everywhere. Maria exclaimed, "Look! Here comes Kyong Suk now! We finished her principle just in time to read it to her."

The scooter raced toward them recklessly, skidding to a rough stop. Kyong Suk screamed, "There's been a murder or something! Leilani, your grandfather's gone crazy or something and shot some people!"

Leilani sat motionless for a second and then ran toward Kyong Suk, "If this is a joke, I will never forgive you!"

"I'm not teasing! He did! He shot some people!"

"Did Grandypa get shot?"

"Yes!"

"Is he alive?! Is he?! Is he?!"

"I don't know!"

Leilani looked up at the black sky and shrieked, "NO-O-O-O!" And she fell into Brady's arms.

Crisco ran to her brother, hugged his waist, and began to cry.

"Where is he?" Leilani cried pitifully as Brady held her.

From the scooter, Kyong Suk said, "The police have him, I think. I don't know. I'm not sure!"

"Grandypa can't go to jail! He's got a bad heart! He'll never live through it! The police can't put Grandypa in jail! They can't!... Grandypa'd never hurt anyone! He doesn't even own a gun! He's the most gentle man in the world. Oh, God! Make this not be true!"

"Leilani! Everybody's looking for you!" Kyong Suk motioned frantically, "Here, jump on my scooter! I can get you out without moving the gate of plants! Coach John, we're going to the police station!"

Speeding through the trees and bushes, Leilani held on tight with one hand and pawed in the denim purse strapped to her shoulder with the other. She found the school-colored condoms. She scattered them through the woods. She found the marijuana and threw it as far as she could. She wanted to pray, and she didn't want anything in her way. She didn't want anything in her possession that was outside the will of God.

SCENE 20

A teenager's world falls apart

TWENTY

WHEN LEILANI saw her grandestmother in the police station, she ran to her screaming, "How bad was Grandpya shot?! Is he going to have a heart attack?! Is he going to live?!"

The gray-haired woman held both of Leilani's hands and said through her own tears, "Yes, he got shot. He's in the emergency room. The police won't let me go there. They want to question me. They think other people are involved."

"Is Grandypa going to die?!"

"They say the bullet only grazed him, and he'll be fine. I haven't seen him yet."

"Did he really shoot somebody?!"

"The police say he was shooting at people. That's all I know. They won't tell me much."

"Did anyone die?"

"They won't tell me," Grandestmother replied. "I tried to get your grandypa to put the abortion behind him and get over it, but he has always stood up for what he believes. He said it was the principle of the thi—"

"What abortion?!" Leilani interrupted. "Whose abortion?! What are you talking about?!"

The old woman fumbled in her pocket and pulled out an envelope addressed to Leilani in her grandpya's handwriting. It was sealed.

Leilani ripped open the envelope but hesitated.

Finally, she unfolded the sheet of paper she found inside. It was a letter written on the stationery of the Continental Association of Retired Individuals where her grandpya served as a volunteer.

To my Princess Leilani from Hawaii,
    Grandestmother found a letter from you to Brady that had fallen between the washer and dryer in the laundry room. You wrote him that you called Dr. Weldon Knight about your spotting. He could not talk to you, but Nurse Ginny Stone said that it was normal, that you did just fine during the abortion, that you

had nothing to worry about. You wrote that you
had tried to contact a Platypus and a Chester
for advice, but it was after school and you
didn't know their home numbers.

Princess, I don't reject you and Brady
for having been sexually active. The world is
shoving sex at kids from every angle. The two
of you remain responsible for your behavior,
but I understand that the pressures are many.
I don't reject you for having an abortion, and I
never want you to hate yourself for it. You were
a little lamb who turned to foreign shepherds
for help. The shepherds isolated you and led you
astray. It was wrong of them not to check with
the shepherds in whose fold you belonged. But it
was as the Bible says of shepherds like them:

"My people have been lost sheep. Their shepherds
have led them astray..." (Jeremiah 50:6, New King
James Version).

"For the shepherds have become dull-hearted,
and have not sought the LORD..." (Jeremiah 10:21,
NKJV).

"...they are shepherds who cannot understand;
they all look to their own way..." (Isaiah 56:11,
NKJV).

Leilani could no longer make out the writing for the tears that
flooded her eyes. She leaned into her grandestmother's hug. "I'm so
sorry," Leilani sobbed. She held the letter up behind her grandestmother's
head and continued to read it as they held each other:

Not knowing better, you listened to the
wrong shepherds and had an abortion. You kids
are too young for the decisions you face these
days, and too many adults have gone haywire.

The tissue they advised you to abort was my great-grandbaby, Princess! Violent people sucked out my great-grandbaby and got rid of him like he was a nothing or her like she was a nobody. They shouldn't have done that. They just have to stop killing people's grandchildren and great-grandchildren.

Leilani held the letter against her grandestmother's back as she began to cry uncontrollably.

Grandestmother said, "I know it hurts, honey. It hurts so bad. It hurts me, too. It'll be okay. Somehow, someway, it'll be okay. Don't think it's all your fault. I love you so much."

After a moment, Leilani was able to read the remainder of Grandypa's letter:

I wish you could have known my world. Things were so much easier for kids then. When I was your age, I was nursing a little fawn to life. I wasn't dealing with alcohol, drugs, sex, crime, gangs, and the wrong crowd. I found the fawn in the woods. I've always loved nature.

I have to stop the guilty shepherds who slipped into my fold and killed one of my sheep and injured you. I wish I could turn to the legal system, but here they will side with the intruding shepherds.

Whatever happens, please know I love you, Princess Leilani from Hawaii, with every inch of my soul.

> *Yours always,*
> *Grandypa*

Leilani went limp in her grandestmother's arms. She groaned with guilt and grief. She said over and over, "I'm so sorry, Grandypa," as if he could hear her.

Other people in the lobby of the police station stared at Grandestmother and Leilani.

Grandestmother tried to console her, "Leilani, your grandypa believed in an old saying that his father told him many, many times: 'If you see a wrong and don't stand against it, you become part of it.' He didn't want to be party to abortion. He says silence is acceptance. Baby, you couldn't have known how strongly he felt."

"Grandestmother, I hid it from you and Grandypa because I respect both of you so much. I didn't want you to know. I didn't want to hurt you. I didn't want you to be disappointed in me."

Leilani sat up and moved to a cold metal folding chair while she said in despair, "Grandpa doesn't have a chance. The world is so weirded out that they'll find him guilty and give him the death sentence." She pulled her knees to her chin, wrapped her arms around her legs, and sobbed.

The door flung open. The coach and everyone from the meadow rushed in. After they'd heard a few details, Grandestmother slipped the letter from Leilani's fingers and motioned for Brady to take it. They made eye contact. Grandestmother dropped her eyes to the letter, again urging him to take it. Brady took it. He read it. He passed it to Kaprice. He moved off to a far corner, and he buried his head in his hands.

Kaprice read the letter with Ray looking over her shoulder. He recited glumly, "Welcome to the world of teenagers, where all is not well."

Kaprice gave the letter to John and Maria before going over and taking Leilani into her arms. Kaprice rocked her friend gently and held her tightly. Brady fled out the door.

John and Maria read the letter and knelt beside the girls, trying to comfort them.

Rumley arrived. The principal grabbed John by the arm and pulled him up and off to the side. He demanded in a loud whisper, "Where were you and the students? People looked everywhere for Leilani!"

"We were talking."

"Where?"

"I can't tell you that."

"None of the parents knew their children were with you! Or where any of you people were! They're madder'n blue blazes! This'll finish you off at Lincoln High School!"

John glared. "You're sick as hell. And I'm not cursing you. You really are as sick as hell itself."

His face fiery red, Rumley lost it and sputtered, "Okay, you rebellious idiot! You have pushed me too far! Your career is in the toilet!!"

John turned away. Rumley, being too mad to deal with anything, bolted out the door.

"If Grandypa doesn't die from being shot, he'll die in jail," Leilani wailed to Maria and Kaprice as John returned to them. "His heart'll never make it."

John gently placed both his hands on Leilani's arms. He said, "Listen to me, sweetheart, I love you, and you know I will tell you the truth. You can make it through this, I promise. I know you can't see how for yourself. You'll just have to let me be *your* cheerleader for a change. I will be with you every step of the way. You will not walk alone. Maria and I will stick by you. And God is with you as well."

Leilani looked into John's eyes and said, "I'm not so sure God is with me. I think He's mad at me."

"God has your baby, and He also wants you. He wants you alive and well…knowing and loving Him right here on this earth. God is your Source and Resource, Leilani. He knows you're a victim of a confused culture, and your abortion was not all your fault. He's not down on you. I know that for sure. A friend named Mat taught me that your value can return even under the most impossible-looking circumstances."

Grandestmother began hyperventilating. An ambulance was called. She was rushed to Memorial Hospital.

SCENE 21

Consequences are everywhere

TWENTY-ONE

WITH FIVE television cameras looking on, twenty-three reporters poised to take notes, and all seats filled with anxious spectators, the black-robed judge took command in the large hollow-sounding courtroom, "The accused will rise. State your full name to the court."

"Sam Summers, your honor," the old man said as he struggled to his feet with the help of his cane, holding his wounded side.

"Is that your full name?"

"Samuel David Summers, sir, is my full name."

The judge stated: "Samuel David Summers, you are charged with two counts of attempted murder, the attempted murders of Dr. Weldon Knight and his nurse, Ms. Ginny Stone. How do you plead?"

I wasn't a danger to anyone, Grandypa thought of saying; but his mouth wouldn't issue the words. With wide eyes, he studied the judge's face. He was bewildered because the charges weren't what he expected. Grandypa said nothing. The courtroom was cold and silent while everyone awaited his reply.

Grandypa was thinking through what he should do. He surveyed the room. He looked at the cameras. He looked at the reporters. He looked at the audience. He adjusted the positions of his cane and legs for better support.

The judge repeated his question, demanding an answer, "Samuel David Summers, how do you plead?!"

Grandypa decided to cooperate with the role the court had prescribed for him. *How many years do I have to lose?* he silently asked himself.

Clearing his throat, he answered the judge in an old and tired voice, "I am not guilty of any attempted murders, sir. If I were guilty of anything of that nature, it would be of trying to perform surgery without medical training. That's because I would have been trying to perform two late abortions on babies that had gotten so large that it would have been necessary to have used a gun instead of the usual instruments of abortion."

Loudly and impatiently, the judge echoed through the courtroom, "Mr. Summers, limit your answer to guilty or not guilty! Do you plead guilty or not guilty?!"

"Not guilty, sir. But the people at the abortion clinic are guilty." Grandypa's voice cracked in grief as he shouted, "They are guilty of abusing my great-grandchild to death! The violent bullies!"

The judge proceeded routinely. "I'm entering your plea of not guilty. Mr. Summers, I advise you to get an attorney. A court date will be set. You will remain in jail unless you can post bond. I'm setting your bond at $125,000 for each offense. Your total bond is $250,000. Mr. Summers, do you understand what I have said?"

"Yes, sir."

"Next case, please," the judge commanded, avoiding looking directly into the TV cameras.

Two policemen grabbed Grandypa by his arms and escorted him slowly through the crowd. A reporter managed to stick a microphone in his face and hurriedly ask, "Do you really want our country to go back to the days of coat hangers?"

While the police officers cleared a path, Grandypa had time to answer, "Don't ask a question like that unless you have the objectivity, as a reporter, to consider the whole picture. Compare the few women killed by coat hangers to the one million grandchildren killed each year by vacuettes, brine water, and brain evacuators. Those instruments rarely miss their targets. If the children were given a choice, don't you think they would choose coat hangers? It would be their only chance to live."

Grandypa leaned heavily on his cane. "Now I have a question for you: How is our country any more civilized than ancient, superstitious cultures? They threw grandbabies to crocodiles to petition their gods to make their lives more convenient. Almost all modern abortions are performed for the same reason. With all of our modern intelligence, we are letting history cycle again. Yet we can stop it. Why don't we? One day an advanced culture will stop it. They will stop the killing, and they will put the abortionists' instruments in museums, representing a violent, self-indulgent culture that will be loathed by museum visitors."

The police officers shoved the old man through the path they had cleared in the crowd as fast as he could move with his cane. The reporters yelled questions at him, but Grandypa was already too far away, hobbling toward his jail cell.

John and Maria had taken Leilani to their apartment because Grandestmother was in the hospital under sedation. Leilani sat in the living room, tears streaming down her pretty face. Suddenly, the TV seized her attention...

> *Normal programming is being interrupted to bring you the following news bulletin. Channel 5 news was the first with an earlier report that a highly respected medical doctor was being stalked at the Women's Clinic. We now are the first to report that a police spokesperson has informed us that this mystery has been solved. Police have in custody an elderly man who objected to a medical procedure performed on a family member by the surgeon and his nurse. The alleged stalker blocked the front door of the clinic with his body and went on a shooting spree. Fortunately, the police moved in quickly, wounding and arresting the alleged shooter.*

The picture moved from a TV news reporter to a video of emergency personnel loading Grandypa on a stretcher and rolling him toward an ambulance. The camera zoomed in for a close-up. He was wearing a blood-stained suit and grimacing with pain. A wrist was handcuffed to the stretcher. His appearance was that of a kind old man rather than a criminal. A policeman was carrying Grandypa's cane like a stick.

> *Police are being congratulated for their quick and efficient response. The alleged stalker was jailed after a brief visit to Memorial Hospital for what a hospital spokesperson described to Channel 5 news as a superficial wound. The alleged gunman, according to a spokesperson for the police department, is Samuel David Summers. Details are sketchy at this time, but stay tuned for updates as we receive them and a complete report on Channel 5's next regular newscast. Now, we return you to scheduled programming already in progress.*

"It's a nightmare! Please, God! Let it be a nightmare!" Leilani screamed. "Someone, please wake me up so this will go away!"

Her cries became more and more hysterical. Her slim body shook violently. After a few minutes, John and Maria rushed her to the emergency room. She was admitted to Memorial Hospital.

John called Brady's house, intending to ask him to come to his girlfriend's side. But Brady's father answered the phone and refused to let John speak to Brady. Instead, he informed John that Brady was busy packing to go and stay with relatives in another state.

Although John asked him to reconsider, Brady's parents refused to let him go to the hospital or even come to the phone. Brady's dad said, "I'm sorry, but I have to think of my own family and my son's welfare at this time. If it weren't for the news coverage that's now getting national attention, he could stay and support Leilani. But the pressure is too great, and I can't let the crush of the media crush my son."

John and Maria remained with Leilani at the hospital throughout the weekend. She was medicated and slept most of the time.

John had plenty of time to think. He thought about what Rumley would do to him Monday, especially after he had told his principal that he was as sick as hell. He figured Rumley couldn't wait to say, "Strike three! You're out!!" John dreaded Rumley's dramatics.

SCENE 22

Coach John is marked for destruction

TWENTY-TWO

DOOMSDAY MORNING came. John asked another PE teacher to watch his class, and he headed straight to the principal's office to get it over with.

Ms. Gibson caught him in the hall and exclaimed in a whisper, "He has Cris 'Platypus' Platt and Evelyn 'Chester' Rouse in there! Buckle your seat belt and give them a ride they won't forget! They'll never change if no one has the guts to stand up to them."

John and Ms. Gibson stepped into her office. She intercommed the principal. "Mr. Rumley, Coach John Bright is here to see you. Shall I send him in?"

"Yes! By all means!" came the reply.

"They are ready for you," Ms. Gibson told John.

John opened the door and walked in, knowing that he might as well be entering a den of hyenas. Ms. Gibson followed, carrying her purse and notepad. She sat in her usual seat off to the side. Rumley had the school nurse and the counselor seated on each side of him behind his hard-rock maple desk. John sat alone in front of the big desk. The scene was cold and had a military feel to it.

Rumley began. "Coach Bright, it's good that you came. I was about to send for you. We have been discussing your inappropriate conduct with students."

John wasn't in a mood to take a lot off anybody. He asked sharply, "What inappropriate conduct?"

"The drinking parties you have been throwing for the kids."

"Drinking parties?"

"We know you have been meeting somewhere in the woods with the students every week. Will you own up to that?"

"We've had meetings. But they were not drinking parties!"

"Are you claiming, Coach Bright, that there was no beer at those gatherings?"

"The kids brought some beer a time or two, but I didn't drink any."

"Did you turn them in?"

"No! I didn't turn them in! You can't win their trust and confidence by siccing the police on them!"

John had said the wrong thing. The trio went for his throat. Evelyn Rouse asked, "Have you been counseling the students about their family problems?"

"Counseling? No. Coaching? Yes. Encouraging? Yes. Being there for them? Yes!!"

Platt stated accusingly, "You've been trying to counsel students while throwing beer parties for them in the woods."

Before John could answer, Rouse pressed, "Wouldn't you agree that there is no difference between counseling and what you've been doing?"

"No, I would not agree. What I've been doing is a heck of a lot better than any counseling the students could get from the treatment center I was at. I know that for sure."

With a gotcha grin opening up across his face, Rumley shot back, "You were in a treatment center?"

John saw his killer teeth and heard his pointed question. He felt almost paralyzed with fear. He knew he had made a major error.

Rumley couldn't have been more pleased at this turn in the conversation. "You were in a treatment center? I don't recall that on your job application. Did you lie when you applied for a coaching position here?"

"No. I left that part blank so we could talk about it in the interview. You must not have noticed the blank. You didn't ask about it."

"I was interviewing several prospective employees during that time. I didn't notice that your application was incomplete. Be that as it may, since we are on the subject of therapy, the school district is under contract with Psychological Services Unlimited in the Professional Building on Frontage Road. We are prepared to give you six sessions with a therapist to see if you can get the help you need. Apparently moving from a college campus to an employment situation has been a difficult adjustment for you. Ms. Gibson will schedule your first appointment if you will cooperate. Will you?"

"Mr. Rumley, I do not need therapy," John replied. "All I've done is try to help some students who have serious personal and family problems."

Rouse cranked up the pressure. "Mr. Rumley has advised us that he has warned you several times not to try to counsel those students. Were you, in fact, counseling them?"

John lost his patience. "Not exactly! I was helping the kids learn how to solve things for themselves! I was—"

"John, that's precisely what counseling is!" Rouse interrupted. "Helping people discover their options and choose the best ones! You've been counseling on a PE degree! And you don't even know the meaning of the word!"

John paused to calm down. Looking directly at Rouse, he said, "The students tell me that you don't take time to talk to them, and that you refer them to places that charge so much they can't afford help. Someone has to be there for these kids."

Rumley said, "I have documentation in your personnel file that proves that I have told you on two separate occasions not to try to counsel students. You are not a professional."

"Not a professional!" John shouted as he jumped to his feet, placing his hands on each side of the desk and bending close to their faces to drive home his points. "You guys are professionals? Well then, I have some questions for you. Did you give Leilani Summers your home phone numbers so she could call if she experienced complications from the abortion? No! Did you do a home study of Leilani's home before you took her to get an abortion behind her grandparents' backs? No! And I've got news for you. Leilani's grandparents would not have rejected her for being pregnant as you narrow-mindedly assumed they would, and they'd have helped her raise their great-grandchild.

"You think you're professional, and everyone who doesn't agree with you is unprofessional. Did you do a psychological test on any member of their family? No! Did you consult with the father to see if Brady wanted his child destroyed? No! Have you set up a fund to help girls who've had abortions behind their parents' backs and suffer complications? No! It falls back on the parents and the grandparents who were left out of the decision to pay for doctor visits, corrective surgery, and medication—the ones you think are too stupid to be involved!

"Did you arrange and pay for after-abortion therapy? No! Did you consult with the baby to see if he or she wanted to die? No! Why not? The child's life was up for grabs!"

John straightened up. With pauses, he said quietly, "Now a child is dead...A doctor and nurse are traumatized...A fine old grandfather, who never committed a crime in his life, is going to die in prison... A sweet old grandmother has been admitted to the hospital, and she's so sedated she looks like a zombie…A girl's life is lying in wreckage at the same hospital…A terrorized boy has been placed in hiding for protection by his parents…You guys call what you did professional? I know better than to do what you've done, and I'm nothing more than a PE teacher, as you make exceedingly clear."

The air was stuffy with anger. Rumley, Platt, and Rouse were speechless. They were totally offended by what they saw as a condemning, judgmental, and holier-than-thou attitude on John's part.

But Platt found his voice, "You can't blame us for what religious bigots do. Leilani's grandfather is so selfish and mixed up that he didn't consider how his actions would hurt his granddaughter. That probably wouldn't have shown up on a psychological test anyway."

"Wrong!" John confronted. "And there you go with your prejudice! So Leilani's grandfather is a narrow-minded, bigoted, religious nut? Don't try to hide behind that! No one is more narrow-minded and shortsighted than you open-minded people are! The likes of you scream against censorship, yet you trash everyone and everything that is not as liberal as you are. You tolerant people are the most intolerant of all!

"Sam Summers lives by a higher law than you do, that's all. He believes school administrators should not arrange to have great-grandchildren killed before they are born. He believes doctors should heal instead of kill. What's so wrong with that?"

"What are we supposed to do?" Rouse probed. "Are we supposed to have psychological tests and home studies done on every student who requests an abortion? That would cost at least $450 per psychological and $1,000 for a home study. And we can't afford to provide post-abortion counseling for every student. That would be no less than $90 per session, and it would require at least three sessions. That's too costly! Besides, the law doesn—"

"Too costly!" John shouted, slapping the shiny desk with a hand. "Too costly!" He pounded the desk again. "What about the child who was killed? And what has it cost a doctor's family? A nurse's family? Leilani's family? Brady's family? What has it cost them?!"

Rumley pushed back from his desk, stood to his feet, and said in his best administrator's voice, "Mr. Platt…Ms. Rouse…I doubt if arguing with a PE teacher is the best use of our time. I will not allow this to proceed further!"

Now at eye level with John, Rumley said slowly and firmly, "STRIKE THREE!"

John was too disgusted to respond.

Suddenly acting casually, Rumley motioned down toward a small framed picture on his big desk, sitting beside a large vase of artificial yellow and red tulips. Picking up the picture, he said, "This is the airplane I'm learning to fly in. Viola Jeffries, from the school board, you'll remember, is teaching me to trust my instruments. At some point, Coach, you must learn the same lesson. You must think of the people in authority over you as fine instruments and learn to trust them. If you learn that lesson from your mistakes here, then perhaps your failure at Lincoln High School will be worth it...and I can feel a little better about all the stress you've caused me."

John just stood there feeling totally grossed out and unamused by Rumley's show-and-tell time.

A smirk appeared on Rumley's face. He returned the picture to its place next to the tulips. "And see this vase of flowers. They're pretty, aren't they? I especially like them because a microphone is hidden in them. Everything you have said has been recorded, and I'll be playing select portions of it to the school board." Rumley turned toward Ms. Gibson and said, "My secretary's notes will serve as a backup to the recording. She is very efficient."

Ms. Gibson didn't look up from her notepad. She was feeling rotten. She didn't know Rumley had bugged his office when she told John to take the trio for a ride that they would never forget.

Turning back to John, Rumley said, "Now, the smoothest way for us to handle your leaving would be for you to quit before I fire you. If you'll resign, I've decided that I'll not forward a bad report on you to the regional office of the Interstate Education Association. Furthermore, if you resign, your employment record will not reflect a firing, and you would not have to appear before the school board for an embarrassing review.

"I promise you, Coach, if you go before the board, *you will be embarrassed*. Board President Robert Means and the three of us will express our concerns, and Ms. Gibson will present her notes. Your attitude problem and your failure to comply with school policy will be confirmed in your own voice when I play selections of the recording made here today. You, sir, are going to testify against yourself."

"No matter how embarrassing it becomes," John vowed, "I will not allow you to force me out in secret. A mentor named Mat taught me that value can be restored." John was surprised that he would think of the mattress at such a stressful time. "I'll go before the school board!"

"It's up to you," Rumley replied. "But don't forget that I tried to be kind and give you a way to save yourself from a lot of embarrassment."

"You are such a nice man, Mr. Rumley!" John said sarcastically. Then he said, "I'm taking a day of sick leave. I am too stressed out to finish the day. I'll be back tomorrow."

"Of course. Take the day off," Rumley said in a condescending way. "Incidentally, the board meeting will not be open to the public. If you turn this into a campaign to save your job, I will personally send a letter against you to every region of the Interstate Education Association. Unfortunately, the first opportunity to hold the board meeting will be two weeks from today due to the business trips of key members...Now if everything is clear and understood, you may be excused."

John left. He felt trashed and insulted. He headed toward the halls, repeating to himself a STRONG WILL from the meadow, "I will not allow open-minded-but-cuckoo-minded professionals to judge me to be a wasteland and make me compromise my positive contribution in life." Then John prayed quietly but sincerely, "Oh, God. Help me make it through this."

The hallway was crowded with noisy students. Bruce passed by and teased, "Hey, Coach, wanna go for another ride on my Ninja?"

"No thanks. I just went on the worst ride of my life," John muttered and disappeared into the crowded hallway.

SCENE 23

Is there a way for Leilani to respect herself again?

TWENTY-THREE

IN THE psych ward at Memorial Hospital, a therapist entered Leilani's room.

He was a distinguished-looking, middle-aged man of medium build, wearing silver-rimmed glasses. His dark hair was accented with gray, and touches of gray highlighted his beard and mustache. Leilani's first impression was that he was a college professor. A name tag on the lapel of his tan blazer included a slogan he taught each and every patient...

> ## DR. CONRAD MOSS, PH.D., L.C.
> There is always hope for those who learn to cope.

"Ms. Summers, I'm Dr. Conrad Moss. I'm your therapist. Your physician explained your situation to me, and he requested that I drop by for a visit. Would you like to talk?"

"Not really."

"You're feeling pretty sad?"

"Yes. Shouldn't I be? I've messed everything up for everybody." Leilani began to weep.

"It seems you are owning all the blame yourself."

"I *am* to blame for everything."

"Are you? May I ask you a question? Did your grandfather have other options?"

The therapist hesitated a moment to accent the question. "Actually, Ms. Summers, he did. Among his options was therapy. If he had come in for therapy, I would have helped him learn to deal with his emotional concerns in nonviolent ways."

"What could you have done? Would you have taught him to care less about me or his great-grandbaby?"

Moss said, "Ms. Summers, you are not to blame, and your grandfather is not to blame. I spoke with the psychologist who saw your grandfather in jail a few hours ago. He told me that he suspects your grandfather is suffering from what is known as organic personality syndrome that may involve or evolve into dementia. That means your grandfather was not responsible for his actions. He's not guilty of doing anything wrong on purpose."

Moss stopped a moment to study Leilani's expression and give her time to think about what he had said before he continued. "To help you understand this, and to help you believe it so conclusively that you can cope with what has happened, I've brought my copy of the primary diagnostic tool used throughout the fields of psychology and psychiatry." He held up a large book with bright capital letters on the cover.

He stepped closer to her bedside. "This volume is published by the professional psychological association of which I am a member. I'll read you what it says about a particular mental syndrome that involves explosive episodes and often affects elderly people."

His eyes scanned the print of the huge book as he held it with both hands. "No, on second thought, I won't trouble you with psychological terminology. I'll just summarize what it says. It says that someone who has the problem to which I'm referring has mental instability, goes into outbursts of aggression or rage, loses contact with appropriate social functioning, is, uh, suspicious and paranoid of normal people. He can be obnoxious, and he can lose his temper beyond what is merited by the negative stimuli present."

Leilani muttered in a monotone voice, "That sounds like the principal of my high school."

Moss let her comment pass. He figured she was merely a typical high school student who liked to complain about administrators, teachers, and cafeteria food.

Moss closed the book with a slight pop and tenderly said, "Leilani, your grandfather—as much as you love the old-timer and as much as he cares for you—has been slowly losing his mind. His values have become confused and distorted. He has been a time bomb ticking his way toward an explosion. The explosion occurred, but it wasn't necessarily his fault or your fault. Do you understand what I'm saying?"

The therapist wasn't sure he was making progress. Leilani's blue eyes were fixed on the bare ceiling, and the look on her face didn't give him any clues.

Leilani spoke slowly, "But I killed his great-grandbaby."

"There wasn't a great-grandbaby. An abortion as early as yours is merely removing tissue that has not yet developed into a baby. You made a decision that as a woman, Leilani, you have the right to make."

Leilani didn't agree. "It was a baby, and the sooner we all own up to that, the sooner I can begin to deal with it. What do you think God thinks about all this?"

"Your Higher Power only wants love for you and for you to feel good about yourself...I study names, and your Hawaiian name means 'heavenly garland.' Your name wears a halo, and your life doesn't wear less. You made a decision that is protected by the laws of our government. Presidents and first ladies have spoken out clearly for a woman's right to choose abortion. A woman's right to choose, might I add, is supported by several religions. Many parents and grandparents in my practice actually encourage their daughters and granddaughters to have abortions.

"Ms. Summers, you, in fact, made a decision that is supported by professionals all over the world. Our nation's most prestigious psychological association, our nation's leading authority on psychological matters, agrees with you that abortion is an appropriate and proper method for dealing with an unwanted pregnancy. Abortions are performed by our culture's most respected medical professionals. Practically everyone agrees that you made a good decision. And your grandfather, at his age and with his disorder, is not responsible for his actions. He is receiving professional services, even as we speak."

Leilani clamped her lips tightly.

The therapist tried to draw her out. "I'd like to know more of your thoughts. Your feelings are of significance to me."

"Are they? Well then, I will tell you my feelings. Grandypa isn't crazy. He is just too good for this screwed-up world. He's, like, sane in an insane society."

Leilani took her eyes off the ceiling and made eye contact with the therapist for the first time. "If I had listened to Grandypa, I wouldn't be here listening to you now. I wouldn't have done drugs. I wouldn't have had sex. I wouldn't have gotten pregnant. For me, personally, my baby was not mere tissue, mister. My baby was Michelle or Michael. My baby is in heaven, not with some kind of Higher Power with no personality. Michelle or Michael is with Jesus Christ. If Grandypa dies over all this junk, I believe he'll be with Jesus Christ, too. Leave! Please!"

"Feelings are neither right nor wrong. They just are," Moss responded routinely. "And I respect your feelings. I know it's hard for you to consider new thoughts at a time like this, but at least think about what I've brought to your attention. I've given you thoughts that can be coping tools for reestablishing your well-being and your ability to thrive."

At the door, he turned and quoted the message on his pin: "'There is always hope for those who learn to cope.' I'll drop back by tomorrow. We will move only at the rate at which you are comfortable."

As he disappeared from her doorway, Leilani yelled after him, "What if your mother had coped by aborting you?!"

The therapist didn't care to answer her anger-laden question. She heard his shoes squeaking against the waxed floor, glad for the distance that every step put between her and him. Leilani cried alone.

Moss resented her insult. Rather than return to her room, he decided to blow off steam to the nurses. He dropped by the nurses' station to do his charting and said, "That patient in room 403 has an attitude problem. Have you ever noticed that the word *ass* is in the middle of sassy?"

He opened his big book, preparing to entertain the nurses with an inside joke. It was shift change time, and two shifts of nurses were present. "I have found the correct diagnosis for that girl's grandfather. It says right here, 'Elderly person who manifests puritanical inappropriateness: rule out bigoted old fart.' But we can't rule it out, now can we?"

One nurse laughed. Five others didn't. Moss defended himself. "Joking a little prevents us from becoming as crazy as the patients we serve. It's a way I've learned to cope."

No expressions changed. They didn't want to agree or disagree with a superior. Moss became more agitated and talked down to them. "You nurses are new at this. I'm not. I've been doing therapy for two decades, and I've learned to be realistically cynical in cases like this. The girl's grandfather has thoroughly brainwashed her, and it would take me two years of therapy to deprogram her from his antiquated values.

"As for Pops, the prognosis is grim. He has dementia, organicity, bigoted values, episodes of rage, and only some psychic knows what else. Dr. Death would serve him better than a therapist. I'm not for capital punishment; but if he were to choose euthanasia, I think society should not interfere with his right to choose. If not euthanasia, then prison. Prison would at least prevent him from endangering other members of society."

Returning to his professional manner, Moss barked an order to the nursing staff. "Monitor Ms. Summers closely. Her shame-based orientation makes her a prime candidate for suicidal ideations—thoughts she is perfectly capable of acting on. I'll see her again tomorrow but don't expect miracles. My only purpose at this point is to stabilize her."

Meanwhile, a janitor, pushing his utility cart, complete with a large, green, plastic, trash can and an array of cleaning products and supplies, entered Leilani's room. He banged things around and sprayed too much disinfectant. He was wearing a pale green, wrinkles-pressed-in uniform with **MEMORIAL HOSPITAL** stenciled across the pocket in black ink that had faded to gray. Leilani ignored him as much as she could until he began to count backward.

"Five, four, three, two, one—five pots of flowers. It seems that a lot of people care for you. Pardon me for counting backward, ma'am," the janitor said as he smiled and approached Leilani's bed. "I learned to count in the ghetto from watching the numbers count down in an old microwave while it was heatin' up pickin's from garbage cans."

"Dale!!" Leilani exclaimed.

"Shhh," he pressed a finger to his lips.

Leilani whispered, "What on earth are you doing acting like a janitor?" To her surprise, she heard a laugh bubbling up inside her and spilling out. She was happy to find that there was a laugh still in her life.

Dale answered, "The jerks wouldn't let me come up to the psycho floor 'cause, like, I wasn't on their precious visitors' list. Well in this janitor uniform, I slipped right by their ditsy rent-a-cop. Do you like my threads? No? Well, I could have disguised myself as a nurse and given you a few shots in your hips while we talked."

"No, I'd prefer you clean my room."

"How are you, Leilani?"

"Where are your street clothes, Dale?"

Dale pointed to his cart.

"In the trash can?"

"They're in a plastic bag, folded nicely. Nothing will get on them. Leilani, how are you?"

"Terrible, Dale! Terrible! I've messed up worse than anybody in the history of the world! I'll never be able to forgive myself for this."

"Forgiving is God's thing. That's what He likes to do more than anything else. And He can help *you* forgive yourself, too."

"God can't forgive all this!" Leilani said, scooting up in bed. "Besides, God's mad at me. I know He is."

"Not. Ever heard of the apostle Paul? He was that most excellent Bible dude. He was worse than you before God got hold of his life."

"He couldn't have messed up this bad," Leilani said, hoping she was wrong.

"Worse. How many innocents did you abort?"

"One."

"The apostle Paul aborted thousands. He was a soldier, and he was in charge of killing new Christians. Although he had killed innocents, when he got his life right with God, God forgave him so totally that He let him write a lot of the Bible, and He let him become one of the best-known ministers of all times."

Someone walked down the hall. Dale busied himself sweeping under Leilani's bed. He saw a doorknob-hanger sign that read: **DO NOT DISTURB. DOCTOR WITH PATIENT**. He held it up for Leilani to read and then hung it outside the door.

"Dale, you're the coolest!" she said, smiling at his antics.

Dale returned to her bed, acting doctorish in his greens. "How might I help you, patient dude, Miss Summers? Tell me all your problems. Sorry about the bed. I requested a couch."

Leilani laughed but stopped abruptly. She felt guilty laughing while Grandestmother was in the hospital and Grandypa was in jail. At the same time though, it felt good to laugh again.

Dale shed the doctor image and laid his hand on her arm. He smiled his beautiful smile, saying, "Leilani, God's not out to get you. God's out to forgive you. He can and will forgive you for everything like He did Paul. Picture Jesus Christ on the cross."

Dale looked out the window as if the crucifixion were happening right then. "There He is, high and lifted up—dying. He is being aborted by a weirded-out system and gang violence. Leilani, He asked God to forgive them even while they were aborting Him. He prayed, 'Father, forgive them for they know not what they do.' Isn't that amazing? Could you echo Christ's prayer right now? Would you pray, 'God, forgive me for I didn't fully know what I was doing'?"

Leilani teared up. She bowed her head, hugged an extra pillow, and prayed aloud, "Please forgive me, God. I didn't realize...Wait, God. That's not true. I did realize, I did know what I was doing, but please, please forgive me for this terrible wrong that I have done and for all my sins, especially my sin of leaving You out of my life. I pray that You will come into my life. I want to be Your daughter, and I'm ready to live like I am Your daughter.

"Oh, God, help Grandypa, help Grandestmother, and help the families of the doctor and nurse. And, God, if You're not mad at me for real, thanks. I need a super powerful friend—not a Higher Power like the doctor guy said. I need no less than almighty God in my life right now."

Dale took Leilani's hand, held it with both of his, and followed her in prayer. "And, God, I thank You for forgiving Leilani. At this moment, she is before You not guilty. You took her guilt upon Yourself. Thank You for doing for us what we can't do for ourselves."

Leilani looked up into Dale's dark brown eyes, moist with tears. "I am forgiven. I really am! This is totally strange. In the middle of the mess I've made, I know God has forgiven me. He doesn't reject me. He's not mad at me. He's going to help me get through this. To tell you the truth, Dale, I was trying to figure out how to commit suicide."

"Offing yourself is way lame. It's a giant mistake that's impossible to correct," Dale replied. "Just keep writing the story of your life, and it won't be a tragedy. It'll be a success story."

"Dale, I didn't know you were a Christian," Leilani said. Then catching on, "Whoa! You've always been different! You're the one who stood up for making Christ a part of our STRONG WILLS. Okay. Okay. Now I am getting a clear picture of you. You don't drink with us. You don't do pot. You don't cuss. You don't mess with girls. You're not full of yourself. You care about people. You live like a Christian. Wait! How did you cut Candace's gramps's face with your switchblade if you're a Christian?"

The subject had suddenly become painful. Dale wiped an insecure look off his face and then responded, "To tell you the truth, I didn't plan to, and maybe I shouldn't have done it. But all at once he represented everything I hate about corrupt men…and I lost it. I might have killed him if Brady and Ray hadn't been there. The scene scares me when I look back on it. I've realized that I've got to do something about all my wounds, all the anger I carry around with me."

"Dale, I'm sure God can help you. Oh, listen to me—I'm counseling you. Ha!…Hey, Dale, you're from the streets. How come you know so much about God?"

"I read the Bible while I listened to my mom fake moans and groans for the johns. I'd listen to her, and I'd pray that God would help me climb out of the mess we were in. I used to pray, 'God, help me heal my limb on my family tree.'"

A big smile spread across Dale's face. "Then there were these minister dudes who were in and out of my life across the years. They were missionaries to the inner city from Campus Life, Teen Challenge, World Impact, people from the church Hope's dad pastors, and others. Most street people and hoodlums wouldn't listen to them, but I would. So we hung out together, and I learned a lot from them. Also, I have an uncle—Uncle Buddy—the director of a counseling clinic. Mom used to let me and my brother stay with him sometimes. I loved the guy and listened to everything he said.

"He tried to get custody of us, but Mom never would give in. After my brother was killed and my mom died, I didn't go to him because I didn't want to leave you guys. Right now, I'm torn. I want a home more than anything. Like I told Hope in the meadow, I'd trade my new truck for it. But I don't want to leave. You guys are my family— the only family I have left. I do have a family, but I'm without a home."

Still holding her hand, he continued, "Leilani, you've got to understand. I've been through most everything anybody could go through. My mom's had five abortions. I used to lie in my bed and listen to her cry in the next room, and I'd try to figure out how she could deal with it."

Dale thought a moment. "You know, this whole abortion thing has made its way from the back alleys where I live to the huge hospitals, and now doctors are making millions off of it. Their front people are guys like Platypus and Chester—people who don't get the big bucks. But I guess their payoff is just getting the attention and approval of the big-time professionals...and feeling like they're important—"

Leilani interrupted with her own thoughts. "Oh, Dale, could I tell you my baby's names? If it was a girl, she was Michelle. If it was a boy, he was Michael. Brady told me he liked those names, too."

"Where is your baby now?"

"With Christ."

"Leilani, do you know what it means when the Bible says that Jesus Christ is our intercessor?"

"No."

"It means that Jesus favors us when we're right with Him, and He takes messages to God on our behalf. Does that make sense to you?"

"Yes."

"Well since Jesus Christ is your intercessor, and since your baby is with Him, don't you believe that Jesus could carry a message to Michelle or Michael for you? Don't you think He could intercede for you with your baby?"

Smiling at the thought, Leilani agreed. "For real...Jesus would do that for me, wouldn't He?"

"He would for real, Leilani. Would you like to pray again and tell Jesus the message you want Him to relay to your son or your daughter?"

Tears filled Leilani's eyes. She took her hand from Dale's and hugged her pillow tightly. She wept and prayed, "Jesus, apologize to Michelle or Michael for me. Tell my baby I'm so very, very sorry."

An attack of grief interrupted her prayer. After crying a moment, she continued, "Tell my baby that I was trapped and confused and didn't know what else to do...and the adults around me seemed to think abortion was the best thing to do. Like Grandypa wrote in his letter, I listened to the wrong shepherds."

Tears of healing flowed from her eyes as if flowing from deep blue springs. "Tell my baby that I would never do that again. Tell my baby to wait for me in heaven. One day there'll be a family reunion. I promise. I am going to live a clean life so I can go to heaven, too, and be there with the two of you."

Leilani sat up and embraced Dale. They wept together.

After a few seconds, Dale whispered, "How do you feel?"

Leilani replied through sniffles, "I feel like Michelle or Michael has forgiven me. I feel like a million pounds have been pulled off my heart. I feel like everything's okay between me and my baby now."

Dale kissed her forehead. "And guess who's the best baby-sitter in the whole universe?"

"Jesus Christ," Leilani said as sadness gave way to joy. She turned to hunt a tissue to wipe her face.

Dale teased, "You're gonna have to get some makeup on that head, girl!"

"I'm sorry. I know I look frightening. I'd hate for Brady to see me looking like this...Oh, I wouldn't care. I wish Brady was here. I love him so much."

"Leilani, Jesus is holding your baby, and together they are saying, 'You are forgiven, and all is well.'...Now, you've got to deal with Grandypa. Can I just tell you something about that?"

Leilani blew her nose. In a nasal tone, she answered. "Go for it, doc. You're doing pretty good so far."

"God's favorite thing is to bring good out of bad, Leilani. I learned that from the streets. If all this hadn't happened, your grandypa would have died one day, and only his family would have noticed. His death wouldn't have meant anything to anybody else. That's changed now. Because he has been brave and stood tall for his values, everyone will realize that the decision for an abortion affects other family members.

"A girl is not an island, alone in a big sea. She is in a network of people who care for her and relate to her. They are the ones who take care of her after the abortion, not the people at the abortion clinic, not Platypus, not Chester, not Rumpley. And, Leilani, the world must be reminded that fetuses are babies, grandbabies, great-grandbabies, nephews, nieces, cousins, brothers, sisters, and they have fathers who should be given a say, too."

Gently stroking her cheek, Dale said, "If Grandypa dies of a heart attack or something, he'll be checking out with meaning. I know you'll continue to worry and blame yourself, but at least know that he has become a man of worldwide influence. He is making a statement. If fetuses really are babies and babies really are people, is it wrong to bear arms to stop the killing of our country's people? That was the question I asked at the end of my debate in speech class last year."

Footsteps sounded outside the door. Dale backed away from Leilani, grabbed his cart, and started for the door. A nurse met him with the **DO NOT DISTURB** sign in her hand.

Dale wondered if he was caught. Their eyes met. Dale studied her expression for a clue.

"Doctors never take down their signs," she complained. "You'll need to step out for a moment while I take my patient's vitals. You can finish cleaning when I'm through."

Out in the hall, Dale felt on display. To avoid someone discovering that he wasn't a janitor, he began cleaning a nearby water fountain.

Even with a blood pressure cuff putting the squeeze on her arm, Leilani couldn't hide her newfound peace. The nurse seemed trustworthy enough—the plump and happy type. Leilani confided in her dreamily, "Nurse, an 'angel' came to my room and visited me. He and I went to God together, and God forgave me! And my baby forgave me! And I feel lighthearted and wonderful. I know I'm okay now. I just want to go home."

As the nurse picked up Leilani's chart, she seemed unimpressed with improvement that was too much, too soon.

"Leilani…let me see…Summers, is it?" The nurse's eyes searched Leilani's chart, then she teased, "The only person I saw enter your room was the janitor. He's handsome as an angel—but an angel with tattoos? I don't think so! I'll note your comments in your chart, and I'll notify your therapist. That would be Dr. Conrad Moss. I'm sure he'll want to get back with you."

The nurse held the clipboard so that only she could see the chart. Beside the time and date, she wrote, "Patient reports a psychotic episode," and scribbled a few notes.

Alarmed, Leilani realized she had misjudged the nurse.

The nurse left, taking Leilani's chart with her. She made a passing comment to the janitor on her way out the door. "Better do a good job in there. The patient thinks you're an angel. Enjoy!"

When Dale returned, Leilani exclaimed, "Quick! Close the door! You've got to get me out of here! I told her that I was well, and she didn't act like she believed me. They're gonna think I've flipped out completely when that nurse tells that therapist guy that I think I had an out-of-the-body experience or something!"

Dale said, "Sneak you outta here? That's right down my alley. Step into my big garbage can, madam."

Leilani jumped out of bed and grabbed her clothes. She stuffed them into the stinking trash. Then she stepped into the container and crouched down. Dale covered her with dirty paper towels.

As Dale pushed his equipment into the hall, he closed the door and hung the sign again: **DO NOT DISTURB. DOCTOR WITH PATIENT.** He stopped at the nurses' station and emptied its trash on top of Leilani. He was trying to act as normal as possible. Then he took the elevator to the third floor where he wheeled his cart into Grandestmother's room and over to the edge of her bed. He scraped the trash back and whispered to Leilani, "You can come up for air now."

She rose slowly until she could see her grandestmother looking back at her with wide eyes. Dale urged, "Quick. Say what you want. We gotta make a getaway."

Grandestmother's medications had worn off, and she was alert. Leilani stood all the way up in the trash can, leaned over, and embraced her grandestmother tightly. A dirty paper towel stuck to her shoulder. Dale grabbed it and returned it to the trash can.

Leilani loosened her hug to see Grandestmother's face. "Grandestmother, Coach John and Maria have been taking care of me… I love you so much, and I am very sorry. Can you ever forgive me? Pleeease."

Grandestmother's chin trembled, "Things are very bad right now. Your grandypa is in jail for attempted murder, and we have our share of huge hospital bills to think about."

Pulling back to talk heart-to-heart, Leilani said, "I prayed, Grandestmother. God has forgiven me. I asked Christ to talk to my baby for me, and my baby has forgiven me. Grandestmother, I'm right with God, and I'm right with my baby. I want to make things right with you and Grandypa. I'll do whatever I can. And I'll try my best to never do anything that would disappoint you again! I promise! I promise! I know Brady will want to apologize, too!"

Racing to a different subject, Leilani said, "Grandestmother, you've got to get me out of here. Those people in the psych ward, they're like wacko! I mean, totally outta their trees! They're trying to tell me that wrong is right so I'll feel better about what I've done. For real, Grandestmother, this therapist guy told me that it wasn't wrong for me to have an abortion. It was that everybody's-doing-it thing.

"And he told me that Grandypa shouldn't be blamed for trying to kill those people because he has become too sick in the head to be held responsible, according to some huge book he had. Get me out, please!"

Grandestmother had heard enough. She reached for a pen and paper from her nightstand and wrote: *I request the release of my granddaughter, Leilani Summers, from Memorial Hospital to the custody of John and Maria Bright.* She signed it, dated it, and handed it to Leilani.

Dale put a hand on Leilani's shoulder, indicating that it was time to hide again. She kissed Grandestmother on the cheek and sank into the trash. Dale covered her up and rolled his cargo to the elevator.

Inside the elevator, Dale kept his thumb on the close-door button while Leilani changed clothes. Leilani did the same for him. Dale dug his street clothes out of the bottom of the trash can, took them out of the plastic bag, and changed into them. Then Leilani pushed the button for the main lobby.

SCENE 24

Dale challenges a doctor for Leilani's freedom

TWENTY-FOUR

DALE AND Leilani found a pay phone. They called John and Maria, and asked them to hurry to the hospital. Dale slammed the phone into its cradle and headed for the business office.

In a businesslike manner, he announced, "I have come to check Leilani Summers out of the psych ward." He presented Grandestmother's note.

The clerk studied the kids—a guy dressed like someone from the streets and one of their patients. *Do these kids think I'm crazy?* the clerk wondered. *What are they trying to pull over on me?* She called the psych ward to check things out.

Seconds later, two male nurses showed up to escort Leilani back to her room. Dale stepped in front of her and took on a karate pose. "Hai! Ya! Touch her, and you're history!"

One of the nurses told a clerk, "Page the supervisor of the Department of Psychology."

A distinguished-appearing psychologist wearing a short-sleeved white shirt with a black tie came in. He was carrying a white lab coat over his arm. He read Grandestmother's note. He gave Dale a look of utter contempt. Mimicking the accent of an Englishman, he sneered, "Well, this is just bloody great!" He followed that with an insulting, "Are you John or Maria Bright?"

"Obviously not!" Dale smarted back. "But I've called them, and they're on their way. I want the paperwork started."

"It doesn't matter to me what you want, son. You are not in control here. I can declare this patient suicidal or homicidal and keep her confined to this hospital. There won't be a thing either of you can do about that."

Dale didn't answer. He was running the doctor's familiar words back and forth through his mind. *Just bloody great!* The words made his skin crawl and seemed strangely familiar. He studied the doctor's bushy eyebrows, the deep dimple in his chin, and all at once, Dale recognized him!

Dale's anger rose to an instant boil, but he hid his feelings and acted as if nothing was wrong. He had learned to be a talented actor on the streets where doing con jobs is the way to survive. So he merely put his Scud missile on the launching pad, waiting for the right time to push the red launch button.

In the meantime, Dale harnessed the energy from his anger to go for the doctor's throat. "Declaring her homicidal or suicidal would make you a scum dog 'cause you can see Leilani is standing here sane. Besides, her family's so crazy, they shoot doctors who make them mad. Have you seen TV news lately?"

Dale turned to Leilani. "Did your grandpa have any brothers?"

Leilani didn't answer. She could tell Dale wasn't really asking. He was driving home a point.

The doctor replied, "The two of you wait here. I need to verify this note."

As he walked toward the door, he said to the office personnel, "I'm going to Mrs. Summers's room and see what the patient's grandmother has to say about this. Don't allow her to leave."

As he passed a clerk, he shielded his mouth with a hand and said something to her. She picked up the phone.

Soon the lobby of the business office began to fill with people. Leilani's physician came in. Dr. Conrad Moss, her therapist, and the plump nurse showed up. Other hospital personnel came in to be sure they didn't miss out on anything exciting. The male nurses and the clerk were still there. The physician, therapist, and nurse tried to talk Leilani out of leaving the hospital.

After a long fifteen minutes, the supervisor of the psychology department returned and took over. He began speaking to everyone in the lobby in an irritated and authoritative manner. "Mrs. Summers, Leilani Summers's grandmother, is too traumatized to make decent, pardon me, uh, appropriate decisions. Therefore if the young lady leaves this hospital, I'm declaring it an AMA withdrawal. That means that the patient is being removed from the hospital against medical advice."

Then looking directly at Dale, "It means her grandparents' insurance may not pay for her expenses here at the hospital, and they will have to pay them themselves. You don't know what you are doing, young man. Therapy is very expensive, and her grandparents will be responsible for thousands of dollars. You are in over your head!"

The staff seemed impressed by how well their supervisor was handling the crisis. Dr. Conrad Moss especially enjoyed watching his boss deal with what he labeled as sociopathic behavior on Dale's part.

But Dale had a lot to say, and he wasn't bashful about saying it. "Doctor, when I was a little kid, the courts used to put my mom on probation and require her to go to family therapy.

"I once heard a therapist say that if you have a belief system that's destroying you like a bad taproot, and you change it, and your new root system stops the pain and helps you cope, and your changes stick, you are well. Would you agree with that?"

"As far as it goes."

"Then, Doctor, Leilani is well, and you should not declare her AME, or whatever the letters were."

"AMA," the doctor corrected impatiently.

Dale pressed on, "I have more questions for you, sir."

Through the corner of his eye, Dale saw John and Maria enter the room. Leilani went to them and stood between them. She welcomed Maria's arm around her waist. John and Maria stayed in the background.

Dale continued his questioning. "You are the main doctor here, right?"

"Yes. I am chairman for the Department of Psychology."

"You're, like, the boss over all these people, right?"

"Everyone except the clerks," he answered proudly.

On the surface, the supervising psychologist seemed confident and competent. But actually, he was out of patience and was disgusted by the scene. Under the watchful eyes of his staff, he was being forced to match wits with what he considered to be a street punk. He was being forced to use his professional listening and communication skills to cope with a sensitive crisis in front of his colleagues. He resented being put on the spot professionally by a smart-aleck kid. The veins in the doctor's temples pounded as if they might break right out of his skin. He licked his thick lips and fiddled with his beeper.

Dale was nearly ready to launch his Scud missile. His finger hovered over the red button. "Okay, here's my final question: What would you do if one of your doctors went down to the ghetto and hired a prostitute and her ten-year-old son to have sex with him?"

The doctor cleared his throat in a nervous way. He was suddenly shaken up inside. *Why would the kid ask me a question like that?* he wondered to himself. *Could he possibly know something?* He tried to dodge the question by bluntly replying, "Your question is not relevant. None of my staff members would do that."

"But what if one did? What if one was that corrupt?" Dale persisted, closing in for the kill.

"It would be handled very professionally," the doctor said. "I would order a hearing before the ethics committee of the hospital, and any action taken would be based on their findings."

Dale pressed the red button. His Scud missile ripped off the launch pad and exploded with revenge. He pointed his finger in the doctor's face and shouted at him, "Behold! You are the doctor! I was the kid! You low-life hypocrite! YOU are that corrupt! You molested me when I was ten years old! And now you stand there calling Leilani sick?! Make her grandparents pay for her lame therapy, and I will bring the Reptiles to deal with you! The Reptiles are a street gang that you can be sure hates the likes of you!"

The doctor turned ashen white. His heart pounded faster than a drummer's solo at a rock concert. He recoiled from Dale. The truth had him feeling naked in front of his staff. Nervously, he put on his lab coat to cover himself, fumbling in the process.

Dale was very pleased that he had succeeded in exposing the man for what he was. The Bible story of the prophet Nathan's meeting with King David had always intrigued Dale. Now he had done what Nathan did. He set someone up to be condemned by his own judgment, and it actually worked.

The doctor turned away from his accuser. In a desperate attempt to discount Dale, he told his staff, "You can't take what he says seriously. He's a druggie from the streets! Hallucinations hit these people without warning!"

"Flashbacks to the truth!" Dale edited.

The doctor ignored Dale's comment and ordered the clerk, "Just release Miss Summers without declaring it an AMA. Who cares who pays the bills?...Just so we get paid."

Dale wouldn't let up. "Doctor Pervert, I once asked my mom how you could do what you did, and I'll never forget her answer. She said psychologists and psychiatrists act holier than thou toward ministers—always brushing them aside as judgmental and condemning— but she said you have to do that because your lives don't measure up to their message. If they're right, you're living wrong. So you have to put them down to try to get rid of them."

The doctor kept his eyes on the clerk as if to hurry her along.

Dale continued speaking loudly and clearly, "I also asked my mom why TV newspeople make such a big deal out of the sexual sins of ministers when therapists do more of the same thing, and it's no big deal.

"Mom said that when ministers do it, it's a big deal because it's an exception to the way they are. Most are good people who really live good lives."

The doctor was grabbing papers from the clerk's desk and clicking a ballpoint pen. Dale crowded as close to him as he could without touching him.

Dale talked loudly, making sure everyone in the lobby could hear him. "Therapists don't have the same code of conduct, Mom said. She said you guys seem allergic to the words *moral* and *Christian*. Having sex with girlfriends, live-ins, and others is not a moral issue with you at all 'cause you base everything on whatever keeps you comfortable and doesn't hurt anyone else. Well, all I can say is that you violated your own low ethics when you involved me in sex with you when I was a child. You did hurt somebody. Me! I got hurt way bad! And I'm still dealing with it."

The doctor stopped trying to sign papers and confronted Dale. "Son, you are lying!"

"Not!" Dale declared. He turned to his audience and said, "Your main man here has two vaccination scars on his left arm. They look like eyes. I used to think they were the eyes of a monster."

Turning back to the doctor, Dale challenged, "Take off that white coat. Pull up your shirt sleeve, Doctor Pervert!"

The doctor just stood there, looking at first one staff member and then another, wondering how he could get rid of Dale and get out of his mess. The lobby was as still as the morgue in the basement below.

Swish! Clunk! Dale's switchblade was in the doctor's face. "Take off your white coat, I said!"

The doctor didn't move.

Leilani screamed a prayer. "Oh, my God! Don't let Dale cut him like he did the other molester!...Dale! I'm already in enough trouble! Let's just go!!" Leilani became weak and leaned into Maria's side.

Her words sent chills up the doctor's spine. Terror swept over his face.

John started toward Dale, then stopped. He wasn't sure what to do. He knew he shouldn't startle Dale when he was so emotionally charged. The orderlies also started toward Dale. John motioned for them to stop.

John said, "Easy, Dale. He's not worth going to prison over."

Moss joined the effort to solve the hostage situation. "Young man, violence is not the only option available to you. If you will put down your knife, I will give you two free sessions with me for learning to cope more effectively."

Dale didn't lose his concentration. He spoke again to the doctor at the tip of his blade, "Look at your audience! They're in suspense! They want to see your arm! Don't keep everyone waiting 'cause I'm obviously in a real bad mood, know what I mean? If you don't take off your coat, I am going to turn it red for you! Do it now!!"

A voice from the audience rang out in support of the doctor, "Prove him wrong! Show him that you have nothing up your sleeve!"

Dale ignored the remark. The doctor slowly removed his lab coat. Dale took it with his free hand and tossed it away. Next Dale tapped the doctor's left shoulder with his knife blade. "Up!"

Slowly, the doctor's right hand moved toward his left arm, but he wouldn't push up his sleeve. His hand became a vise that clamped down on the cloth.

Dale placed his knife tip against the back of the doctor's hand. The doctor grimaced and held his head away from Dale. His green eyes almost crossed as he tried to keep Dale's blade in view.

"Up!" Dale directed as he guided the doctor's hand with the point of his knife.

As the curtain was raised, two vaccination scars made their appearance, staring wide-eyed at the spellbound audience.

Dale touched each scar with the tip of his knife as if it were a pointer, and he, a teacher. "See! The eyes of a monster! How could I know they are there unless I am telling the truth?! This man is guilty beyond any reasonable doubt!"

Dale loosened his grip. The embarrassed and humiliated doctor, appearing as if he was going into shock, turned away from his colleagues and bent over a counter, still afraid the street kid might cut him.

Dale closed his knife and launched another Scud. "My mom died of AIDS. Doctor Pervert, I'd recommend you get yourself an HIV test."

The hospital staff were stunned. They started drifting toward doors.

Dale's final accusation rang out, "Doc, you've got a much bigger problem than Leilani here has. You have to live with yourself. That, like, must be really hard, Main Man!"

Dale took Leilani from Maria. As he held her, she sighed, "Whoa, Dale. You have more guts than ten gladiators. I'm glad that's over. Like, I'm so relieved!"

John stepped up to the doctor to collect the paperwork. Dale and Leilani left, holding hands, promising to drop by John and Maria's apartment later.

Since Leilani was no longer a psych patient, and Dale and Leilani were over fourteen, and since no one else wanted to tangle with Dale, they were free to visit her grandmother's hospital room.

They went to Chick-fil-A, bought Grandestmother her favorite sandwich, and returned to her room. They talked for an hour or so.

Despite her own problems, Grandestmother was concerned about supporting Dale. Dale was upset. A lot of old memories had flooded his mind when he saw the man who had paid his mother for sex and molested him.

"I'll tell you this much," Dale said, "being able to nail that guy helped me get some hurt out. Revealing to everybody what a hypocrite he is was great therapy for me. I wish Mom could've seen that."

The plump nurse poked her head in the door and said, "I thought I might find you kids here. I just thought you'd like to know that the hospital administrator called the police, and your allegations will be investigated. Also, I want to apologize for how insensitive I was earlier."

"No problem," Leilani said.

"Thanks," Dale followed.

Leilani's grandestmother decided that she wanted to go home, too. Her family doctor came by to check on her and agreed to release her the following morning if she continued to show improvement.

Later that night, Leilani wanted to mellow out on pot. She asked Dale to drive her by her house for a moment. Dale, being streetwise, caught on quickly and refused to provide transportation for that purpose. He taught her the Scripture that says she has to put off the old person with her old habits and put on the new person who is being created anew in Christ Jesus.

Smiling his magnetic smile, he asked Leilani, "What was that I heard you pray in your hospital room?" Then he quoted her prayer to her so she'd know which part he was talking about. "You told God, 'I want to be Your daughter, and I'm ready to live like I am Your daughter.'" He grinned affectionately and said, "Leilani, as my friends on parole say, 'If you talk the talk, you gotta walk the walk.'"

Leilani blushed. "You're right. And I did mean what I prayed, Dale. I guess you think it's pretty stupid of me to want to do drugs after today's events. But it has been my way. If I was happy, I liked to smoke pot. If I was depressed, I liked to smoke pot. Now I'm both happy and depressed, and I'd like to smoke pot."

"Don't be too embarrassed, Leilani. Bad stress or good stress triggers the desire to do drugs. Just page me if you get shaky in your commitment to be clean. I volunteer to be your support person during weak times."

Dale took Leilani to John and Maria's apartment. The coach and his wife congratulated him for the way he stood up to the head of the hospital's Department of Psychology. But John cautioned him, "Dale, I'm afraid that switchblade is going to get you in big trouble. It's illegal for you to carry it. Zorro was successful in movies, but acting like Zorro in real life will eventually cause you some serious problems. The only reason you aren't arrested now is because the hospital staff didn't press charges. They could have, and you'd be dealing with a felony. I'd like to see you get rid of the knife."

Dale said he'd think about it.

After they enjoyed hot peach cobbler topped with ice cream together, Dale returned to the inner city for the night.

SCENE 25

Hope kisses who?

TWENTY-FIVE

RUMLEY WAS like a bulldog guarding a bone. He was growling orders and doing his best to keep the special board meeting a secret.

However, Ms. Gibson felt it was important for everyone to hear about the way John was being treated. She had a mother-daughter talk with Kaprice.

"Sweetheart, I know Mr. Rumley like the back of my hand," she began. "The man is controlling and scheming, and I can tell you exactly what he's up to. He's playing school politics. He's treating John with dignity in public so his faculty won't find it believable that he's being a jerk to John behind closed doors. And he's going from board member to board member to win the support of each before they come together in the boardroom.

"He's keeping the board meeting a secret, Kaprice, because he knows the students love Coach John and would campaign to keep him. John can't tell about Rumley's threat to fire him or about the board meeting because it would put him in deeper jeopardy with Rumley and his pals on the board. So I wonder, dear daughter, how it could leak out?"

"Mom, all we have to do is tell the school's blabbermouths, and they'll flap their lips all over the place, know what I'm sayin'?"

"And their wagging tongues can do something good for a change," Kaprice's mom mused. "But how can we hide the fact that it came from me? If that gets out, I'll be fired, and it'll be nearly impossible for me to get another job."

"No problem, Mom. I'll just get Leilani, Candace, Franco, and Ray to plant the rumor without telling the blabbermouths where they heard it. Trust us, Mom. We're good!"

It worked. Within two days, every student at LHS knew about Rumley's plan to fire John and the private board meeting.

Rumley, plenty irritated, called Ms. Gibson into his office. "John told about the board meeting! There's no other way it could have gotten out. All I need is proof, and that's where you come in. When students are in your office, ask them how they found out about the meeting. Document everything they say. Get me proof, Ms. Gibson! Get me proof, and I'll present that appetizer to the board and doom John at the beginning of the meeting!"

Rumley calmed down a bit and decided to assure himself of her support. "By the way, did you notice your raise was on your last check?"

"Yes, I did. Thank you."

The week went by at a snail's pace. The teenagers and John and Maria wanted and needed to go to the meadow to talk. At last, it was Saturday afternoon and time for the second Teens With Wisdom Society meeting. They met at six o'clock.

Everyone except Brady came. Four trucks were circled up on the sunny side of the meadow. John backed in his Mustang convertible and put the top down so some of the kids could kneel in the backseat, facing the group.

Maria had baked brownies to brighten things up a little. As she served them to the kids on the tailgates and in the Mustang, John began with a few comments about Leilani's situation. "I'm glad Leilani's grandfather didn't hurt anyone at the abortion clinic. He apparently didn't intend to hurt anyone. He has pleaded not guilty to attempted murder. Leilani's grandmother is home from the hospital and doing well. Leilani is doing better, too, and we're glad she's able to be with us this evening."

He flashed a big smile to Leilani and said, "Leilani has something to tell you. She has invited Christ to become the head coach of her life. And she is going to do what her head coach says. Right, girl?"

"Right!" Leilani joined in. "God has forgiven me for everything. I have gotten right with God, and He is helping me wade through the giant mess I've made for my family."

John thought Leilani might want to volunteer additional comments, and he allowed a long silence in case she wanted to say more.

In the quietness...

Franco hoped his mom would get right with God and start acting right.

Ray hoped his dad would get right with God and stop beating him, and he prayed that his mom would get right with God and stop having an affair with Fred's dad.

Fred hoped nothing. He was too turned off to hope. He again wondered if the meadow meetings were turning into nothing more than a Sunday school class.

Candace felt guilt she didn't deserve. (It wasn't her fault her stepdad's father was a child molester.)

Kyong Suk hoped for a miracle. She wished her mom and dad would stop divorce proceedings.

Terence hoped something different. He wished his parents would get less right with God—become a little less religious—so they would stop being so strict.

Leilani wished that Brady had been at the hospital with her when she prayed. She thought about how different things could have been if her dad's drinking and her mom's snorting hadn't destroyed their relationship with her. *If only they had gotten right with God,* she thought.

Hope jarred all of them out of their thoughts. She yelled across the circle, "Leilani! After the meeting, I need to talk about some of the things you've dealt with. Could I come over to your house?" During the silence, Hope had been troubled about her abortions. She felt that she and Leilani might find comfort in each other.

"Sure," Leilani replied.

Leilani was sitting next to Dale. Hope spoke to him, "Dale, I want to apologize to you in front of everyone. I'm sorry I said I saw you in the soup lines. That was totally rude of me, okay?"

Dale signaled forgiveness with a nod. He wished she hadn't brought it up again.

Hope continued talking to him as the others listened. "I haven't been able to get what you said out of my mind. You said that everything we do will always be with us. You said that we are all playing for keeps. You said that my parents would become the grandparents of my children. You said that my getting into the New Age stuff wasn't surprising since I wanted to be different from, uh, opposite of my parents. What else did you say?"

Gathering her thoughts, she continued, "Oh, yeah. You said that I was like a robot that had been programmed by rebellious attitudes, but that I could choose to correct my programming and be my own person…it went something like that. But the thing you said that got my attention the most was that my rebellion was betraying me. Dale, I was majorly mad at you that night, but I later realized that you were pretty much right in what you said."

John felt uncomfortable with the words "everything we do will always be with us." *Although Maria has said she has forgiven me, she will never forget about me wetting the bed and making a fool of myself?* he thought. *I'll never be able to forget that night, either?*

John wondered how Leilani was feeling about those same words: "Everything we do will always be with us." John thought of Dale and Candace. *Always may not be very long for them if they had contracted HIV...as far as life on earth is concerned.*

Hope's attitude was completely different from before, and it was easy for John and Maria to see that a miracle had happened in her heart. Everyone noticed.

Maria asked about it. "Hope, you have a different attitude. What has happened?"

"Let me think," Hope replied. "It was Friday night when Dale mouthed off at me, and I got so mad at him. Dale, I was mad at you all weekend. Then on Monday, I got this card in the mail from my dad."

She pulled a greeting card out of her purse and held it up. "It's one of those cards that has a pretty scene on front but is blank inside."

She opened it. "My dad supplied his own words. He wrote: 'I love you more than I hate what you have done wrong. Love, Dad.'"

Hope pressed a tissue to her eyes and handed her card to Maria to pass around.

When the card reached Leilani, she said softly, "I want my grandparents to feel that way." Then she bowed her head as if she were praying.

"If I could, I'd tell my mother that," Dale said. "I'd say, 'Mother, I love you more than I hate what you did wrong.'"

The circle grew quiet, so quiet the noisy crickets seemed disrespectful. John swallowed a giant-sized lump in his throat as he thought about what Dale had said. That statement had come from a kid whose mom's prostitution sentenced him to live on the street and worry about having HIV.

Dale said, "Maybe some of the rest of you could think about applying it to your parents. In your heart, you could say to them: 'Mom and Dad, I love you more than I hate any mistakes that you've made.'"

Maria leaned close to John and whispered, "I love you more than I hate anything you've done wrong. Do you feel the same toward me?"

To say yes with a nice gesture, John kissed her cheek. Maria's words finally made him understand that their love was greater than any ugly mistake he had made. He relaxed.

"After my father's card came," Hope said, "I could see for the first time that my mom's and dad's anger was sitting on top of their hurt.

Like, their hurt was the fire, and their anger was the smoke."

She forced a shaky smile. "But they love me, so it was kind of like they were sending smoke signals of love. I just had to learn how to read smoke signals," she laughed.

A few kids laughed with her.

Hope composed herself and said, "Soon after the card came, we began to come up with our STRONG WILLS here in the meadow. When I accepted the first two, I could feel myself changing."

She pulled a crumpled-up piece of paper out of her jeans pocket and read from it: "I will do right no matter what I think is wrong with my parents or guardians. I will be responsible for myself and not try to use my parents' or guardians' problems to excuse my own stupid sins."

Looking up, she said, "Our STRONG WILLS taught me that even if my parents were a mess, I'm supposed to be mature enough to do what's right." She waved the paper for emphasis as she said, "Well, I've changed a lot since we wrote these."

Then with delight on her face, she added, "But no one can brag about straightening me out. Our STRONG WILLS straightened me out. The STRONG WILLS are powerful, very powerful. They can change lives. They can make miracles!"

Hope fought back tears and continued, "I was in biology class one day, and the teacher was teaching that we inherit things like alcoholism. I have an uncle who is forty-one and has never grown up. A grandfather of mine was an alcoholic. After that class, I sort of gave up. I decided I was doomed, before I was born, to be an alcoholic or a druggie. I was so-o-o depressed."

She stopped a moment to keep from crying. Then she said, "It was our STRONG WILLS that lifted me out of that despair. They say I can do what's right no matter what is wrong with my genes. With the STRONG WILLS, I don't have to obey my DNA. I don't have to be a copy of some loser in my past and robot his genetic programming."

Kyong Suk offered her a tissue. The tissue seemed to give Hope permission to cry, and tears flowed freely. Her makeup got messier and messier. "To tell you the truth, my old friends made me want to change, big time. I discovered something very ugly about them. They are full of themselves, stuck on themselves. That adds up to selfishness, and I've learned that sin and selfishness run in pairs, like old people say about snakes. They say snakes run in pairs. My friends hurt me again and again…and they never even looked back. They were using me and trashing me, huh, Dale?"

Candace added to Hope's observation, "That's a good point, Hope. Sin and selfishness do run in pairs like snakes. My stepgrandfather was both sinful and selfish. That's for sure."

Franco said, "That's the way my mom and her studs have been. They sure haven't cared about us kids."

Crisco cupped her hand behind Franco's ear and asked, "Do you think Mom and Dad will ever get married again?"

"We'll talk about that later," Franco said, patting her leg.

Nodding at Hope, Dale added, "Mom's customers used to ask her, 'Why would a nice girl like you do something like this?' They were so full of themselves that they asked her that after they had crawled all over her. Those maggots actually thought they were better than my mom!"

John made eye contact with Hope. "When I was your age, I went through something like you have gone through. I hurt my mother, and all she was trying to do was love me and keep me out of trouble. But I swapped her for the wrong crowd and went the wrong way in life anyway. I'm still trying to win the respect of Maria's parents."

Hope blotted her soggy makeup. "I'm sure I should have known better. I mean, the proof of how selfish those so-called friends of mine were was right there in front of me. They didn't care about God's opinion of what they were doing, or their parents', or my parents', or our church's, or our country's—that's extremely selfish! They didn't give a dam—uh…darn about anyone but their pitiful little group of friends. Only two of them have come to see me at the youth home, and they came only once.

"I look back now and wonder how I thought that people who were so pathetically selfish with the rest of the world would somehow treat me unselfishly—treat me right, treat me with respect, make me their one and only exception. I came to the conclusion that it was never going to happen. Building a relationship on we-all-think-our-parents-suck is pretty weak. Being in the wrong crowd didn't turn out to be as cool as I thought. It's not cool at all. It's losers ganging up against decent people. That's immature. That's, in fact, worse than immature. Now I understand why my parents invaded my privacy. They were trying to figure out where I was going wrong so they could try to stop me. Anyway, they were just responding to what I had taught them. I had taught them that I needed closer supervision and they were just responding to that, huh, Dale?"

Hope stuffed the wet tissue in a pocket of her jeans. "Dale, I realized you were right. My rebellion really was betraying me. After I received my dad's message that he loved me more than he hated anything I had done wrong, and after I got into the STRONG WILLS, I called my dad and asked if I could come over. He and Mom agreed. I didn't exactly apologize to them then, but I did tell them that my new goal was to teach them to trust me again. They said they'd be open to that...Well, to make a long story short, we are going to family counseling with a therapist who respects our faith. He's wonderful, and he is putting our family back together." A radiant smile streaked across Hope's face.

Applause broke out softly. It got louder as Hope slid off the tailgate, walked across the circle, and gave Dale a long, tender kiss on his lips. The kids howled, "Whoa! Dude! Woo! Go, Hope! Go, Dale!"

Hope ignored them and said, "Thanks, Dale. I want you to know that I am very, very, very sorry that you haven't had a real home. I've been praying that God will give you one." With a grin, she said, "And I'm praying that you won't have to trade your new truck for it."

Hope sat down on the tailgate beside Dale. She put her arm around him and rested her hand on his shoulder. Her sweet-smelling perfume accented her presence. She reached up and whispered in his ear, "And you also have some healing to do, counselor-on-call. You need to dump your anger by forgiving the johns who used your mother, the gang who killed your brother, and the straight people who haven't accepted you and won't give you a chance. You are going to hurt somebody if you don't get your anger under control."

She paused to give him a quick kiss on the cheek. "Dale, I once heard my dad say in a sermon: 'If you want to be like Christ, you have to be forgiving like He is.' Okay?"

"I haven't been out of control, Hope," Dale objected mildly.

Leaning nearer, he whispered, "If I had been, I would have shoved my blade through Rumpley's navel by now."

He checked her face for a response. Hope's expression didn't change. Dale gave in. "Okay, I know you're right."

At another edge of the circle John squeezed Maria's shoulders with a powerful hug. "It's all been worth it!" he told her softly. "They are solving their own problems. I am so proud of them."

"You are completely right," Maria agreed, returning his hug and planting a big kiss on his lips.

The kiss didn't go unnoticed. "Get it on, Coach! Whomp! Whomp!" the boys bellowed.

At that moment, Maria's attention was drawn to Leilani. Leilani was picking apart a wildflower. Maria read her lips: "Brady loves me. Brady loves me not." Maria thought, *I wish Brady were here to kiss Leilani. She needs to be kissed by him.*

Ray cleared his throat loudly and started talking as if he was using a megaphone. "What are we going to do about Rumpley's big bad plan to fire Coach John? We can't let Bongo Buns be as bad as he wants to be!"

Franco spoke up, "Coach, after all you and Maria have done for us, we're going to totally take up for you."

John replied, "I don't think there's anything you guys can do. Rumley's got everything stacked in his favor. He's got the school board in his back pocket. It looks like I'll be gone in a few days."

Leilani observed cynically, "This stupid world isn't fair!"

"You can't quit!" Kaprice warned John. "Mom says that if you quit, Mr. Rumpley won't have to answer for his actions, and he'll just keep doing other employees the way he's done you. She told me that if you take a stand against Rumpley, you'll be doing something that no one else has ever had the guts to do. Mom says that you won't be alone. She says that she has a surprise that will take the sting out of Rumpley's stinger. What do you say, Coach?"

John doubted that any kind of surprise from Ms. Gibson could solve his huge problem, but he planned to fight anyway. "Oh, I'm not going to quit. I'm not letting Rumley sweep this under the rug."

The meadow erupted into cheering and clapping. Kaprice grabbed Leilani's hand and pulled her into the middle of the circle to do a special cheer they had practiced together. "One, two, hit it!" Kaprice began. But Leilani wasn't in the mood. She returned to her place on the tailgate.

Kaprice yelled to Crisco who was writing "wash me" in the dust on the back window of Dale's truck, "C'mon, Crisco! Help me do this cheer!"

In a flash, Crisco jumped to her side as if she knew what she was doing. She followed along in the cheer, sounding more like Kaprice's echo than her partner.

Who you gonna yell for?
Coach John! Coach John!
Whatta you gonna yell?

We won't let Rump dump on you!
We're the ones who'll see you through!

Fire Coach John? No, he will not!
Bongo Buns can go to pot!

Hey, Coach John! Yeah, you're so fine!
Thanks for putting your neck on the line!

Yea! Yea!

Kaprice did high kicks, and Crisco jumped up and down. Their audience yelled a variety of victory sounds.

Franco said, "We've got to make plans. Let's make an effigy of Big Rump and burn it on campus."

"What's an effigy?" Crisco quizzed.

Terence answered, "It's a dummy or a statue that you make of someone you hate. Then you burn it to show how pathetic you think that person is."

Dale said, "Do you mind if I furnish an effigy of a perverted doctor?"

"How about if I toss in an effigy of my stepgrandfather?" Candace yelled.

"And I'll furnish one that looks like my mom's present significant other," Franco joined in.

"Why don't we just shoot Bongo Buttface like Leilani's grandfather tried to waste that doctor guy?" Ray smarted off.

Leilani screamed, "Ray, have you been attacked by a brain-sucking bat?! That was a terrible thing to say!"

John became worried about where the conversation was leading. He cautioned, "I don't want you to return evil for evil. I've become a true Christian now, and I want us to do the right thing the right way."

The kids had puzzled looks on their faces. John accepted their cue for an explanation. "I made a serious commitment to Christ here in your meadow. It was that Saturday morning that Maria and I camped here in our camper."

"So if you are going to get involved," Maria urged, "we want you to do it in a wise way. After all, you are not just mere teenagers anymore. You are the Teens With Wisdom Society, right?"

All at once, they heard a roaring sound overhead. An airplane buzzed the treetops just beyond their view.

Kaprice screamed, "I bet that's Rumpley and Viola Jeffries! He has a flying lesson today! They're looking for us!"

Dale yelled, "Get off the trucks! Get out of the Mustang! Get the vehicles out of sight! Move them under the trees!"

"Crisco!" Maria yelled. "Take my hand!" They ran to the woods.

Drivers jumped into vehicles. Engines roared, and the fleet lunged for cover.

In seconds, the meadow was deserted. The plane circled back, its engine noise growing louder and louder.

Kaprice shouted, "They're looking for our secret meeting place because Rump Face thinks we're having drinking parties with John and Maria!"

John watched the plane through the branches of the trees. He didn't want to believe it, but Kaprice was right. John yelled back, "He's looking for the final nail to drive into my coffin when he gets me in front of the school board!"

"You got it!" Kaprice said. "The man won't stop at anything!"

The plane dipped toward the meadow so low that the pilots were clearly visible.

Ray yelled, making fun of Rumley, "Look, it's the *rear* admiral! He's wearing his shades! He thinks he's Mr. Cool!"

"Not!" the kids yelled in unison.

Rumley and Jeffries didn't make another pass. They hadn't discovered the secret meeting place…or had they? No one knew for sure. The possibility added to the stress that was building.

Coming out of their hiding places, they reassembled in the woods beside John and Maria's Mustang and talked about how overly dramatic Rumley always is.

"Bongo Buns is a real pot head, and I'm talking commode here," Hope said to sum up everyone's comments.

Ray's truck was nearby. He opened his ice chest and passed around soft drinks. No beer. He had left it behind this time. Somehow, it didn't seem to fit in with how serious things had become.

Kaprice got things going again. "Now, Maria, what were you saying before Rumpley so rudely interrupted?"

Maria took up where she left off. "Since you have become the Society of Teens With Wisdom, if you develop a plan for defending John, it has to be a wise plan. Only wisdom will bring positive results. Anything less will only contribute to our problems."

Daniel said, "Well, if you ask me, I think Coach John and Maria need to leave and let us figure out what we'll do on our own. That way, no one can ever accuse Coach John of putting us up to doing what we decide to do."

SCENE 26

There is life after rude teachers and other problems

TWENTY-SIX

ALTHOUGH THE teenagers agreed that John and Maria should leave so that they could make plans among themselves, Maria held up both her hands in protest. "Before you chase us away, let's finish our work on your STRONG WILLS for the Teens With Wisdom Society."

"Maria is right," John said. "I may be out of the picture soon, but before I leave Lincoln High, I'd like to know that you kids have a set of dynamic principles that will steady you after I'm gone."

"Coach, you're not going anywhere!" Terence yelled.

"Maybe not," John replied, "but still we need to get this done. I have read over your STRONG WILLS again, and I'm excited about the maturity in your work. If you really will follow your new STRONG WILLS, you will succeed in life, for sure, in spite of what terrible things people have done to you, in spite of any awful mistakes you yourselves have made. Truly, your STRONG WILLS are your life preservers. Right, Hope?"

"Right, Coach!" Hope responded, proud of her success.

With a compassionate look at her husband, Maria asked the teens, "Do you want to make up one to deal with any damage that has been done to you by school administrators? Maybe some of you have had your feelings hurt by faculty members."

The response was mixed. Franco and Leilani were much more interested in help with family problems. But Kyong Suk spoke up in her cute accent, "My feelings have been hurt. Last year, a history teacher was teaching about World War II, and he looked at me like I personally flew kamikaze missions or something. I was born in our country, not Japan. I am as much a citizen of our country as he is. He needs to remember that his ancestors weren't from this continent, either. He's not a native of this area. Besides, I'm Korean."

Terence joined in. "When I was in the first grade, I picked up a book to read. And right in front of everyone, the teacher jerked it out of my hands and said, 'Gimme that. You don't know how to read that.' But I did know how to read it. I had one like it at home, and I had learned to read it. It was like someone had labeled me a poor student while I was still in the first grade."

Dale added, "I could tell worse stories, but here's one that bothered me in junior high. When I was in the seventh grade, I was making lousy grades, and I was feeling stupider than anyone else in my classes. I was acting funny to get a few laughs when the teacher stormed at me, 'I don't know why you bother to come to class, Dale! You're never going to be anything but a trash man anyway!' I can still hear him yelling that."

Maria gave everyone a chance to talk, but no one else could remember having had feelings hurt by a teacher. She patted John's leg and said, "Honey, you teachers have a pretty good record. Only three out of eleven students have painful memories." Then she asked the kids how they wanted to word the principle.

Kyong Suk took a stab at it, "I will not allow rude comments... uh...attitudes...uh...or actions of teachers to turn me away from respecting myself."

"And from believing that I can achieve good goals with my life," Dale added forcefully. "I will prove that insensitive teachers are wrong about me."

Maria wrote fast. "Okay, that's a long one, but I've got it all on paper. Now how about a principle concerning—"

Leilani interrupted, "We need one about God! I think we teens need to take a stand on this. If God isn't for real, then my baby's not in heaven, and I'm not forgiven, and Jesus isn't going to be there to receive Grandyppa if he has a heart attack and dies in jail."

"Evolution apart from God is depressing!" John said, being very impressed with Leilani's reasons why God *has* to be real. John put his arm around his wife and said to the young people, "I'd like to share something with you that Maria taught me here in the meadow when we stayed out here in our camper. She taught me that trust goes both ways. God wants us to trust Him, but He's also trusting us. He is trusting us to live on a best-friends basis with Him and treat Him right. Ever since she told me that, I have felt closer to God."

John gestured toward heaven and said, "The thought of God's trusting me is awesome! I'm important to God. I'm not *just* a PE teacher. I have eternal value. I have immortal significance. I am a significant other to my heavenly Father. I'm not a mere mortal jellyfish floating around in the sea with the tide among zillions of other creatures that are hopelessly cooperating with the evolutionary process. I am a human being in whom God is uniquely interested. I am best friends with my own Creator!"

"Thank You, God, for trusting me with a new start," Leilani said softly for no one's ears but God's. "I promise to be more careful not to let You down. Please be with Brady, wherever he is tonight. Does he have a good heart like I thought? Does he even care about what I'm going through? Is he stepping out of my life? Help me make it through this."

"Are you okay?" Maria asked Leilani.

"I'm fine."

Maria said, "How about if we keep this principle short: I will honor God's trust of me in our best-friends relationship. That says everything."

Dale wanted more information included. He said, "This guy who used to minister on the streets would always teach people to say: 'The opportunities in my present and future are God's gifts to me; how I succeed with those opportunities is my gift to God.' He taught me to say, 'God votes for me, the pull of sin votes against me, and I am breaking the tie by the way I am voting with each decision I make.' Let's add those."

Among a general show of approval from his peers, Maria said, "That's just perfect, Dale. Good for you."

Leilani prayed even more quietly. "Dear God, I won't be careless with Your gift of my life ever again. I will live clean so that I can have my family reunion in heaven. And, God, I pray that You like Grandypa's gift of his life. I think he may be presenting it to You soon, in person. Amen."

John nudged Maria and stood up. "These kids have done a super job. I think it's time for us to go."

Hope objected. "No, we need a STRONG WILL for dealing with selfish friends."

John sat back down.

"Go for it," Maria said to Hope.

"Well, I messed up bad, I mean real bad! I rebelled against my parents because I wanted to be independent. Then I did whatever my self-centered friends wanted...and I became self-obsessed like them. That's not being independent. Why did I give in to my peers when I wouldn't give in to my parents? I don't know. Maybe my brain took a vacation or something."

"Okay, you guys," Maria said, waving her pencil. "I will not let my peers, what?"

Terence spoke up, "Allow my peers to pressure me away from what I believe is right."

Hope took over, "By hassling me, by putting down my parents or decent friends, or by threatening to leave me out if I don't conform to what they want."

"You can always tell who the wrong crowd is," Dale explained. "They are proud of what they should be ashamed of. They are driven by lust, addictions, and sinful desires. They have to sneak around behind the backs of decent people 'cause what they do is wrong."

Leilani's mind drifted back to the time when she had left condoms in school colors for Maria and to the time she had acted proud in front of Maria for having sex with Brady. She thought of how she and Brady had tricked John and Maria into letting them set up their camper so that they could party in it. And she remembered how cool she thought it was when she smoked dope in front of her friends.

Hope's mind wandered for a moment, too. She thought of how proud of lying she had been. She used to be on an ego trip about how easily she could fool her parents because she was such a good liar.

Several of the kids remembered how they had given tours of their bedrooms to show off all the stuff they had shoplifted.

"Hypocrites!" John exclaimed without warning. He captured everyone's attention with his sudden exclamation. He sounded as if he had just discovered something new.

He put his hands together, applauding his revelation. He stopped clapping to say, "The wrong-crowd types are the worst hypocrites. They act decent in public and act indecent behind everybody's back. They act like good citizens in front of everyone, but on the sly they lie, cheat, commit crimes, and do drugs. The *wrong crowd* and *hypocrites* are synonymous terms. The hypocrites are the wrong-crowd types! The wrong-crowd types are the hypocrites! Most hypocrites are not in our churches! They are sneaking around doing wrong! They wouldn't go to church if their lives depended on it!"

Maria winked at him. "Their lives do depend on it, John. And I am so glad to see you finally get victory over that hypocrite hang-up you've had."

Dale said with authority, "The big hippos are in a lot of trouble. Hypocrites were the only people that Jesus got tough with. And the Bible actually says that they are enemies of Easter."

"For real?" Hope probed. "Enemies of Easter?"

"For real," Dale responded. "Just wait a minute. I'll get my Bible out of my truck and read it to you."

Hope repeated Dale's words slowly, "Enemies of Easter? That sounds about as serious as serious can get. Who would want to be an enemy of rising from the dead and going to heaven?"

Dale returned with his burgundy New Testament and said, "These Bible verses talk about the wrong crowd and then the right crowd. It's the apostle Paul writing here."

As Dale opened his Bible, John noticed from the cover that it was Today's English Version.

Turning pages, Dale said, "The apostle Paul was a wrong-crowd-type guy who killed Christians till God got hold of his life. That's when God changed his name from Saul to Paul and trusted him to preach all over the place and write a lot of the Bible."

Dale read from Philippians 3:18-21: *"I have told you this many times before, and now I repeat it, with tears: there are many whose lives make them enemies of Christ's death on the cross."*

Dale stopped reading and tapped the page in the Bible with his finger, saying pointedly, "See, they are enemies of Easter!"

He read more, *"They are going to end up in hell, because their god is their bodily desires."* Dale stressed, "They are bossed around by appetites!"

He read on, *"They are proud of what they should be ashamed of."* Dale looked up and explained, "That's how I knew that the wrong crowd is proud of what they should be ashamed of. The Bible says it clearly."

His eyes returned to scanning the sentences, *"And they think only of things that belong to this world."* Looking up again, he said, "Like, where the next party's gonna be."

"We, however, are citizens of heaven." Dale made eye contact with several of the kids and then said, "I may live in the slums, but I'm actually a citizen of heaven."

"Cool!" Leilani said. "My citizenship is where my baby is!"

I like the sound of that, Hope thought as applause filled the meadow, celebrating Leilani's words.

As the applause quieted, Dale read, *"And we eagerly wait for our Savior to come from heaven, the Lord Jesus Christ. He will change*

*our weak mortal bodies and make them like his own glorious body, using
that power by which he is able to bring all things under his rule."*

Dale looked at John and asked, "Coach John, do you know what
that means?"

"You tell me what it means, Dale."

"When the Bible says that all things will be brought under His
rule, it means that even the knees of the professionals will bow before
Christ. Every knee includes their knees."

Kaprice questioned, "You mean the people who are against
talking about God are going to have to kneel before Christ? Whoa, man!
Are they ever going to be in a bind! Know what I'm sayin'?"

Hope held up her hand shyly, as if she was still feeling out her
thoughts, but wanted to go ahead and share them. "Dale, what bothers
me about that Scripture is that not only was I *in* the wrong crowd, but
I was a *leader* in the wrong crowd."

Candace was more bold with her observation. "Our group here
has been the wrong crowd in the past. We've been proud of what we
should've been ashamed of, and we've done things behind people's backs,
and we've been chasing shameful appetites."

Everyone was uncomfortable with that and tried to take off the
pressure by joking around.

"Not me," Fred said. "I just run the video library and take a bold
stand against censorship."

"Not me!" Ray hollered. "I've just been the beer distributor!"

The comments kept coming. They were all making fun of
themselves, trying to come to terms with reality at a digestible rate.

"Not me," said Leilani. "I just hung out at the pharmacy."

"Not me," said Kyong Suk. "I've been trying to help the tobacco
companies turn a profit."

"Not me," Daniel said. "I've just helped stores move out old
merchandise, like most of you have."

"Not me," Hope joined in. "My grand mission has been to show
other adolescents how not to act."

"Not me," said Franco. "I've just cruised all day long and stayed
away from my mom and her studs."

"Not me," Crisco said.

"Not me," Terence said, grinning. "I just hung out with
hoodlums and tried to be a good example to you."

"I'm with you, Terence," Candace said.

"Good grief," Ray said. "We've been a bunch of thieves, beer guzzlers, druggies, smokers, sex mongers, and porno fiends. If we haven't been the wrong crowd, who has?"

"Most teenagers have done at least some of the things we've done," Dale said. "That's just how bad things are now."

Ray said, "Welcome to...

Before he could get the words out, the others joined in, "the world of teenagers..."

"...where all is not well," Ray finished on a negative note.

With sudden inspiration, Dale flipped through the pages in his Bible. "I have another Scripture to read. I think it will help us stop putting ourselves down."

Dale read 1 Timothy 4:12, *"Do not let anyone look down on you because you are young, but be an example for the believers, in your speech, your conduct, your love, faith, and purity."*

"I like that," Kaprice said. "Our STRONG WILLS can make that happen for us. I think that verse should become our main verse for our Teens With Wisdom Society."

They unanimously adopted the verse.

John announced, "I, for one, am getting back into church. I am going Sunday with Hope. Anyone want to meet us at her dad's church? Or if you want, you can meet Maria at St. Andrew's Catholic Church."

Maria added, "Whatever you do, don't forget to pray for Brady. It's hard to be away from home and not know what's going on."

As John and Maria got ready to leave, Fred stood up and announced, "You won't be seeing me at no church service. You guys are turning into true Christians. Next thing you know, you'll be wanting to burn the videos, and no one's getting a lighter near my videos. In fact, I'm taking them to a party tonight. Wanna go, Hope? Lance, Kathy, and Zack'll be there. They've never done you wrong. Ah, come on, you can stay away from the bedrooms and the booze. It'll be fun."

Hope got up and said, "If I go, will you help me resist temptation?"

Speechless, Maria stared in disbelief. How could Fred and Hope go to that kind of party from a meeting that had meant so much to everyone?

John wasn't so surprised. He knew how on again and off again people can be who have been in a partying lifestyle. He took the clipboard from Maria and began to read one of the STRONG WILLS: "I will not allow my peers to pressure me away from what I believe is right by putting down my decent friends."

Hope thought about her respect for the STRONG WILLS. Her eyes moved from John to Fred and then back again.

John told her, "You are having a mood swing, Hope. It's normal. It will happen to you for a while. One minute, you'll be against your old friends and your old ways. The next minute, you'll want to party again. I know, I used to be in the wrong crowd. To break away from old friends and old habits and make it stick, you have to pray a lot, use a lot of self-control, and receive a lot of support from your friends here…and control old appetites. When sinful appetites control wisdom, that's immaturity. Maturity is when wisdom controls appetites. You're getting there. We're all getting there."

"Coach John's right about mood swings," Leilani said. "After I got out of the hospital, I wanted to smoke a joint. That was totally crazy!! Drugs and sex put my Grandypa in jail and me and Grandestmother in the hospital, and I wanted more? Can you believe that?! Dale wouldn't take me by the house so I could get some. Instead, Dale gave me the support I needed to stay clean that night."

Kaprice stood up beside Hope and locked her arms around her waist. "She ain't goin', Fred! Ain't gonna happen!"

Fred said, "Well, I'm going, and I'm dropping out of this group. I don't like what this is turning into. Outsiders are going to see you as strange, and I don't want them to think I'm weird, too. Later, people!"

Petite Kyong Suk called after Fred, "We're not being weird. We're learning what it means to be wise. Wisdom will look weird only to those who don't have it. I can already tell you the names of the kids who'll think we're strange, but it'll be because our stand will remind them that partying is more important to them than doing right. Fred, please don't leave!"

"Careful, Fred," Dale cautioned, "there's a Scripture that warns against what you are doing: 'A wise man fears and departs from evil, but a fool rages and is self-confident' (KJV). I got that verse from a street preacher."

Fred headed for his truck.

As she was feeling stronger, a Scripture came to Hope's heart to go with Dale's. *"'To do evil is like sport to a fool, but a man of understanding has wisdom.'* I think that's Proverbs chapter 10 verse 23" (NKJV).

Maria reassured the others, "Some friends will think you're strange. The 'have-nots' will always put down the 'haves,' especially when the lives of the 'haves' are more mature than the 'have-nots.' Your maturity will remind them of their immaturity. The more responsible you get, the more irresponsible they'll look. They'll hate you for that, and they'll try to blow out your light by putting you down. That's guaranteed. Expecting it will help you not feel so rejected when it happens. As Kyong Suk says, you already know who's going to do it. But remember, people who are drawn to evil are to be pitied, not hated. Sin is humiliating and robs them of dignity."

"Maria!" John shouted. "That's it! You just said it! Rumpley, Platypus, and Chester...they can't like me! It's impossible for them to like me. I stand against what they stand for. They either have to change or get rid of me. They're getting rid of me!"

John and Maria caught up with Fred at the gate. John jumped out and helped him move plants.

As they worked together, John said, "Don't think anyone was condemning you back there. People sometimes misinterpret why Scripture is used in situations like that. Our minds were like computers searching our memories for something to say to warn you, to appeal to you. We were trying to say something that would make sense to you so that we could keep you. We just don't want to lose you—I like you! And we don't want Hope to risk what she's gaining."

"Thanks for saying that, Coach."

"Maria feels the same way. She likes you, too. All the kids do. I've heard them talking."

John walked Fred to his truck, saying, "Man to man, friend to friend, Fred, I can tell you, from personal experience, that the author of evil will suck you in, promising you pleasure, but then betray you and bury you beneath his filthy consequences—the consequences you've brought upon yourself. A friend named Mat taught me that...And when consequences come, it won't be God punishing you; it'll be the consequences of your own wrong choices punishing you. Believe me, I know.

I've been there. I've learned that sin is like a honey bee. It has honey in its mouth and a stinger in its tail…I wish you wouldn't drop out, Fred. You've been valuable to what we're doing. You've helped these young people think up your STRONG WILLS."

"Not mine, Coach. I didn't make them mine. They're theirs. Knowing about them is not the same as committing your life to them. They do. I don't," Fred said, reaching for the door of his truck. "And it's not that I don't like you and Maria and everyone. I'm just not ready to give up the stuff I like to do. When I'm old, I'll get right, and I'll ask forgiveness for what I'm doing now. That way I can party now and be forgiven later. I can have it all! Everything'll be fine. When we all get to heaven, the rest of you will realize how much fun that you guys missed out on. Do you remember…no, you weren't at LHS then. Last year, a bunch of adults spoke at our assembly on the dangers of drugs. They did loads of stuff when they were kids. But they're healthy today. They're respected today. They're speaking at high school assemblies now. I'm doing what they did."

"Fred, there are at least two problems with that. First, you are gambling with your soul. You could die or be killed before you get around to repenting. Second, God is not wimpy. He won't be manipulated. The Bible says, *'Be not deceived; God is not mocked: for whatsoever a man soweth, that shall he also reap.'*" John was grateful that he remembered Galatians 6:7. He had memorized it in vacation Bible school when he was a child.

"Also, Fred," John kindly said, "remember what was said back in your meadow: God is trusting you not to be an enemy of Christ's death on the cross. You don't want to be an enemy of Easter. You are too smart for that."

Fred started his engine. John shut his door for him and said through the window, "Fred, even if you stick to your decision to drop out of the group, I care about you. Stay in touch. Okay? Give me a call in a few days, and we'll grab a burger together."

The teens who stayed behind moved their trucks back into the meadow to form a triangle of tailgates. There were only three. Brady's truck wasn't there, and Fred had just left in his truck. Tiki torches provided flames of light after the sun sank beyond the tall trees. The teenagers talked about how they could help John and Maria.

Hope said she had discussed the problem with her father. "I asked him what we could do. He said that we should act like no one would expect us to act. He said Mr. Rumley and the school board would expect us to be angry and hateful and carry signs. He said we needed to be more professional than that. Professional—Dad used the word *professional*, can you believe that?"

While her friends chuckled at her remark, she said thoughtfully to herself, "Why did I say that? Dad himself is a professional, and he's respected by a lot of people. Professionals aren't bad. They just have to be tested for quality."

Ray smarted off, "You mean we're not going to piss on Mr. Rumpley like so many other students have?"

The majority agreed that they would take the advice of Hope's father and also honor John and Maria's request for them to be wise in what they planned to do.

Franco said softly, "To me, the whole thing looks hopeless. Our coach is in the last two minutes of the fourth quarter, and the score is 28 to zip. What can Coach John do? The man is going to lose the game."

Crisco began to chant in her wee voice, "We will win! We will win!"

"I pray that you're right," Franco said, squeezing her small hand.

Kaprice was more optimistic than Franco. "My mom, like, acts as if she knows something that's going to help Coach John, but she won't tell me. Maybe it's going to be like a Hail Mary pass at the last second or something. Anyway, I think we ought to give Coach John our best shot. If we lose, at least we'll know we've done our best for him and Maria."

Dale was ready to fight for right. "Tonight is Saturday night. The board meeting is not this Monday, but the next. So we have one week and one weekend before the board meeting. That's plenty of time. Let's get some plans made."

At first, there was dead silence. Then ideas began to flow. Plans began to take shape.

SCENE 27

*Together
at
the
jail*

TWENTY-SEVEN

THE NEXT day being Sunday, John took Leilani and her grandestmother to see Grandypa. Visiting hours at the jail were from 1:00 to 4:00 P.M.

John approached a heavy-set man in police uniform sitting behind a counter with two others. "We're here to see Samuel Summers."

"Are you family?"

"No."

"Then you're not seeing anybody. Only family are allowed in."

John stepped aside and motioned toward Grandestmother and Leilani, "They're family."

"Have 'em sign in," the jailer ordered.

As they signed their names, the jailer, without looking up, mouthed memorized words, "Rules state that only one visitor can see a prisoner at a time, and that'll be for fifteen minutes. Whoever's first, step through the metal detector and follow me."

Grandestmother urged Leilani to go in first because she knew Leilani wanted to apologize to her grandfather. Grandestmother stayed behind praying for her husband and their granddaughter. She held a lace-edged handkerchief to her mouth and nose.

A loud buzzer sounded, and the steel door opened with an echoing clang. Leilani stepped in. The big door slammed behind her with another eerie bang. Leilani followed the huge jailer into the bowels of the jail, winding through hallways. The jail smelled sweaty. Everything was painted pale brown. Leilani suddenly realized she was alone with the jailer. She was under his mercy. He could do anything he wanted to her and no one would know. Frightened, she nervously tried to make conversation. "Why is the air-conditioning turned down so low?"

The jailer wasn't interested in conversation. He barked, "Keep 'em cold, wrapped in blankets, trying to stay warm, and these caged animals fight less, cause less trouble. Jail ain't meant to be cozy, kid."

Arriving in the visitors' room, the big jailer motioned for Leilani to sit down on a round metal stool that was welded onto a steel post sticking out of the concrete floor. The stool felt freezing cold to her bottom. Leilani began to shiver. She noticed cold steel was everywhere—walls, doors, bars, and the cabinet top where she rested her arms. She sat facing a large glass that had wire mesh molded into it—mesh that looked like fencing for chickens. Through the glass, she could only see a blank steel wall.

Suddenly, Grandypa hobbled into view, leaning on his cane, holding his bandaged side. He took a seat on the cold steel stool opposite his granddaughter.

Seeing Grandypa—his face framed in steel, his beautiful gray hair and beard ungroomed—broke Leilani's heart. Over a bright orange shirt with **COUNTY JAIL** stenciled where the left front pocket should have been, Grandypa wore a loosely wrapped grungy old black wool blanket.

Leilani couldn't speak. She laid her head on her arms and sobbed.

In an unconscious gesture, Grandypa reached for her. His hand hit the cold glass with a thud.

Startled, Leilani jumped and looked up. She picked up the phone on her side of the window. She cried out, "Grandypa, I'm so...so sorry! You fought for me, and you took me in, and look what I've done to you! I love you! I love you! Please forgive me! Please, please..."

"Hey, teenybopper!" the mean-looking visitor at the next window exclaimed. "Control yourself! There's other people here!"

He was a heavily bearded middle-aged man who looked like a bad guy from the cartoon world. He was trying to talk to a prisoner about posting bail for him.

Still sobbing, Leilani tried to apologize, "I'm sorry. I can't help it. I caused my grandfather to go on a shooting spree! Grandypa is here because of me!"

A guard came over and ordered, "Keep it down, young lady, or you'll have to leave."

The grizzly man leaned over and peered through the window at Grandypa. "Oh, you're the old goat that shot up the Women's Clinic! I saw you on television!"

"He shot up the place 'cause they did an abortion on me, and—"

"Oh, yeah?" the grizzly man interrupted. "They didn't say that on the news. You're dead meat, Pops. You gotta commit crimes that don't upset people, like selling drugs or ripping off houses. The law's gonna make an example outta ya. Personally, I'm for abortion. It's wonderful. It keeps me from having to pay child support!" Having had his say, he returned to talking to his friend.

Grandypa wanted to explain his side, but the grizzly man didn't give him a chance.

Leilani controlled herself as best she could, "Grandypa, can you forgive me?"

"Princess, didn't Grandestmother give you my letter?"

Leilani nodded yes. Tears fell faster than she could wipe them away.

"I explained in that letter, Princess, that I am not holding anything against you. I forgave you as soon as I found out about it."

"What will they do to you, Grandypa?"

"Oh, I reckon I'll be going to prison, Princess. But so far, it's not been too bad. The guards and inmates here are treating me well enough."

The grizzly man eavesdropped.

Leilani was afraid to ask, but she felt she had to have an answer. "Grandypa, uh, do you believe that, uh—"

"What I did was right?" he finished the question for her. "Princess, my Princess, God created the womb to be a sanctuary, not a death chamber; to be the place where life begins, not death row. Abortion is child abuse at its worst—sudden, catastrophic, and deadly. To tell you the truth, though, I was running on emotion. I just wanted to block the door and prevent them from killing anyone else's grandchildren. All I had to use was my body, and that's what I used."

Grandypa took a deep breath and asked, "Leilani, is it right that the womb is the most dangerous place a baby can be these days? Is it right for Dr. Knight and Mrs. Stone to violently kill children, and yet have me locked up for merely blocking the door? I'm not a member of any group that fights abortion. They can't shove me into that mold. I'm just an old man who wanted to hold his great-grandbaby before I die of this heart problem I have."

"I'm sorry, Grandypa."

"Oh, Princess, I didn't say that to hurt you. I love you so much, it would be impossible for me to hold a grudge against you. I don't blame you."

Grandypa wiped tears from his eyes. "But before abortion can be stopped, we have to have a revival that will convert people from being so self-seeking, so selfish, and so self-indulgent, or else thousands of precious unwanted children, those spared from abortion, will be abused at the hands of frustrated parents.

"Princess, our culture needs a revival that will give us a fresh transfusion with the unselfish blood of Christ. This revival would convert people from being self-focused to God-focused. They'd learn fresh and new how to be devoted to others. They'd stop being ruled by their wants and appetites, and they'd return to the wisdom of the Ten Commandments and the Golden Rule.

"Then we'd have the moral fabric necessary for embracing unwanted children rather than aborting them. We'd have the moral fabric necessary for loving them and for nurturing them throughout their young lives. Women who don't want to raise their babies would carry pregnancies to full term so that thousands of people praying to adopt children could see their prayers come true. We'd have the moral fabric necessary for actually taking care of the homeless children of the world rather than ignoring them while they dig in trash cans for food."

Grandypa folded his hands and stared down as he continued, "What's the difference between physicians, who have taken the Hippocratic oath, men and women who have dedicated themselves to healing, snuffing out the beating hearts of grandbabies, and me, dedicated to justice, blocking the door of the abortion clinic, trying to prevent fully formed adults from being violent against miniature humans? Why am I considered bad and arrested on the trumped-up charges of trying to abort a big balding human? There is no difference except for the warp in our culture's thinking—a culture that will block hundreds of lumberjacks from earning their living to save spotted owls while too few environmentalists even notice the unborn children who are losing their habitat to surgical steel."

He looked up into Leilani's moist eyes and said, "Princess, our nation is in deep trouble. It has become allergic to correct answers. Our culture is plagued with indecent behavior and unwise 'solutions.' Our culture is corrupt."

Grandypa's gaze wandered beyond Leilani as if he was seeing God in the distance. He quoted a Bible verse. "*'If My people who are called by My name will humble themselves, and pray and seek My face, and turn from their wicked ways'*—their self-serving and corrupt ways," Grandypa added, "*'then I will hear from heaven, and will forgive their sin and heal their land.'*" Grandypa's Scripture was from 2 Chronicles 7:14 (NKJV).

Leilani's mood swung to sudden pride. "Grandypa, you look like Moses, except that Moses didn't have John Lennon glasses to wear back then. Your tattered blanket makes you look like a holy man."

"I was quoting the Bible, sweetheart," Grandypa said. "That's where the right answers are. No one should ever be allergic to God's wisdom."

"But what will happen to you, Grandypa? That guy next door says you're dead meat." Leilani placed the palm of her right hand to the cold glass on her side. Grandypa, mirroring her hand, placed his left hand on the cold glass on his side.

"I reckon I'll be spending the remainder of my life in prison. Christopher Columbus once said, 'Nothing is achieved with unanimous consent, and those who are enlightened before the others are condemned to pursue that light in spite of the others.'* For the record, Princess, you know I don't own a gun. The shots were fired by—"

The guard broke in. "Your time is up, young lady."

Grandypa and Leilani pulled their hands away from the window. "Just one more minute, please," Leilani pleaded. She began speaking as fast as she could through the phone. "Grandypa, your great-grandbaby is with Jesus, and Jesus apologized to my baby for me…and Jesus forgave me for what I did…Brady's parents moved him to relatives in another state…Hope's moving back in with her parents…We're starting a Society for Teens With Wisdom…Things are going to be better…Oh! Rumpley's gonna fire Coach John! What can we do?"

The guard placed his hand on her shoulder. Grandypa didn't have time to answer her. "I love you, Grandypa. I'm leaving some cookies I baked for you with the guard out front."

"I love you, Princess Leilani from Hawaii, and don't worry about me. I'll be just fine. Tell Grandestmother to leave me a comb."

"Grandypa, how's your heart? Are you having chest pains?"

"No. No. I'm fine."

The guard pulled Leilani away by an arm. He demanded gruffly, "Come on! There's been a problem in one of the cell blocks! Visiting hours have been canceled!"

Leilani glanced back to get one more look at Grandypa. He smiled at her. The guard escorted her out of the depths of the jail.

Leilani hugged both Grandestmother and John at the same time and said, "Grandypa has forgiven me. Have you forgiven me, Grandestmother?"

*Roselyne Bosch (author). Mimi Polk Sotela and Iain Smith (executive producers). *1492: Conquest of Paradise*. California: Paramount Pictures © 1992.

"Of course, I have. I just needed to get past the first shock wave.
My love for you is stronger than any mistake you can make."

Grandestmother didn't get to see Grandypa.

SCENE 28

The countdown begins

TWENTY-EIGHT

MONDAY

MONDAY AT school, John wondered if he had caught some kind of deadly disease that other faculty members were afraid they might catch. They stayed away from him. When he put his tray down to eat lunch, the teachers at the table got up and moved to other tables. He sat alone, not understanding what was going on.

What he didn't know was that Monday morning, Rumley had held a brief faculty meeting before classes began. Rumley chose a time when John would not be able to attend. John was unavailable because he was showing videos of Friday night's football game to his team.

Rumley said to his faculty: "In the few minutes we have together, there are two matters about which I need to advise you. The first one is an employee review and the other matter is that one of our students has a grandfather who is in jail for attempted murder.

"First, many of you have heard by now that the administration is having major concerns about one of its coaches, Mr. John Bright. The worst is confidential, of course, but I will tell you what I can. Mr. Bright has admitted to me to being in attendance at drinking parties with students. He has held secret meetings with them in the woods without parental consent, and I have taken calls from parents who were more than a little concerned."

The teachers were glued to their principal, absorbing every juicy word.

Rumley continued, "We're not sure what all Mr. Bright is involved in, but I assure you that the matter is under investigation. Your school counselor, Ms. Evelyn Rouse, and your school nurse, Mr. Cris Platt, have sought to help Mr. Bright reconsider his relationship with the students and his attitude within this work environment. Unfortunately, their noble efforts were met by Mr. Bright's unprofessional behavior. But I do want to thank them for trying to help me salvage this employee."

Platt and Rouse nodded their heads in acceptance of Rumley's grattitude. Ms. Gibson became nauseated.

Rumley continued, "As I said, the worst is confidential, but I did want to tell you enough to clue you in on how complex and serious this matter is and let you know that it is in your best interest not to be seen in off-to-the-side conversations with this particular employee. As you've probably heard, the school board will be meeting next Monday night in a closed session to examine the findings of my investigation and decide the appropriate course of action concerning Mr. Bright's employment with this institution."

Rumley shuffled his papers to find his place and spoke again. "The second matter I want to cover is the recent crisis in our community involving two attempted murders. I'm sure you've seen it on TV news and on the front page of the newspaper.

"An elderly man by the name of Samuel Summers objected to a surgical procedure performed on a member of his family and allegedly took the law into his own hands and tried to murder the doctor who performed the surgery and the nurse who assisted him. His granddaughter is a student here at LHS. If you don't know who she is, she is the cheerleader with the dark complexion—Leilani Summers. Some of the students refer to her as Princess Leilani from Hawaii.

"Leilani has received professional therapy at the hospital and is hopefully stabilized at this point. However, if you see any problems, report them immediately to Mr. Platt or Ms. Rouse, and they will do what they can for her and notify me. I will take appropriate action. By the way, when the crime occurred, the police could not find this student because she was in the woods with Mr. Bright...Are there any questions?"

There were no questions from the stunned audience. Ms. Gibson was stunned right along with them, but not for the same reason. Picking up her purse, she made her way to the bathroom. She blamed Rumley for her vomiting and diarrhea.

The only change the members of the Teens With Wisdom Society noticed on Monday was that the principal, counselor, and nurse monitored the halls between classes to see if they could pick up on any trouble that was brewing.

Monday evening, telephone lines sizzled and E-mail sped from computer to computer as the teenagers prepared to put their plans into action.

When John got home from football practice, he told Maria how the other faculty members had given him the cold shoulder. "Something terrible is happening, and I can't find out what's going on. No faculty member will sit by me or talk to me, even about the weather, much less about what Rumpley's concocting behind my back."

TUESDAY

The cheerleaders wore their uniforms to school and sold two ribbons. The first was for Friday night's game. It was a purple ribbon with white letters that said, "Defang the Tigers." Beneath the words, a cartoonlike tiger wearing a football helmet was seated in a dentist's chair, losing its fangs, obviously in pain.

The other ribbon was for the school board meeting. It was a gold ribbon with purple letters. The message on it asked: "If we do right, will it turn out wrong?" In a cartoonlike drawing, a puzzled student looked up at a question mark over his head.

Word got around that the second ribbon was for the school board meeting, and it was selling fast...until the cheerleading sponsor got wind of the matter. She flatly ordered the girls to stop selling it on campus. The sponsor had heard Rumley's speech, and she was afraid for the cheerleaders to have any connection whatsoever to the coach.

From then on, the cheerleaders told all interested customers to meet them after school at 5:00 P.M. at the mall near the fountain.

Leilani and Kaprice popped into John's office in the gym. Kaprice asked, "Wanna buy a ribbon, Coach John?"

He read the ribbon and hugged both girls. "Sure, I want to buy a ribbon."

"Sorry, you can't!" Leilani asserted. "Our sponsor has made us quit selling them on campus."

"Are you serious?"

"Serious as can be," Leilani said. "But if you really, really want one, we'll be selling them at the mall at five after school."

"You will?"

"Then everyone can wear them to school tomorrow! Give us five, Coach!" They slapped hands above their heads.

"How did you girls get the money to have these ribbons made? That must have cost a lot."

"More than a hundred bucks. Hope's parents put up the money for us. We promised to pay them back after we sell the ribbons."

"Well, make my day! You guys are great! I needed some encouragement. But go now. If they catch me with you girls, they'll probably try to make something out of it."

As they left, Kaprice and Leilani turned and did a quick cheer in a whisper.

Fire Coach John? No, he will not!
Bongo Buns can go to pot!

They laughed, stuffed a ribbon in his shirt pocket, and were gone.

Ribbon sales at the mall were brisk that evening. They sold out in two hours.

WEDNESDAY

Students drove into the parking lot with signs on their cars that read, "If we do right, will it turn out wrong?"

The lot monitor rushed a report to Rumley.

Ribbons with the same message were all over the school. Some of the boys wore one on the outside of each pant leg, and the ribbons blew in the breeze as they walked. Dale had Leilani pin one to each sleeve of his T-shirt.

After lunch, Dale and Hope went to Rumley's office and asked Ms. Gibson if they could speak with him.

Ms. Gibson intercommed him.

Rumley asked Ms. Gibson to come in his office for the reply. He told her to tell the students to check back tomorrow, and he'd see if he could find time to see them. She relayed his words. Disappointed, they went to class.

THURSDAY

"If we do right, will it turn out wrong?" was still on the cars.

Buses came rolling in bearing the same message on posters taped to back doors. Student passengers quietly pressed signs against the windows at their seats for people to read.

Teachers found photocopies of the message in their mailboxes. When Rumley checked the fax machine for a fax he was expecting, it was there, too. He checked his messages on his answering machine. A message was recorded there as well. Rumley called Ms. Gibson in and made her listen to it. "See what they're doing! See what John has caused by leaking the meeting! This message is all over the school! There may be a riot!"

Ms. Gibson cautiously replied, "You asked me to tell you if any student mentioned to me that Coach Bright told them about the board meeting. None have. I'm sure it got out some other way."

"Yeah, right!" Rumley said sarcastically.

Rumley was correct about it being all over the school. The message was written on every marker board in every classroom and on napkins in the cafeteria. The message was in the bathroom stalls, over the urinals, and in front of the wash basins. The school had been blitzed. The student body loved John, and they didn't want to lose him.

Rumley held a hasty meeting with Cris Platt and Evelyn Rouse. They discussed when and how the volcano of emotions might erupt.

Dale and Hope dropped by the principal's office at lunchtime. Again they asked Ms. Gibson if they could speak with Rumley. She handed them a written message from him. It read: "If there are no demonstrations in the pep rally tomorrow morning, I will grant you an appointment during the last period of the day."

Dale wadded up the note. "I can see through this. Mr. Rumley is buying time. He is putting us off to run out the clock. He's also trying to put pressure on us not to screw up his precious pep rally."

"Dale, you are wise beyond your years," Ms. Gibson observed.

FRIDAY

The signs had been ripped from the buses. Rumley had ordered the buses inspected before they began their routes. The messages had been wiped from the marker boards and removed from the halls, the bathrooms, and everywhere else.

Platt had borrowed a button maker from a printer friend and made several dozen large buttons to compete with the students' ribbons and signs. Only a few teachers wore the large badge that read: "If you do wrong, it will turn out wrong!" Most teachers refused to wear it, saying it lowered wearers to the students' level and was unprofessional...but a few did.

John saw the buttons on the teachers, and he was crushed, believing that all the teachers had turned against him. The merciless rejection of his peers bewildered him. He still hadn't heard about Rumley's secret meeting with the faculty on Monday.

The time for the pep rally arrived. More than a thousand students crowded into the school's largest gym. Security guards stood at each end of the gym. Rumley, Platt, and Rouse were there, patrolling and nervously putting their heads together every few moments.

The pep rally was wild and loud. The cheerleaders had all of the students screaming for their team and acting as if they were shooting Tigers. Coach John spoke about the goals for the game, the improvements he felt the team would make. Team captains told how they were going to skin the Tigers and bring back a couple of rugs for Coach John's office.

After three more cheers, the cheerleaders stopped. One handed Leilani a microphone, and Leilani walked to the middle of the gym floor. The other girls moved to the left edge of the floor in close formation.

A thousand students began to chant, "Princess! Princess! Princess! Princess! Princess!" Their chanting was soft and affectionate. Most had heard about what she was going through, and they, with warm words, were embracing their beautiful Princess Leilani from Hawaii.

Rumley fidgeted and tried to get the security guard to read his lips as he mouthed: That girl with a mike in her hand could mean trouble.

Leilani's voice soared through the gym, echoing into every corner.

> As all of you know, my grandfather is in jail for two counts
> of attempted murder, and I suppose you know that it was
> over an abortion I had last year.

Rumley started toward Leilani. The cheerleaders raced over and blocked him, pleading, "Please don't stop her. She has to get this out. Don't worry. It's not going to be about Coach John."

Rumley stopped, surrounded by cheerleaders. He was unsure of what to do. He decided to wait and see if the cheerleaders were right.

Standing alone in the middle of the gym floor, in the circle marking the center of the basketball court, Leilani appeared tiny as she faced the thousand students. She was beautiful in her purple and gold uniform with white trim. Her long jet-black hair framed a sincere face and flowed down her back. She nervously pulled some strands of hair over her right shoulder. Her Polynesian complexion made her appear as if she had a fresh tan. Her blue eyes scanned the ocean of students as they waited anxiously for her next words. She had plenty to say. She had lain awake nights thinking of things. She had prayed for God to inspire her as she spoke. Leilani's voice cracked and then grew clear and strong as she said:

> I just want to tell you...I just want to tell you that our heroes are doing us wrong. I think many celebrities have gotten so open-minded that their brains have fallen out or something. They are pushing sex and alcohol at us and acting like there are no consequences.
>
> I was in the library thumbing through a *Therapy Issues Today* magazine, and I read where it said that sex is mentioned on TV every four minutes on prime-time programs, and it almost always happens between unmarried people. It's crazy! Many celebrities host fund-raisers for helping people with AIDS, while they promote immorality to us every four minutes on the tube. Does that make sense to you guys?
>
> The magazine said that TV presents sex as pleasure without consequences. That's lame! That's totally untrue! I'm here today to tell you that there can be very serious consequences to having sex outside of marriage. Because of my abortion, my womb became a death chamber instead of a sanctuary, and my grandypa is in jail for protesting the violence that happens in wombs. When I visited him in jail, Grandypa told me that a mother's womb is the most dangerous place a child can be. How did our country come to this? Why?

Leilani bowed her head to collect her thoughts. Whispers rippled through the gym.

Rumley didn't like what was happening, and he was puzzling with the question: *How can I stop Leilani without looking like*

an insensitive and heavy-handed principal to the student body and
faculty? That's probably what John Bright has been saying about me
behind my back. I don't want to do anything that might make people
think he's right about me.

Leilani made eye contact with the student body, and she spoke
louder:

I'd be more embarrassed to say what I'm saying if I didn't
know some of your secrets.

Some of you have had abortions, too. You are still
worried sick that your parents will find out. A few of you
are waiting for your HIV test results to come in. A few of
you have herpes. A few of you have genital warts. And
some of you have had other sexually transmitted diseases.
A few of you guys are so low that you've used date-rape
drugs. A few of you girls have received them, and now
you don't know who all has seen you without your clothes
on or what they've done to you. Some of you have
already been in drug or alcohol rehab. When are we
students going to wise up?

Part of the problem, I think, is what we listen to on
our CD's, our radios, and music television. Too much of
the music industry is designed to increase our feelings
of rebellion so bigwigs can make money off us. Celebrities are leading us on. They are betraying us. And we are
mindlessly following along like puppets who have handed
our strings to them.

Do you know what the sobering truth is? It's this:
Right now in our society, the children we don't abort,
we corrupt! Meditate on that the next time you're
daydreaming in class: Many of the children our society
doesn't abort, it corrupts!

To drill home the point, Leilani paused, her eyes searching the
bleachers. Her audience was motionless. The huge gym was ghost-town
quiet.

Look around you. See the trouble your friends are in.

Ask yourself, "Is partying with sex, alcohol, and drugs pleasure without consequences?"

Students of Lincoln High, I think we ought to rebel against the wrong crowd—the one that's on the TV shows, the movie screens, and the music charts—the electronic wrong crowd!…the crowd that baby-sat us when we were children and our parents worked or partied…the crowd we first learned about in our children's newspapers and magazines. We were weaned on celebrities, but the more we act like many of them, the more we destroy our families. We've got to stop letting them tell us that it's okay to use our minds and reproductive systems as party toys. We've got to be smarter.

Actually, *we are* smarter than they are. How many of you would invite over the children and their parents from Martha Washington Elementary and take off all your clothes and have sex in front of them—all for a few bucks? I hope none of us would do that. Celebrities do it! That's what they do on the movies and on the TV! They're not stupid! They know children will be watching! They do it to be popular, to have fame! They do it to make money, to get rich! They are selling themselves!

We teens, even with our problems, have better morals than our role models do. And those celebrities think it's a bother to give us autographs? Those celebrities ought to be asking us for autographs! We are the least corrupt. We are the most intelligent. We are better people!!

Leilani stopped speaking for a moment to deal with a conflict that came to her mind. She realized that she needed to change what she had just said.

On second thought, are we better influences than corrupt celebrities?

Maybe not. We influence our little brothers and sisters to become sexually active, and we influence them to drink, and to do drugs, and to hate their parents, and to rebel against their families. Is that better? Is it?

Like baby elephants behind adult elephants, we are grabbing the tails in front of us and joining the parade into corruption. Our little brothers and sisters are grabbing our tails, and we are leading them into corruption. We are passing corruption on to the next generation!

Leilani began demonstrating what she was saying. She stuck out her left arm in front of her and let it flop around limply like an elephant's trunk, her hair almost touching the shiny floor. She stuck out her right arm behind her hips like an elephant's tail. The mike was in her right hand and the cord trailed along behind her. Twice she walked around the circle in the middle of the gym floor like a mindless elephant parade. As she demonstrated, she held the mike to her mouth and said, "You can't see around an elephant's behind. It's the blind leading the blind!"

Laughter was sparse. The students didn't laugh much because they knew Leilani was seriously appealing to them to resurrect from letting the morally blind lead them while they misled the children coming up behind them. All laughter faded. Only the shrill sounds of Leilani's tennis shoes scuffing the gym floor could be heard. She had drilled home her message, and they got the point.

Leilani stopped, turned to the students in the bleachers, stood at attention, placed the tip of a finger to her head, paused to emphasize her point, and brightly said:

I have a better idea! We teens like to be rebellious! Why don't we rebel by fighting adult corruption? Why don't we just say no to adult corruption? Why don't we stop the stupid cycle of corruption?

Something Terence wrote in a paper for journalism class this week deserves to be said here: "A corrupt culture cultures corrupt kids." Say it with me: "A corrupt culture cultures corrupt kids."

The gym came to life with a mild roar. The student body repeated the sentence to be polite to Leilani.

Let's say it together one more time: "A corrupt culture cultures corrupt kids." Thank you.

Adults are wacko if they think they can get us to make all the right choices while we live in the middle of a corrupt culture. Hello! It's the culture, stupid! Our shepherds are corrupt! They are leading us astray! Hello! I refuse to take all the blame for what's happened in my family. I refuse to believe my grandfather is worse than those who lead us down mined trails.

We are all the time hearing about how messed up teens are, but my very good friend Dale once told me that the reason there are so many juvenile delinquents now is because there are so many adult delinquents. Dale doesn't let the adult world blame everything on us teens. He says adults are the ones who manufacture and deal drugs. They are the ones who manufacture, advertise, and demonstrate how to use alcohol and tobacco. Adults are the ones who produce and distribute TV shows and movies that promote and demonstrate sex to children. Adults are the ones who produce the wicked and violent video games, and they are the ones who animate filth into cartoons.

Why don't we stop the stupid cycle?! Why don't we fight adult corruption instead of joining it? Why don't we stop relaying it to younger children? Why don't we just say no to adult corruption? Why don't we?!

Students, I challenge you to let go of the elephant's tail in front of you! Be your own person! Take a better path in life! Be a decent influence!

I would like to start a crusade here this morning! I would like to start a crusade against adult corruption! The Good Book says in Acts 2:40, "Save yourselves from this corrupt generation" (NIV). (I didn't mention God, Mr. Rumley!) Let's do what it says! Let's save ourselves from this corrupt generation!

Rumley, being paranoid, was unnerved by the word *crusade*. He moved in the direction of the microphone. Two cheerleaders grabbed him by each of his arms, leaned into him, sandwiching him between them, holding him tightly. Rumley impatiently tried to pull away. The girls held their ground. "Wait! Mr. Rumley, please wait!" one exclaimed.

"It's not what you think! The crusade Leilani wants to start will be good for our school!"

Leilani was nervous, and she was unsure of how well she was presenting her thoughts. She wasn't following an outline. She was speaking from her heart. She backtracked.

> Who taught us teenagers that getting drunk is the way to be the coolest? Why did we believe them? Are we wimps or what?
>
> Temporary insanity, that's what getting drunk is. Drunk kids act disgusting and have sex with people they'd never even look at if they were in their right minds…and kids who are temporarily insane from alcohol don't even remember to apply what they learned in sex education.
>
> Teens like to be in control, and drinking causes us to lose control…Well, all I can say is: We've really swallowed the advertising. We teenagers, too many of us, would rather stand in a field and drink a beer than go to a school dance or go skiing or play sports. Well, I have a very important announcement to make—

Rumley broke free of the girls and headed toward Leilani. She caught sight of him and shouted into the mike.

> We are not Mr. Cool or Ms. Cool when we drink or do drugs! We are nothing more than mindless disposal sites for dangerous chemicals that are owned by people who count their money while we suffer pathetic consequences.

The principal backed up and blended again into the group of cheerleaders. He had suddenly thought of something that made sense to him. He decided to count Leilani's speech toward meeting his state-mandated requirements for providing drug education.

Leilani continued with so much intensity that she held the attention of every person in the gym:

> So what is our standard for cool? Is it how much beer we can drink? Is it how many drugs we've done? How much

sex we've had? How much stuff we've shoplifted? What gang we're in? That's what cool is?

Again I ask: Who told us that? Why did we believe it? What are we going to do now? Stay stupid? Or wise up?

Some of us are wising up. Someone recently told me that "there is hope for those who learn to cope." I agree. And we are learning to cope in ways that come with lifetime guarantees. We students are starting a new organization. We're calling it the Teens With Wisdom Society. It's for students who have the guts to be independent individuals and stop slipping around in celebrity slime and adult corruption. It's for you students who want to stop holding onto the tail in front of you.

As Leilani said the name of the organization, she realized she needed to be clearer about its purpose:

But I don't want you to get the idea that our new society is about not drinking or doing drugs or having sex. It's positive. It's about—

Her speech was interrupted by applause and kids screaming, "Whoop! Whoop! Whoop!"

One of the most popular kids on campus had stepped onto the gym floor and was walking toward Leilani. Terence had a sheet of paper in his right hand. It was the STRONG WILLS. Hope had typed them into her laptop computer and printed them on beautiful paper. Terence handed the paper to Leilani.

Leilani saw what it was and handed it back to him. "Would you read it?" she asked. She motioned for Kaprice to join them.

Terence reached for the mike, saying, "Here's our purpose, and Kaprice would like to read it for you." Terence passed the STRONG WILLS and the mike to Kaprice.

Kaprice understood his fear of reading in public due to his dyslexia, and she was happy to read the purpose of the new organization for him: "'Our Teens With Wisdom Society is a fellowship of teens who have formed an oasis of friendship and support in a stressed-out and confused culture. Our purpose is to help each other muscle up and rise above his or her problems, frustrations, or mistakes, and build an invincible life. Our common goal is to be truly independent—to live quality-controlled lives based on the wisdom of Chri…uh, the wisdom of the ages.' We three are members!"

Terence took the STRONG WILLS and the mike from Kaprice and held the paper up to the students. "This document contains our new standard for cool! Through these, you can let go of the tails of the elephants in front of you! You can step out of the cycle! You can stop following big butts!!"

Leilani placed her hand on Terence's wrist and said softly into the mike, "Those interested in joining the Teens With Wisdom Society, contact one of us. Thanks for listening. I hope you liked my speech. When you're not at school, please pray for my family. Thank you."

The student body applauded politely as Terence escorted Leilani off the court and out a side door and as the cheerleading squad joined Kaprice on the gym floor.

Out of sight, Leilani began to cry from the stress and leaned into Terence's hug. "That was so-o-o difficult," she said through sobs. "How did I do?"

"You did perfect. The Force was with you," he said, smiling. "Actually, it was you know Who, but I'm not supposed to say the G-word in school."

Leilani smiled with him. "You're right. The Almighty was with me. I felt strong because of His presence."

The cheerleaders closed the pep rally with a final cheer, but few students participated. Most were thinking about the many things Leilani had said. The band played the school fight song softer than usual as the students exited with less talking than normal.

The principal met with Dale and Hope during the last period of the school day.

Ms. Gibson escorted them into his office and seated them in two of three chairs in front of Rumley's huge shiny desk. She sat down off to the side and dug in her purse for a pencil. Rumley looked over the students' shoulders as if expecting another guest.

After an awkward couple of minutes, during which Dale and Hope waited uncomfortably, not knowing when it was okay to start speaking, a man wearing a business suit rushed in to take the empty seat. The newcomer asked, "Are you just beginning?"

Rumley nodded yes.

"Good. A meeting at the investment firm lasted much too long."

Rumley began the session by addressing Hope, "It's good to see you." He forced a grin. "Have you decided to behave for a change and stop embarrassing your old man?"

Hope sizzled inside but replied politely, "Our family is in counseling, and I'll be returning home soon."

Rumley shifted his eyes to Dale. "How have you been doing? I know the loss of your mother and brother has been hard on you. Are you still living in the projects?"

Without waiting for Dale's answer, Rumley introduced the other man with an apology that seemed fake. "Oh, pardon me. Do the two of you know Mr. Means? He's president of the school board. Mr. Means, this is Dale, and this young lady is Hope."

Means shook Dale's hand and then reached across him to shake Hope's. Rumley continued, "These students are here to talk about Coach John Bright and the board meeting Monday. They are the ones I mentioned to you earlier on the phone."

Hope said, "We just came to ask you to be fair with Coach John. We students like him a lot, and he's helped us a lot."

Rumley ignored Hope's comment and spoke directly to Dale. He asked, "Dale, may I speak plainly without fear of retaliation coming at me or my family or this school from you and your friends on the streets?"

Dale was disgusted by the way Rumley trashed him in front of the others in the room, but he held his temper. "Me and my hoodlum friends will try to control ourselves, Mr. Rumley. I came here to seek justice for Coach John, not to cause trouble."

"In that case," Rumley began, "I must tell you that I think it is inappropriate for you to come in my office and tell Mr. Means and me that you suspect that we are going to be unjust and unfair. I see that as an insult to our characters."

Rumley cocked his head, raising one eyebrow to make his point. "Furthermore, I don't think you and Hope are in any position to instruct us on being responsible people. Stop and consider your own reputations."

Hope responded, "Okay, I've been a sorry person. That's no big secret. And that's the point. The meetings we've had with Coach John helped me change my attitude and helped me want to go back home to make things right. Coach John didn't counsel me. He and Maria only guided the meetings. Our new STRONG WILLS changed me...and Dale counseled me...oh, and my dad reached out to me again. What has Coach John done wrong? Why do you want to fire him? He cares more than anybody in this school. Why can't doing right turn out right for him?"

Rumley was ticked. He leaned toward her and hit her with a series of rapid-fire questions: "Has Coach Bright met with students when beer was present?"

"Yes, but—"

"Has Mr. Bright met with students without parental knowledge?"

"Yes, but—"

"Was Mr. Bright hiding out in the woods with the students when Leilani Summers's grandfather attempted to murder the medical professionals?"

"Yes, but—"

"Get out of her face!!" Dale screamed angrily.

Rumley leaned back in his office chair. A sly smile played around his lips as if he were enjoying himself. "Dale, there has been a rumor that you brought a gun to school. Is there anything to that rumor?"

Dale responded, "Mr. Rumley, that was two years ago. Since then, I have—"

Means interrupted, "Look, kids, we appreciate your concern for your coach, but Mr. Bright needs to learn some lessons in being a proper employee. He needs to learn how to work with his superiors and the importance of following established policies. He'll likely do better in his next position."

Hope felt benched.

Dale thought a minute and said, "So we have failed in our mission to get you to give Coach John another chance. Then I've got something to say to you, Mr. Rumley. When me and Hope came in here, you put her down about her past. Then you brought up my mother and brother and pointed out to Mr. Means that you assume that I'm an outlaw from the city's gutters. You threw up our old reputations to us—our *old* reputations," he emphasized.

"You got in Hope's face and talked down to her when she was doing her best to stand up for what she believed. You made me look like the worst person on your campus by mentioning the gun incident."

Dale glanced at Mr. Means to be sure he was listening, too. "I just want to say that Coach John wouldn't have done that to us. He respects us. He believes that adults have to respect what there is to be respected in us if anything more is to become respectable."

Dale stood up and motioned for Hope to join him. "Come on, Hope. This is a lost cause."

The principal sent Dale a look of contempt, but kept silent. He didn't want to give Dale anything more to hold against him.

Hope followed Dale out, stopping long enough to say, "Mr. Rumley, what you do will always be with you."

They bumped into a security guard who had been stationed outside the office door. Neither student knew he was there. He took his position after they entered Rumley's office. Both were insulted even more.

After the students left, Means said, "Alfredo, I don't understand your purpose in putting those kids down and making them angry. You hit 'em too hard. I think things are going to get downright nasty now. You had better double up the security officers for Monday night."

Disappointed in what he had witnessed, Mr. Means left. Ms. Gibson went back to her office. Rumley slumped in his chair and put one hand to his forehead as he thought, *Maybe I shouldn't have rubbed Dale's and Hope's faces in the gutter since it bothered Means, but I wanted to squelch any support for that upstart coach. Those students get on my last nerve. They're nothing but troublemakers. If it weren't for students like them, my job would be fulfilling.*

He sat up and intercommed Ms. Gibson to return to his office. "Ms. Gibson, you are supportive of my action with Coach John, but I just want to tell you that if any faculty member shows up at that board meeting to stand up for Coach John or to speak against my leadership, it will be very damaging to his or her future in this school district. So if there happen to be any faculty members like that and you know who they are, do them a favor and encourage them *not* to show up at that meeting. This whole situation has become extremely explosive."

MONDAY

A large number of students came to school wearing their ribbons in support of John. Most teachers remained against John, and a few wore Platypus's buttons.

As planned by the students, at the beginning of all second-period classes, someone in each class raised a hand and asked the teachers: "Do you think that doing right should turn out wrong?"

In most cases, the teachers allowed time for discussion. They agreed with the students that right should turn out right, but they wouldn't comment on whether or not John had done right. One of the social studies teachers said, "From what I've heard in the teachers' lounge, most of us believe it is best for John to be forced to take some time off from coaching and enter professional therapy. The majority of our faculty members support the administration."

SCENE 29

Coach John goes before the firing squad

TWENTY-NINE

MONDAY NIGHT

FOUR POLICE cars were already parked in front of the school district's administration building when Rumley and Means arrived for the board meeting. They happened to drive into the parking lot at the same time. Stepping out of their cars, locking them, and checking to be sure they locked them, they shook hands and walked together toward the building.

To their surprise, they found the campus orderly. They had expected rowdy students to be marching with signs and yelling in John's defense.

Instead, the student body appeared and acted as if it was attending a church service. The guys were dressed in suits or blazers. The girls wore beautiful dresses that were nice enough for Easter Sunday. Leilani and Kaprice were the only exceptions. They chose to wear their cheerleading uniforms to show the board members that student leaders were involved in the protest.

Some teens were near the police cars, visiting with police officers. Others introduced themselves to board members.

More and more students arrived until there were at least 150 neatly groomed, well-behaved young people in attendance—all wearing those gold ribbons with purple print: "If we do right, will it turn out wrong?"

A little bewildered, the police sergeant chuckled and asked Rumley and Means, "Are these the kids you want us to protect you from?"

Means replied, "Just hang in here. The fat lady hasn't sung yet."

"And the worst kid in school has yet to arrive," Rumley anxiously said.

"Dale? No, I saw him." Means nodded in Dale's direction. "He's over there. He looks as nice as any of these kids."

"Any bulges in his clothes?" Rumley sneered. "Is he carrying a gun?!"

"I don't see any bulges from here," the sergeant said. "I'll drift over and check him out more closely."

The sergeant approached Dale, "Pardon me, son. I need to check you for a weapon. I don't have probable cause or a search warrant, so I'll need your permission. If you refuse, you'll not enter the building."

Dale was offended, but his greater priority was to be with his friends and John. "Sure. Why not? But I'll bet I'm the only person that you search," Dale responded, playing it cool, yet showing his resentment.

Dale held out his arms and spread his legs apart. The officer's searching hands began to explore Dale's body.

Dale—embarrassed, insulted, and trapped—looked at those looking at him as the officer doubted his decency and invaded his privacy. Everyone was watching—board members, faculty members, students, and other policepersons. Dale was glad he had decided to leave his switchblade in his truck. The officer turned to Means and Rumley and showed them empty hands, meaning that he had come up empty-handed.

The exchange of looks didn't go unnoticed by Dale. Dale contributed a drop-dead look to Rumley. Means also saw it and thought Rumley was pushing their luck again. Means knew that street people have friends, dangerous friends.

Means told Rumley, "There's no way I can exclude these students from the board meeting. I am president of an investment firm, and I can't afford a reputation of being rude and inconsiderate to high schoolers. Some of these students' parents invest with me, and some of these kids already have their first accounts with me. There is more at stake here than whether or not you'll get to fire a coach." Means emphasized, "Besides, these kids are acting like young adults, and they deserve to be treated accordingly. I'm inviting them in. After a brief introduction, in which I'll humor them, we can retire into a private chamber to discuss the real issues."

Rumley felt his stomach wrench and sink to his feet. "This has been planned as a closed meeting, Mr. Means. You can't let the students get their way! You are letting them be controlling! That's below you!"

Means replied, "You worry too much, Alfredo." He turned and walked toward the boardroom.

Rumley and the board members took their seats behind microphones at a long, highly polished, blond wooden desk that was slightly curved into a large C so the board members could see each other and their audience. The desk was on a platform elevated above the audience.

John and Maria were seated on the front row of the audience section. It was unusual for spouses to attend a firing, but Maria wanted to be at John's side, and John wanted her there with him. Maria squeezed John's arm, showing support. He hadn't been able to eat dinner. His stomach churned. They both suspected that John's employment records were in the stack of papers in front of Rumley.

They saw that Rumley had one of Platypus's buttons in his right hand—"If you do wrong, it will turn out wrong!" He fidgeted with it as he waited for the board meeting to begin. He was wearing his skinny black-rimmed reading glasses, looking over the top of them, watching people come in, offering gestures of greeting to various individuals.

Means brought the meeting to order. "We are here to discuss matters of concern relating to one of our employees, Mr. John Bright. We will begin by calling roll."

The secretary of the board began to call out the names: "Robert Means."

"Here."

"Bill Wycoff."

"Here."

"Estelle Rutherford."

"Here."

A quiet wave of laughter traveled through the audience. The students thought it was funny to hear adults answering roll call like they had to answer it in school. A couple of policemen gave them dirty looks.

"Elaine Simmons."

"Here."

"Viola Jeffries."

"Present."

"Yours truly, Donald Bundik, is here, too. Alfredo Rumley is present. John Bright is present. Thank you."

During roll call, John had noticed board members scanning their young audience. He was proud of the students—the care they had taken in dressing for the occasion and the way they were conducting themselves. A few of the board members seemed to sit a little taller, too, as they made eye contact with the young people. Some students had important parents, representing a lot of votes in school board elections.

Means took over again. "Ladies and gentlemen of the school board, we have guests with us this evening for the introductory portion of this meeting. Members of our student body are here, expressing interest in these proceedings."

Then he addressed the students, "Thank you for coming, students. We want you to know that our board is dedicated to expressing justice in all matters, including this one. We want to be fair with all parties. We have been elected to do what's right and to uphold justice for the student body and for Lincoln High School. You may not fully understand our decision since you won't be included in hearing the facts—facts that will be revealed in a closed meeting. However, we trust that you will realize that the school board members seated before you are dedicated citizens who freely give of their time in service to our community. We hope that you each will be mature enough to support whatever decision we arrive at. It's our country's way, due process, at work."

Not familiar with how board meetings are conducted, Terence raised his hand before audience input was permitted by the president of the board. He had been appointed to be the spokesperson for the students since he was so well liked by both students and faculty. Plus Terence, being an African-American, had minority status, and the students didn't think the board would put him down in front of everyone.

Means called on him.

"Sir, we students have a request to place before the school board," Terence began, trying to speak with confidence. "We have come to this meeting in an adult manner. We are not here to be against anyone. We are here to try to understand what's going on. If your evidence clearly shows that Coach John is guilty of doing wrong, we will understand why he must leave, and we will help you keep the student body from getting radical about it. If evidence does not show that Coach John has done enough wrong to get fired, we don't believe the board will fire him. Sir, could we be included in your meeting and watch justice at work? It will be very educational for us."

Estelle Rutherford said, "Mr. Means, I make a motion that the students be included."

Donald Bundik said, "I'll second it if Estelle will amend her motion to read: 'I make a motion that the students be included if it meets with Mr. John Bright's approval.' The coach up for review is the only one who may be put in an embarrassing position. He should have the right to have input in whether this meeting will be public or private."

"I'll amend the motion," Rutherford said.

Means said, "I have a motion and a second. Any questions or discussion?"

Viola Jeffries said, "I won't vote for it. These well-dressed and well-mannered students have expressed extreme prejudice against Mr. Rumley throughout this past week. Even now, they are wearing ribbons of protest."

Bundik replied, "Their ribbons don't say: 'Flush the principal!'"

A nervous laugh spread through the board members and audience.

Bundik continued, "Their ribbons ask a fundamental question: 'If we do right, will it turn out wrong?' We don't have to be worried about students who want right to turn out right and wrong to turn out wrong, do we?"

Means replied, "Viola, Mr. Rumley doesn't have anything to fear. As a professional, he wants only what's fair and just, and he will carry out anything this board decides. We all know him well. I agree with Mr. Bundik that Mr. Bright is the only one here who might not want confidential matters to go public."

Jeffries said, "Well, our principal should certainly have a say in this."

Rumley had relaxed some. He had reminded himself of how well prepared he was. He had his recordings ready. He had his speeches ready. And he prided himself on his public speaking ability. Ms. Gibson was set to testify in his behalf. Means was on his side. He had spoken with each board member privately and convinced each one that he was right. He was confident things would go his way, and the students would learn a lot from watching him apply his skills as a well-prepared and highly experienced administrator. But he wasn't eager to give in.

Means asked Rumley for his opinion. Rumley stated, "I think it would be highly unusual, and it would break with normal procedures."

Means scribbled Rumley a note. The other board members passed it along to the principal.

Rutherford said, "These young people have witnessed some of the things we will be questioning. I think they can be helpful to us as we try to sort things out. No one's down on anyone. We are going to do only what we have to do."

Rumley silently read Means's note: Let Dale and Hope see for themselves. That will settle them down. You don't need Dale and his street thugs or Hope's father against you...or me.

Rumley decided it wasn't a bad idea. He responded to the board and audience, "I don't mind if the students are included. Perhaps it will be beneficial for them to see a glimpse of the real world."

"Any more discussion? Any other questions? All in favor say aye. All opposed say no. The ayes have it."

Only Viola Jeffries voted against it.

Means addressed John, "You've heard the discussion and the vote. It's up to you. Are the students to be included or excluded?"

"I would like them included."

Jeffries said to Means, "Well, since the students are included, I think it would be appropriate for someone to educate them on how this works. May I?"

"That'll be fine, Viola."

"We want you students to understand that the school board has complete faith in Mr. Rumley. He has been in education for almost four decades, and his record speaks for itself. Mr. Rumley has recommended to the school board that Mr. Bright be fired. We will honor that recommendation unless extremely important reasons are presented why we should overturn our principal's recommendation, which, to be honest, I personally don't anticipate. In other words, as far as I'm concerned, Mr. Bright will not be employed as an employee of Lincoln High School after tonight. Furthermore—"

Means butted in. "But, Ms. Jeffries, I think we should stress to the students that we are open to any evidence that is properly presented on Mr. Bright's behalf. We favor Mr. Rumley's recommendation, no doubt, but we aren't close-minded about anything Mr. Bright has to say."

"Well," she shot back, "the burden of proof is certainly on Mr. Bright!"

Means asked, "Do you students understand that?"

"Yes, sir. We understand," Terence answered, acting as the spokesperson. However, he thought to himself, *But it seems Coach John is being considered guilty until proven innocent.*

Means said, "You know, young people, when you work for someone, you have to do what he or she says. If you don't, that by itself is enough reason to fire an employee. According to Mr. Rumley, Mr. Bright has not been responsive to his direction or correction."

Means addressed the principal, "Mr. Rumley, would you like to present your reasons for Mr. Bright's dismissal?"

Rumley cleared his throat and said, "You gave the first. All the other teachers are responsive to my authority. Mr. Bright always argues, and most of the time he defies my policies. In three meetings with him—one of which you attended, Mr. Means—I warned Mr. Bright that his failure to follow orders would cost him his job. The meetings are fully documented, and the records have been placed in his personnel file, which I have here."

Means spoke to the board and the audience. "That's true. I did attend one of those meetings. I was disappointed by Mr. Bright's attitude in the meeting. I also warned Mr. Bright. I told him that his principal had had more patience with him than members of the school board would probably have. Okay, Mr. Rumley, what else?"

"Mr. Bright is careless with the separation of the church and state issue. He called one of the parents on a school phone during school hours and told her that he would be praying about their family. It angered her, and she told me to tell him to keep his prayers to himself. I relayed her words to him, and Mr. Bright was defiant about the matter."

Franco stood up. "Mr. President, sir, that was my mom who called, and our family does need prayer. We are a dysfunctional family! Coach John has—"

Means interrupted and said, "Young man, you are out of order. Students will have the opportunity to speak later."

Franco sat down.

Then Means said to the student body, "But in passing, let me help you students understand something. The issue here is not prayer. I think everyone on this panel attends a church or synagogue and prays. The issue is that of separation of church and state. Mr. Bright broke school policy and wasn't open to correction. That's the problem."

Rumley continued, "I'm not sure Mr. Bright knows what career he wants to pursue. He's a PE teacher, but sometimes he acts as if he wants to be a therapist or a psychologist, without proper training, without being a professional. Again and again, I have reminded him that his place is to teach physical education and coach in our sports program. But he has been on what has appeared to be an ego trip and has said that he could help the students more than Ms. Rouse, our school counselor, or professional therapists."

Hope sprang to her feet. "The professional counselors didn't help me, but what happened in the meetings with Coach John and Maria did!"

Jeffries said impatiently, "Mr. Means, I make a motion that all students be excused from this meeting!"

Means answered, "Before I entertain a second to that motion, I will again ask that the audience stop interrupting and cooperate."

Hope sat down. Silence fell over the spectators.

The motion died because of a lack of a second.

Means said, "Continue, Mr. Rumley."

"What Mr. Bright does on his own time is his business, unless it is illegal or reflects poorly on our fine institution. And that is the case. Mr. Bright has been in the company of adolescents who were drinking alcohol. I have tried to talk to him about that subject, but he avoids discussing it with me."

Rumley paused to make eye contact with each of his school board members. "Actually, we don't know what has been going on between this coach and our students. On several occasions he has hung out with them in the woods, holding secret meetings without parental consent.

"In fact, at the time of the unfortunate incident wherein a doctor was allegedly almost shot by Leilani Summers's grandfather, Leilani was with Mr. Bright in the woods. No one knew where they were, and Mr. Bright refuses to say. I tried to support him at the police station, and he met me with rudeness, saying that I am as sick as hell. I think Mr. Bright should be required to tell the board what he's been doing in the woods with our students."

Leilani was bitterly angry. She wanted to scream at Rumley, but she kept her self-control for the sake of John and Maria. She thought, *He heard me speak at the pep rally. He heard me introduce our Teens With Wisdom Society. Is the man blind and deaf? What is he thinking? What is he up to?*

Means spoke to John, "Have you been in attendance when underage kids were drinking?"

"Yes, I have."

"Did you stop them?"

"No, I wanted to win their trust, and you don't do that by putting them down. You have to respect what there is to be respected before anything else can become respectable."

Means scratched his head. "I can't think of anything more strange than a teacher having a hideout for himself and a group of students and allowing the kids to break the law by drinking underage. That's enough to get you fired by itself. What have you been doing in the woods with those children?!"

John answered, "The students are here. May they tell you?"

Means addressed the students, "Those of you who have been a part of the secret gatherings out in the woods with Coach John Bright, please stand."

The ten members of the Teens With Wisdom Society rose to their feet.

Rumley frowned at Kaprice Gibson, then caught Ms. Gibson's eye as if to ask why her daughter was among the rebels. She gave him a don't-ask-me look. He thought that it was poor parenting on his secretary's part not to know her daughter was involved.

Means inquired, "Is there a spokesperson for the group? Who wants to tell the school board about these secret meetings with Mr. Bright?"

"Terence is our spokesperson," Hope replied, "but I want to say that Mrs. Bright has always been there, too."

"That's encouraging," Means acknowledged with a touch of sarcasm in his voice. "Now will somebody tell us what has been going on in the woods?"

"We've been trying to figure out our problems," Kyong Suk blurted out, in her accent.

A wide smile broke out on Rumley's face. "You see, board members! I have made it extremely clear to Mr. Bright that he is not a professional therapist and has no role in counseling students. So what does he do? Instead of responding to my leadership, he hides out in the forest where he can play psychologist and group therapist and puts the whole school district at risk of being sued for malpractice! He has exhausted my patience!!"

SCENE 30

The teens stand up for what they believe

THIRTY

WITH THE students still standing in the boardroom, President Means said to John, "Do you wish to speak in your own defense? Can you explain your behavior?"

John replied, "Mr. Means, Mr. Rumley says he has grounds to fire me. I've tried to talk to him about that, but he won't listen to me. He can't seem to accept the fact that I am only interested in helping the students, and that I am not interested in being a professional therapist for them. Whatever I say to him is twisted and used against me. I've concluded that I don't know how to defend myself in a way that will make a difference to him…or to you…or to his other friends on the school board."

"Then why did you want this hearing?" Means asked, with a barb of sarcasm in his voice.

"It's the principle of the thing, Mr. Means. I haven't done anything wrong enough to get fired over. That's why I've chosen to go through the whole process rather than seeing Mr. Rumley sweep everything under the rug and go on as if no one got hurt. I'm getting hurt! And there are students who are getting hurt!" John glanced at the students.

Addressing the board again, John said, "And even if I don't save my job, perhaps because of this experience you'll believe the next person who is hurt by Mr. Rumley and has the courage to bring it to your attention. Perhaps then A plus B will equal C to you board members…Oh, and there's one more reason. A friend named Mat taught me that things can turn out right for you even when you can't say a thing that matters, even in the worst of circumstances. Besides, I don't want to give up and walk off the field before the game's over. I wouldn't let my team do that."

John sat back down, unsure he had said anything of real value. Maria leaned into him and whispered a Scripture. "Wait on the Lord, sweetheart, and He shall renew your strength."

Means, having gotten little usable input from John, impatiently turned to the students who remained standing in the audience. "All right, you've been hiding in the woods, trying to figure out your problems. Would you care to explain that further?"

Terence looked around at the others. He shifted his weight from one leg to the other and began, "It's different for us than when you guys were coming up. Things are more difficult for kids now. There are ten teens standing in front of you. One of us has been living in a youth home. One has been molested by a family member. One has been molested by a psychologist. Both of them are waiting to get HIV tests to see if they are HIV positive. Two others have had abortions. Several have been sexually active. One has been beaten many times by his father. One has watched his mother get beat up by her live-ins and one-night stands. One's parents are getting a divorce and shoving her into the middle of it. Two of us have a weirded-out relationship because our parents are having an affair. One of our moms died of AIDS; a brother was killed by a gang in a turf war. One of us is living with her grandparents because her father is an alcoholic and her mother is a cocaine addict. One of our grandfathers is in jail for attempted murder. Only three of those standing before you have homes like most of you grew up in."

Terence summed it up, "These are the problems we've been trying to figure out how to make it through. We have been trying to figure ways to help ourselves and to help each other. I don't know. You may not be impressed. You may think we're, like, just a bunch of problem kids—"

"Now that you brought it up," Jeffries interrupted, "that is precisely what I think. You have more than your share of problems. Professional research shows that only 10 to 15 percent of the student body is like you."

Terence turned around, faced the students, and said, "Everyone who has one or more of the problems I mentioned, please stand."

Suddenly, the audience was alive with movement. All but a few of the students stood up. Terence said, "If you don't think that almost all teenagers are dealing with serious issues, then you are out of touch with our world. Lincoln High School is full of kids who are going through all kinds of bad things. Welcome to the world of today's teenagers!"

Hope spoke up, "Terence didn't mention the other side of this story. Some of our problems are our own fault. Most of you know my dad and mom. I can tell you that they are good people. I've treated them like hel—heck, and I couldn't see it until Dale became my eyes. I saw it through his eyes! Teenagers can easily get confused among all the bad influences, uh, corruption we come in contact with, and we need someone who will love us, like John and Maria have, and help us see, like Dale has, even while we are still being butthea...pardon me, rebellious persons."

Leilani added, "If Coach John and Maria and Dale had gotten to me earlier, I could have avoided everything my grandparents and I have gone through, and we wouldn't be on TV news now!"

Jeffries said, "This school district has always had a counseling program. There was help here before Mr. Bright came riding over the hill. Ms. Rouse and Mr. Platt are experienced professionals, and I know they make referrals to community agencies."

Franco said, "Ms. Rouse is too busy with schedule changes to do counseling. She refers us to people who charge $90 an hour to talk to kids. Can you believe that, $1.50 per minute? Where are we supposed to get that kind of money? Sell drugs?"

"Turn tricks?" Hope added tartly. "We can't afford to pay professional therapists! We haven't had anyone before Coach John came. Remove Coach John, and we won't have anyone. But Coach John and Maria haven't counseled us. All they've done is be there for us."

"We have decided that it's pretty much up to us to figure things out for ourselves," Dale added. "Adults aren't going to solve our problems. It's up to us. And we are succeeding! And we believe that one day we will be able to pass along what we are learning to other teens, and they, too, will be able to help themselves."

"Your sincerity is to be admired, of course," Jeffries said bluntly. "But sincerity will not solve complicated psychosocial problems. Mr. Bright has you children believing that you can develop therapeutic techniques that psychologists and psychiatrists have been developing since Sigmund Freud pioneered psychoanalysis in the early 1900s. That's impossible!! Mr. Means, can we move on?!"

Kaprice said, "Mr. Means, sir, could I just read to the school board what we teens have come up with so far? We are calling them our STRONG WILLS because they all begin with 'I will,' and they all represent choices that will save our lives...It's only one page. Could I? You'll see what we've been doing in the woods, okay?"

Leilani held up the sheet of paper that contained the STRONG WILLS. "This is our new standard for cool."

Jeffries objected, "Mr. Means, we are way off the subject. Whatever these kids have on that paper does not change the fact that

Mr. Bright refused to follow established policies and refused to respond appropriately to correction."

"I don't agree that we're off the subject, Viola. We asked the students what they've been doing in the woods with Mr. John Bright. They may read us what they've come up with."

"Thank you," said Kaprice nervously. This was the first time anyone besides their group had heard more than their statement of purpose. Kaprice hoped the board members would like what they had done in the meadow and feel better toward John.

The scene was one to memorize and cherish. Leilani and Kaprice stood together in their beautiful cheerleading uniforms—purple and gold with white trim. Their makeup was perfect. Each placed one arm around the other, and Leilani whispered to Kaprice, "Let's take turns reading. I'll go first."

Leilani read the title, introduction, and the Scripture verse: "The STRONG WILLS of the Teens With Wisdom Society. Our Teens With Wisdom Society is a fellowship of teens who have formed an oasis of friendship and support in a stressed-out and confused culture. Our purpose is to help each other muscle up and rise above his or her problems, frustrations, or mistakes, and build an invincible life. Our common goal is to be truly independent—to live quality-controlled lives based on the wisdom of the ages. *Do not let anyone look down on you because you are young, but be an example for the believers, in your speech, your conduct, your love, faith, and purity*' (1 Timothy 4:12, TEV)."

Kaprice read the first STRONG WILL. After that, she and Leilani took turns reading: "I will do right no matter what I think is wrong with my parents or guardians. I will be responsible for myself and not try to use my parents' or guardians' problems to excuse my own stupid sins. I will do well even if my parents or guardians have a lousy opinion of me. I will succeed even if I'm not favored for success. I will not give my brothers or sisters or my parent's significant other's children the right to ruin my life forever. I will not allow open-minded-but-narrow-minded professionals to judge me to be a wasteland and make me compromise my positive contribution in life."

With a look at the school board, the girls exchanged uneasy smiles. They hadn't thought of how that one would sound in front of administrators. Quickly they continued: "I will finally leave the sins of offenders in the past where they belong. I will make it through the storms and disappointments of family life. I will not allow rude comments, attitudes, or actions of teachers to turn me away from respecting myself and from believing that I can achieve good goals with my life. I will prove that insensitive teachers are wrong about me."

Kaprice grimaced as she read that one. It stepped on the toes of school officials. The girls looked up and saw cold stares beamed in their direction from board members. "Oops," Kaprice said, "please don't be offended. We believe that most teachers are okay. Only three out of eleven of us had been hurt by teachers." Her eyes dropped back to the sheet of paper.

"I will not allow my peers to pressure me away from what I believe is right by hassling me, by putting down my parents or decent friends, or by threatening to leave me out if I don't conform to what they want. I will honor God's trust of me in our best-friends relationship. The opportunities in my present and future are God's gifts to me; how I succeed with those opportunities is my gift to God. God votes for me, the pull of sin votes against me, and I am breaking the tie by the way I am voting with each decision I make."

Kaprice whispered to Leilani, "Let's read together."

Leilani whispered back, "Let's read with feeling."

They read with great resolve: "By making the above choices and living loyal to these choices, we teens will succeed in life, although bad things have happened to us in the past, although we've made mistakes ourselves, and although there are pressures on us now. Our STRONG WILLS are our life preservers!"

As Kaprice and Leilani finished, the meeting room was quiet and still. The girls looked up and waited for a response. More than a hundred students were still standing in front of the school board.

"Thank you, girls," Means said. "Please, all of you, be seated."

Obviously impressed by their STRONG WILLS, the board president said, "I congratulate you on the work that must have gone into developing those strong choices, er, wills. It's clear to me that such resolutions will help you deal with the problems with which you are trying to cope. I noticed a few that could be beneficial to my staff at Carlton and Means Investments. I think we may owe you students an apology."

Before the students could react, Jeffries reacted, "Hold on, Means! How about the booze?"

Ray found himself on his feet again. "Ms. Jeffries, did you drink when you were a teenager?"

Bursting out laughing, Bill Wycoff roared, "Yes, she did! I went to high school with her!"

The students broke out laughing, too. Other board members couldn't help but join them.

Means tried to stop laughing to restore order. Leaning into his mike, he said, "As I was saying, we owe you students an apology."

Means looked around to give board members an opportunity to show agreement. He returned his attention to the students. "We apologize for suspecting that you were up to no good. I encourage you to keep developing your material. You will truly receive help from it, and I commend you on your plan to pass it on to other young people."

Hope held up her hand to speak. Means called on her. "Mr. Means, we students are happy that you approve of what we've done, but how about Coach John and Maria? They have been, like, our coaches for developing our new standard of what it is to be cool. Since they've done right, why should it turn out wrong for them?" Hope sat down.

Rumley said, "Mr. Means, I have an answer for that."

"Yes?"

"What has come to light here is that Mr. Bright is in the wrong business. He should work for Young Life or, better yet, the Fellowship of Christian Athletes. He has not succeeded in the public school system, and I cannot let him remain on my staff."

Rumley pulled a recorder/player from his briefcase. John flinched, remembering how Rumley had gloated over secretly recording the meeting in his office. Rumley told the board, "I have a recording that illustrates Mr. Bright's attitude. This segment was made during a conference in which Ms. Rouse, Mr. Platt, and I were trying to reason with him. The recording will speak for itself."

He pushed a button and cranked up the volume.

(*Rouse*) "Wouldn't you agree that there is no difference between counseling and what you've been doing?"

(*Coach John*) "No, I would not agree. What I've been doing is a heck of a lot better than any counseling the students could get from the treatment center I was at. I know that for sure."

(*Rumley*) "You were in a treatment center? I don't recall that on your job application. Did you lie when you applied for a coaching position here?"

(*Coach John*) "No. I left that part blank so we could talk about it in the interview. You must not have noticed the blank. You didn't ask about it."

(*Rumley*) "I was interviewing several prospective employees during that time. I didn't notice that your application was incomplete. Be that as it may, since we are on the subject of therapy, the school district is under contract with Psychological Services Unlimited in the Professional Building on Frontage Road. We are prepared to give you six sessions with a therapist to see if you can get the help you need. Apparently moving from a college campus to an employment situation has been a difficult adjustment for you. Ms. Gibson will schedule your first appointment if you will cooperate. Will you?"

(*Coach John*) "Mr. Rumley, I do not need therapy. All I've done is try to help some students who have serious personal and family problems."

(*Rouse*) "Mr. Rumley has advised us that he has warned you several times not to try to counsel those students. Were you, in fact, counseling them?"

(*Coach John*) "Not exactly! I was helping the kids learn how to solve things for themselves! I was—"

(*Rouse*) "John, that's precisely what counseling is. Helping people discover their options and choose the best ones! You've been counseling on a PE degree! And you don't even know the meaning of the word!"

(*Coach John*) "The students tell me that you don't take time to talk to them, and that you refer them to places that charge so much they can't afford help. Someone has to be there for these kids."

(*Rumley*) "I have documentation in your personnel file that proves that I have told you on two separate occasions not to try to counsel students. You are not a professional."

(*Coach John*) "Not a professional! (*scuffling noises*) You guys are professionals?"

Rumley stopped the player. "Need I play more?"

"No. We have heard quite enough," Bundik said.

Rumley stated, "Men and women of the school board, the recording documents the fact that I have been careful to meet all criteria necessary for firing this employee. I gave him three warnings in front of witnesses, I properly documented those warnings in his file, and I offered six sessions with a professional therapist. Mr. Bright will have no ability to appeal this decision, legal or otherwise."

Means addressed the students. "You heard the same thing we did, Mr. Bright screaming at his supervisor and refusing to cooperate with efforts to help him save his job. That wouldn't do in any work situation. If he worked for me, I'd be firing him, too."

Terence raised his hand for permission to speak. Having been acknowledged, he rose to his feet and said, "There is something wrong here, sir. The coach that Mr. Rumley is presenting here is not the coach we students know." He sat back down.

"Son," Means said, "there is something you have to learn in life, and the earlier the better: Everything that glitters isn't gold! People aren't always as together as they seem on the surface. I'm sorry this has been such a difficult lesson for you students to learn tonight. You came here with the best intentions."

With a pompous smirk, Rumley said, "Thank you, Mr. Means. Mr. Bright got so angry and out of control during our discussions that the shuffling noise you heard on the recording was him jumping out of his chair at me and nearly knocking me down. Ms. Gibson, my secretary, was present. She is prepared to confirm the incident. Mr. Means, do you mind if she reads her notes?"

Means nodded approval. "Fine. I think it's important to remove all doubt from the students' minds that their principal has made a proper decision in firing Mr. Bright. Ms. Gibson, please come forward."

Kaprice's mom stood. In her hand, she held a recording. "May I play this? I think it will help clarify matters."

"Of course. Bring it forward. I'm sure Mr. Rumley won't mind if you borrow his player."

Rumley reluctantly motioned toward his player with a gesture that gave his permission.

Kaprice whispered to Leilani, "So now we find out Mom's surprise."

John squeezed Maria's hand. Rumley appeared puzzled. Tension mounted in the audience.

Avoiding Rumley's questioning stare, Ms. Gibson walked quickly to the front, high heels tapping the floor loudly, emphasizing every step.

Rumley reluctantly pushed the player toward her and tried to make eye contact with her to gain a clue to what she was doing. Ms. Gibson kept her eyes on the recorder, placed the recording in the machine with a snap, and pressed the play button. She swung by John and Maria on her way back to her seat and whispered to John, "The cavalry is about to ride over the hill!"

Rumley watched her.

And she whispered a Scripture to Maria, "What is done in secret shall be shouted from the rooftops."

Rumley saw her. He was getting worried.

She went over and sat down by her daughter, Kaprice, and they held hands. A moment later, the player came to life.

An angry voice boomed over the speaker. It was Rumley.

(*Rumley*) "Let me give you a little coaching, Coach! I am an administrator who has forgotten more about education than you will ever know, and you'd do well to listen to me! The kids you're losing your job for aren't worth it!"

Rumley grabbed the player, and his fingers searched for the stop button to make it shut up. He pushed the button so hard, it made a loud pop that echoed throughout the boardroom. Speaking with a shaky voice, he said, "Mr. Means, I would like to personally request that this not be admitted as evidence. This conversation happened after Mr. Bright had pushed me too far."

The audience was quiet, but alive with fresh hope.

"Press play," Means replied.

Jeffries said, "I make a motion that the board go into closed session."

"I second it," Bundik said.

Means sucked in his breath deeply. "Okay, I have a motion and a second, any questions or discussion?"

Rutherford said, "We've heard Mr. Rumley's side in front of the students. Why would we go into closed session when Mr. Bright's side is presented? Mr. Rumley has nothing to fear unless his behavior was unprofessional."

Elaine Simmons said, "I agree with Estelle Rutherford. What's fair for one is fair for the other. Mr. Rumley has set a precedent that makes recorded conversations appropriate to play at this hearing."

"Any other discussion?"

There was none.

"In that case, all in favor of going into a closed session, raise your right hand."

Jeffries's and Bundik's hands went up.

"All against going into closed session, same sign."

Rutherford and Simmons raised their hands.

Wycoff hadn't made up his mind and didn't vote.

Means was obviously angry at discovering this new side of Rumley's character. He felt like he was about to choke on his own words: "Everything that glitters isn't gold."

And a secretary blowing the whistle on an administrator was weird enough to arouse suspicion. Perhaps everything wasn't as tidy as Rumley had presented it. Means declared, "When there is a tie vote, it is the responsibility of the president to cast the deciding vote. I vote by saying: Mr. Rumley, press play!"

Rumley's hand didn't move. He was trying to think of a way to escape. Thinking of none, his finger slowly journeyed to the player. He slowly pressed play until the tiny click was heard throughout the quiet room. The player came to life with plenty of volume on Rumley's obnoxious voice.

(*Rumley*) "Kids like them have peed on me time and time again! And they will pee on you, too! Pardon my language, Ms. Gibson."

The students who weren't members of the Teens With Wisdom Society and hadn't heard about his comment before, found it more pathetic than funny. Only a few chuckles rippled through the audience and didn't interfere with anyone's ability to hear the recording.

(*Rumley*) "I'll ask you about it in twenty years, Coach. If you know what's good for you, you'll get off your savior kick! Do you know why Means was here? Because I'm getting everything lined up to fire your butt!"

Rumley pushed stop again. "I plead the Fifth Amendment. I should not be asked to testify against myself."

Means replied, "Mr. Rumley, you are the one who played the first recording. Now we will hear the second recording. Press play!"

Rumley had no choice. He pressed play. His booming voice returned to the player.

(*Rumley*) "All the members of the school board are always on my side because I know how to work them! I've got them in my back pocket. In a few hours, Means and I will be at the driving range with Bundik, and we'll brief him on this meeting. Bill Wycoff and I are in Lions Club together. Estelle Rutherford is on a Chamber of Commerce committee with me. Elaine Simmons and I are going to a seminar together next Monday. Viola Jeffries attends the same church that I do, and I'm taking flying lessons from her. So if you're stupid enough to try to talk to board members behind my back, you'll be terribly sorry you did. They are turned off by people who go over their supervisor's head! At Lincoln High School, we do everything strictly by the book. I make no exceptions, and I stay out of trouble. Your coaching career is just about over! I've got friends all over the state! You'll wish you had never taken me on before this is finished!" (*Shuffling of feet heard on the recording*)
(*Coach John*) "No. I won't give you strike three. You can't strike me out. I'm walking."
(*Rumley*) "Grow up!"
(*Rumley to Ms. Gibson*) "I want to read those notes after you get them typed. That brat is not going to act like an immature and rebellious teenager and get by with it. Ms. Gibson, your notes will not include my private comments to that, that, that embarrassment to the evolutionary process!"
(*Ms. Gibson*) "I understand."

(*Rumley*) "Ms. Gibson? I may need to call on you to tell the school board that you saw Mr. Bright lose his temper and almost knock me down."

(*Ms. Gibson*) "I saw everything, and I hope you do include me in any board meeting of that nature."

This time Means stopped the recording, shaking his head in disgust, by saying in a commanding voice, "Turn it off, Mr. Rumley!"

The room was deathly quiet. Rumley laid his glasses on John's file and rubbed his eyes with his open palms, trying to hide his face in his hands.

John whispered to Maria, "I always wondered why she brought her large purse to our meetings in Mr. Rumley's office. That's where her recorder was hidden."

Kaprice and Leilani walked up to the front seats, and Kaprice sat by Maria and put her arm around her. Leilani sat by John and rested her hand on his shoulder, the shoulder that was next to her.

Rumley looked at the board members helplessly. He remembered Mr. Platt's button lying in front of him: "If you do wrong, it will turn out wrong!" He picked it up and stuffed it into the pocket of his suit coat to get it out of sight.

Means announced, "I will entertain a motion that this portion of our meeting be moved into a closed session."

"I make that motion," said Rutherford.

"Second," said Wycoff.

"Any questions or discussion?" Means paused a moment and continued, "Being none, all in favor of moving into a closed session, say aye. All opposed, say no. Motion carried."

The board president came down to where John and Maria sat. "Mr. Bright, I would like to offer you my sincerest apology. I obviously was wrong about you."

Kaprice removed her gold ribbon and carefully pinned it to Mr. Means's lapel. Leilani followed Kaprice's example and pinned her ribbon on Ms. Rutherford's blouse.

The audience of students remained quiet.

Rumley slumped back in his chair and watched with dismay. He mumbled in thoughts to himself, *This is like watching the other team celebrate their win at your homecoming game.*

Maria was thinking about how beautiful it was for the teenagers to get the correct answer to their question in purple letters—the color of the robe of Jesus Christ: "If we do right, will it turn out wrong?" *No, it will turn out right,* Maria thought happily. The young people are learning a lesson in life that will last a lifetime: If you do right, it will certainly turn out *right*. If you do wrong, it will surely turn out *wrong*.

Hope pinned her ribbon on Ms. Simmons. Kyong Suk went to Mr. Bundik. Candace approached Ms. Jeffries, but Jeffries pulled away from her, saying, "I don't need a ribbon to remind me to do what's right." So Candace pinned her ribbon on Mr. Wycoff's shirt pocket instead. The girls returned to their seats.

With his ribbon waving on his lapel, Means returned to the mike. "Before the board goes into closed session, I want to thank you students for the maturity you have shown. Your input into this process has been powerful. Ms. Gibson, I know it took a lot of courage for you to stand up for what you believe. I assure you that this school board respects your action. Members of the audience, you can feel free to leave or wait, but I anticipate that we will be meeting for quite some time."

With that, the board filed into a private room. Rumley shoved his papers in his briefcase and hurried out of the boardroom, escaping into the night.

John and Ms. Gibson decided to wait for the board to return with their decisions. Of course, Maria stayed. The students of the Teens With Wisdom Society and a few of their friends waited, too. They talked excitedly about how pleased they were with the way things had gone.

Ray said gleefully, "Well, welcome to the world of teenagers where things are getting better!"

After about thirty minutes, a man walked briskly through the boardroom. He was still wearing the clothes he had worn to play golf that afternoon. He entered the private room in which the board was in closed session.

Only Ms. Gibson knew who the man was. "He's the school district's attorney," she informed everyone.

Another man entered the room. He appeared to be about forty years old, a handsome man, a little taller than most men, and he was wearing a suit. He sat down beside Hope and said, "I got here as soon as I finished performing the wedding. How are things going?"

"Perfect. Coach John is safe, and Mr. Rumley is in jeopardy," Hope said, eyes sparkling. "Hey, you guys! This here's my father."

John, Maria, Ms. Gibson, and the students were delighted to tell the minister about how wonderfully well everything had gone.

About two hours later, the board members returned to their seats in the board meeting room. The attorney was with them. He sat in the seat that Rumley had vacated. Each board member appeared very stressed. Their mood wasn't what the remaining audience expected. Tension began to mount again.

Means spoke first. "I apologize for the long wait. The board now has some decisions to announce. But before I tell you what they are, I want to say that the world is very complicated now. Nothing is easy. The decisions we are about to unveil to you are not ones that you will agree with completely. However, these are the decisions that our attorney has advised us are legally in the best interest of this school district."

Means began to announce the decisions. "Ms. Gibson, you will be transferred to the administration building, and you will be in charge of desktop publishing and maintenance of our Internet page. You will receive a 10 percent increase in salary. Each board member realizes that you are the only reason we are fully aware of all issues in the matter brought before us tonight."

Addressing the small audience, Means said, "Mr. Rumley will be given a choice of being fired or resigning. Either way, he will keep all his employment-related benefits."

Speaking specifically to the Teens With Wisdom Society and their small group of friends, he said, "Sometimes, when a lot of things have gone wrong and a lot of damage has been done, it is better for each person and the school district to be given a fresh start. That fact has gone into our decision about Mr. Bright, and we hope you will handle it maturely."

Looking directly at John, the board president said, "I want to say to you, Mr. Bright, that the decision we are about to announce to you may or may not express the feelings of individual board members. However, our attorney advises us that due to the possibility of a lawsuit from Mr. Rumley or a lawsuit from the student's parent concerning the separation of church and state issue, the school district must put itself in the best position for defending itself in court. To do that, we must be able to testify in court that we took all corrective action humanly possible. Therefore, we cannot allow you to continue to coach or teach at Lincoln High School."

Maria jumped to her feet and screamed, "¡No puedo creerlo! ¡No pueden tratar a mi esposo en esa manera! ¿Cómo pudieron frustrar a los muchachos y tener la cara de nombrarse los líderes de la comunidad? Su abogado no se dio cuenta que los muchachos se hubieran madurado. No escuchó las grabaciones. No entiende que John arriesgo su carrera por los estudiantes. ¿Qué les pasó en ese cuarto privado? ¿Por qué se redujeron como individuales a la opinión de un sólo abogado?"

The teens, fascinated by a side of Maria they hadn't seen, stared at her with shocked looks on their faces. Kaprice yelled, "You go, girl!"

Catching her breath and slowing down enough to speak English, Maria said in a demanding tone, "At least, place John on probation under another principal, and see for yourself that he can be a good employee!"

John was reacting in his thoughts: *Do you think I'm too young or too poor to sue? I'll show you that you can't treat me like I'm a nobody! I'll show you that I, too, have rights and can play hardball!*

Silence. The board members didn't respond to Maria's angry outburst. She realized there was nothing more that she could say or do.

Having repaired her self-control, Maria softly asked, "May the students have their ribbons back? It is hypocritical of you to keep them if you are not going to have the courage to make right turn out right like it's supposed to."

The board members who had ribbons laid them on the desk. As solemn as a mourner at a funeral, Kyong Suk collected the ribbons.

Taking his eyes off Kyong Suk, Means said, "Mr. Bright, the school board voted to pay your salary for sixty days while you find another job. We will also give you an excellent letter of recommendation."

Finding it hard to believe what he was seeing and hearing, Hope's father rose to his feet.

"Reverend, do you have a comment?" Means asked, granting him permission to speak.

Hope's father thoughtfully and courteously said, "Men and women of the school board, if you carry through with what you are doing, one day you'll remember this day as the worst day in your political careers. You don't want to turn your backs on justice while your students watch you. You don't want to tattoo their minds with this memory. We adults must set a better example than this for them. They deserve better than this. I urge you to return to your private meeting and reconsider your decision to fire this coach. Base your decision on what's right rather than on what's convenient and expedient. When we know to do what's right and don't do it, we are sinning. In theology, it is called a sin of omission. I urge you to return to your meeting room."

"Is there a motion to reconsider our decision?" Means asked his board members.

Silence.

"As much as I respect you, Reverend, I don't have a motion or a second. I can't reconvene the private session."

Hope's father responded, "Men and women of the school board, again I urge you not to carry through on this mistake. Your meeting isn't yet adjourned. There is still time to make this night turn out right. These young people have had a lot of class in the way they have protested. They deserve an honorable response. As community leaders and administrators—"

Jeffries interrupted and smarted off, "Reverend, you had better stick to preaching! We're not meeting again, got it? The man is out! And he has cost us the best principal this school district has ever had! And it's obvious to me that Mr. Rumley was set up! Gibson and Bright formed a committee of two to get him ousted! John Bright knew she was hiding a recorder! I'm convinced of that!"

"Okay, Viola, I'll stick to preaching." Hope's father replied as he stepped into the aisle, "You school board members are choking on a gnat while you are swallowing a camel! You stand up for what will keep you out of a lawsuit while you wimp out on a just cause! At the same time, you do nothing about the parent bashing and immoral leadership being dealt out by some of your key faculty members—faculty members who aren't being fired this night! You are not acting as cool, spring-fed rivers of living water. You are acting as rivers who have compromised themselves into paths of least resistance. You are lost in that you are fighting the wrong cause. Coach John Bright is not a part of the problem; he is a part of the solution."

Speaking more calmly, clearing his throat, holding back tears, he said, "This coach, his wife, and the kids from the meadow gave me a new beginning with my daughter. I love her so much."

Hope stood up and moved into the aisle beside her father. They faced each other in a quick father-daughter embrace. Tears began to trickle down both their faces. "We respect each other again. We enjoy each other again. We *have* each other again!"

"Prayer is a neutral term," Hope announced. "Coach John didn't tell Franco's mom that he was going to call Rev. Jimmy Falderal, and they were going to call down the Holy Ghost to heal their family!"

Without allowing anyone to get a word in edgewise, Hope hurried and said, "If you want to know the truth, I think Coach John's comment bothered the woman's conscience. She knows she's living a corrupt life in front of her children. When I was living a corrupt life, it made me hot and bothered when people told me they were praying for me."

Hope's father regained the attention of the board members, saying, "Hope has shown me the STRONG WILLS that she and her friends are writing. She has them on her laptop. Do you people not realize that these young people are presently the most positive force we have in our city? Perhaps in our culture? The Bible says that truth will come out of the mouths of babes—these kids—but you don't have ears to hear them. You aren't listening to them. These young people have had a revival in maturity and morality, and they have already risen above many adults."

He put his arm around Hope's thin body as she put her arm around him. With her other hand she discreetly pulled on her necklace until the thin chain broke. She slowly lowered her hand to her side and let the crystal fall to the floor. Her dad held her close to his side and felt anointed of God to proclaim: "In the name of Jesus Christ, I prophesy that healing rays from their Teens With Wisdom Societies will spread like lasers piercing night skies! They will bless every community! Every church! Every school! They will—"

Drowning him out, Jeffries sarcastically shouted, "Reverend, you are no Isaiah! Aren't you feeling just a little too special?!"

Without waiting for a reply, Jeffries impatiently cut her eyes to the president of the school board and said, "Mr. Means, I make a motion that we adjourn this meeting before things get more ridiculous!"

Hope tried to speak again in support of her dad. Dale jumped to his feet, saying, "You people have bowed to adult peer pressure."

Means ignored Dale's words and Hope's bid to speak. "Our decisions are final! Is there a second to the motion to adjourn?"

"So moved!"

"All in favor, say aye!"

"Aye!"

"All opposed, same sign!"

"This meeting is adjourned!"

The board members exited through a side door. Viola Jeffries walked beside Means saying, "If that preacher's a prophet, I'm a jack-ass! His values are from the Dark Ages and have him retarded! And those kids, they don't know the difference between psychology and a rat's behind! A board meeting is no place for children, Robert!"

Means didn't reply. No one in the boardroom heard her.

John and Maria and the kids held one another and cried—disappointed by the injustice and brokenhearted by the thought that John and Maria would have to move away.

Hope's father held her while she sobbed, "Dad, we prayed. Why didn't God answer our prayers?"

SCENE 31

Will Grandypa rot in jail?

THIRTY-ONE

THE NEXT day, Ms. Gibson cleaned out her desk. John cleaned out his small office.

The school board asked John to be off campus by Tuesday afternoon. The school board needed John out of the picture as fast as possible so things would settle down as quickly as possible. In quiet protest, students wore their gold ribbons upside down, meaning: If you do right in this school district, *it will turn out wrong*.

The teens called, visited, and comforted John and Maria throughout the week. Hope and her parents had them over for a meal. Terence's parents sent Terence to John and Maria's apartment with sandwiches and a delicious cheesecake.

A high school, in a neighboring state, 375 miles away, was looking for a coach. John drove up and interviewed on Thursday and was hired on Friday. Mr. Means kept his promise and gave John a positive recommendation when the principal of the new school phoned him. His new position paid two thousand more per year than he had been earning at Lincoln High School. John planned to start driving back home early Saturday morning so he could be back in town in time for Saturday night's meeting in the meadow.

John and Maria's teenage friends were happy that John had landed another job so quickly. They were thrilled that he'd receive a better salary. They were disappointed that he and Maria would move so soon.

Meanwhile, the doorbell rang at Leilani's home at 8:00 P.M. Because it was dark, Grandestmother and Leilani answered the door together.

A big man filled their doorway. "Remember me, young lady?" he asked Leilani.

It was the grizzly man from the jail. Leilani told her grandestmother who he was.

The grizzly man said, "Well, I think I have something you may want."

He moved his huge body to one side, and they saw Grandypa standing there! He was leaning on his cane, all smiles. He hobbled up to hug his family.

Leilani lunged to embrace him and exclaimed without thinking, "Oh, Grandypa, did Grizzly break you out of jail? Did he?"

"Grizzly?" the man said.

"Oops, sorry, I have nicknames for everyone," Leilani said. "Could we introduce ourselves?"

"The name's Hank," the man said firmly.

"Mine's Leilani."

"Princess Leilani from Hawaii," Grandypa corrected, giving her another quick hug.

Grandestmother got them inside and seated them in the living room. She sat next to Grandypa, and they held hands.

Hank explained everything. "Me, I'm a jailhouse lawyer. That's a guy who has been in jail and prison so much that he's learned to use the twists and turns of the law to beat the system and get himself out of trouble. I just made a few phone calls, that's all—no big deal."

"It is a big deal!" Leilani protested. "Grandypa's home! Who did you call? What did you say?"

"I called the abortion clinic's law firm. I suggested they keep the case out of court so it would stay out of the news. I warned them that more media coverage would only help Samuel Summers focus attention on his cause, and they didn't want that. I warned them that more attention could result in new legislation being passed that would require family members to be included in abortion decisions, and they didn't want that. And I warned them about what's called copycat crimes—that's when other people copy the crimes they hear about on TV, and they didn't want that. In fact, they seemed unusually eager to cooperate. I'm still puzzled by that."

Hank continued his explanation, "I called the doctor and nurse and explained the same stuff to them. They didn't want to risk more public exposure. They really, really wanted the reporters to leave them alone. I'm telling you that they just wanted their lives to return to normal. They were eager to cooperate. In fact, they were too eager. I think there's a mystery that's yet to be solved."

He went on, "The district attorney's office cut a deal with Mr. Summers since the abortion clinic and the doctor and nurse had stopped cooperating with the DA. They agreed to reduce the charges against him and give him probation. That is, if he would agree not to continue his campaign. He agreed—not because he felt differently about things, but because he says he never had a campaign. He told them he just wanted to let the abortion people know that he didn't appreciate them killing his great-grandbaby, and he wanted to block the door to protect other senior citizens' grandchildren. Your grandfather almost screwed things up for me, though. He kept saying he wasn't the shooter."

Then with a big scruffy smile, he teased Grandypa, "You're not getting a little senile, are you, old feller?" Turning to Leilani and Grandestmother, he said, "Keep a close eye on him and see if you can keep him out of trouble."

"Grandypa, you don't have to defend yourself," Leilani said as she hugged him. "The Bible says every knee shall bow before Christ, and that includes the abortionists and the people who support what they do. I'm so glad you're home."

Leilani turned toward Hank and searched his face to find a spot where there was no hair. She kissed him there and said, "You're Grizzly Angel. That's my nickname for you. Thank you for bringing Grandypa home."

Grandestmother gave him a warm handshake and thanked him as well. Still looking at Leilani, Hank said, "Lose the name, girl. I'm a zillion miles from being angelic. I only freed your grandfather because the guys in jail didn't like having an old man in there who was so gentle and good. It made them terribly uncomfortable." Hank laughed, "They said it was like being marooned on an island with a saint."

The electronic tweeting of a phone interrupted their good-byes. Leilani answered it. It was Dale. Leilani blurted, "Grandypa's home, and he's not going to be charged with attempted murder!"

"That's for sure, Leilani. There's been a break in the case. I have scheduled a press conference in the conference room of the police station tomorrow morning at ten. Have Grandypa there. Be sure he's in a suit."

"You scheduled a press conference? How can a teenager do that? You don't have the authority! Are you for real?"

"Leilani, I'm tired of justice being bullied by injustice. I'm tired of adult corruption. Just be there with Grandypa. I'm calling all the members of the Teens With Wisdom Society."

"Dale, you're amazing!"

"If there's a change in time, I'll call you."

Click. Dale was gone.

While Dale called the other eight members of the TWW Society and asked them to come in the same dress clothes they had worn at the board meeting, a forty-seven-year-old con artist Dale knew from the streets, who specialized in phone scams, went to the police station and placed several phone calls from the pay phone in the lobby.

With the sounds of the police station in the background, and sounding very official himself, he first phoned the executive director of the abortion clinic at home and told him that he was to be at the police station by ten the next morning to help finalize the investigation of the violent demonstration at his clinic. He told him to wear a suit because the newspeople would likely want to file their final reports. The executive director agreed to be there.

Having secured that commitment, the con artist called the news bureaus. Speaking with distinction, he announced the press conference to the news departments of the TV stations, radio stations, and newspaper offices. He announced it as an update on the ongoing investigation of the shooting spree at the abortion clinic. They said they'd see about having reporters in attendance.

At 9:30 Saturday morning, TV news crews began setting up their cameras in the police station's conference room.

Office personnel were bewildered. A dispatcher told the news crews that she didn't think that the police chief or the public relations officer had scheduled a press conference. However, the Channel 5 crew wouldn't pack up and leave. They told the dispatcher, "There's something going on here; and if it's newsworthy, you can be sure Channel 5 will be the first to have it on the airwaves."

Having overheard the comment, the other TV crews continued setting up. They didn't want Channel 5 to be the first to break another story. Newspaper reporters arrived. They also were told that no news conference had been scheduled by police personnel. Although skeptical, they decided to hang in for a few minutes.

Well-dressed teenagers began walking in. Grandypa hobbled in with his cane. Grandestmother and Princess Leilani from Hawaii were beside him. Maria came in alone behind them. Reporters recognized Grandypa as the alleged shooter. They then suspected that something worth reporting was definitely in the making. The entry door swung open fast and wide. In walked Hank. He walked over to Leilani.

"Grizzly Angel!" Leilani said too loudly, smiling, giving him a high five.

"Wrong!" Hank said, warmly returning her smile, as his hand touched Leilani's above her head.

Grandypa and Grandestmother both reached out to shake Hank's hand as if their new friend was an old friend.

Dale arrived escorting two women, wearing fancy masks that matched their tight, short dresses. Their masks were like ones worn to elegant masquerade balls. Both masks were brilliant in color and adorned with sequins and feathers: one red, the other turquoise.

At five till ten, the Teens With Wisdom Society members were all present. They were sitting toward the front of the room with Leilani, Hank, Grandypa, Grandestmother, Maria, and Crisco.

Three police officers greeted people and asked questions, trying to figure out what was going on. The police chief arrived and questioned each of his officers. The executive director of the abortion clinic walked in and took a seat in the back of the room, without speaking to anyone, not wanting to make a point of his presence.

The time was ripe. The cameras were ready. Pencils were poised above the reporters' skinny spiral notepads.

The police chief stepped to the microphone. Blinding video lights were switched on. "Ladies and gentlemen, I apologize for the inconvenience, but I have checked with all key personnel, and I can assure you that no one in this department called a press conference. I do not understand how there could be a misunderstanding of this magnitude."

Pausing, not knowing what to do, he scanned his audience: sharp teenagers, an eight-year-old girl, a young Hispanic woman, a jailhouse lawyer, the alleged shooter, the executive director of the Women's Clinic, two masked women, reporters and cameras from every news source in the metroplex, three police officers standing at the back and the sides of the room.

Looking at the masked women, the chief quizzed, "Would anyone like to shed some light on what's going on here? Someone's behind this. This meeting is well organized. Who set this up?"

On cue from Dale, the ten teens stood together with the two flashy women in masks. The atmosphere became electric with anticipation. They walked to the speaker's stand at the same time. Crisco stayed with Maria. The police officers watched every move. Anxious reporters were excited that something big was unfolding before the lenses of their digital cameras.

As the teens formed a line behind the microphone the police chief—curious as everyone else—stepped to the side of the room. He didn't feel a need to stop the proceedings because he had already issued his disclaimer. Reporters knew that he wasn't to be blamed for anything that happened in the next few moments. Besides, he was intrigued by the ten teens who appeared refreshingly mature. He was anxious to see what they were up to.

Dale and the women stepped to the mike. Dale said, "Jayla and Myrna here are prostitutes. They were in the abortion clinic for their HIV tests and pregnancy tests when Samuel David Summers supposedly shot up the place. They have something they want to tell you."

Dale stepped aside. The two masked women centered themselves behind the mike. Jayla pulled the mike down toward her mouth. Feedback screeched through the public address system. "The elderly man didn't have a gun," she announced. "He only blocked the door and screamed that the clinic must stop the violence against grandchildren."

Myrna leaned into the mike and said, "The shots were fired by the clinic's executive director. He shot at the old man several times."

Jayla added, "The police didn't fire a shot. They got there a few moments after everything was over. The elderly man was already down, bleeding on the floor. The executive director hid his gun."

Dale stepped back to the mike. "Is the shooter in this room?"

Jayla said, "Yes."

Jayla and Myrna pointed to the executive director of the abortion clinic in the back of the room.

Reporters suddenly converged on him, sticking microphones and cameras in his face. The police chief looked on in amazement.

Several reporters fired questions at the executive director at once. "Is what they say true?"

"Did you do the shooting?"

"Why the cover-up?"

"Why didn't you come forward?"

"There was no cover-up," he countered. "You newspeople jumped to conclusions, and I didn't correct your reporting. I have a right not to incriminate myself."

"Why didn't you come forward with the truth?"

"I didn't want abortion providers to be classed with radical pro-lifers."

"Why did you shoot the elderly gentleman?"

"Why didn't you just call the police?"

"Why did you take the law into your own hands?"

Becoming obviously irritated, the executive director replied, "With that stalker out there after one of my docs and with abortion clinics being bombed across the nation, I was edgy. Wouldn't you be? I saw the lower portion of the old man's cane, and I thought he was carrying a rifle...I have no further comment. You'll need to contact my lawyer."

The members of the Teens With Wisdom Society, Hank, Grandypa, Grandestmother, Maria, and Crisco slipped out the doors. Although tired from the stress, Grandypa and Grandestmother walked arm and arm, smiling all the way. They knew the whole world was going to know that he was a sane person who wasn't guilty of felony charges for attempted murder.

In the parking lot, everyone thanked Jayla and Myrna. Myrna said, "We did it for Dale's mother."

The women quickly stepped into a car and took off their masks as they drove away.

"Everybody's gotta meet Grizzly Angel!" Leilani yelled excitedly. "He's a jailhouse lawyer man! And he got Grandypa out of jail!"

Tossing a friendly frown in Leilani's direction, he responded, "The name's Hank. You kids did a great job in there."

Leilani's grandparents were slowly getting into their car. "Careful where you point that cane," Hank teased Grandypa. "It might be loaded."

The police chief kept the executive director of the Women's Clinic for further questioning.

The reporters rushed to the window of Grandypa's car. The teens stayed near, feeling protective of the elderly gentleman. Grandypa lowered the window halfway to respond to the reporters.

"What group are you a member of?"

"None."

"What pro-life group do you contribute to?"

"I don't."

"Why did you block the entrance to the Women's Clinic?"

"They killed my great-grandbaby, and that's all I could do. I wanted to stand at the location where he or she had been killed. That's the closest thing to a funeral I will ever get. Also, I wanted to stop them from killing the grandchildren of other senior citizens."

"Why are you against a woman's right to choose?"

"Because they aren't giving great-grandbabies the right to choose. The babies are the only ones whose lives are in jeopardy, and they are not included in the choice-making process. That is radically unjust, I'd say. And it is also unjust for grandparents not to be included in the choice-making process. And furthermore, it is unjust for those who were not aborted to choose to abort others. That is far too controlling and manipulative."

Rolling down the window all the way, Grandypa said, "Now let me ask you a question. Is an unborn baby girl a miniature woman or a grasshopper? If you say a grasshopper, you are a nincompoop! If you say she's a miniature woman, then what about women's rights for her? Over half the babies they are snuffing out are girl babies!"

The reporters didn't have an answer, so they opted to fire another question at him, "If your opinion is the only correct one, why are there so few who share your view and crusade?"

"I've told you I'm not a member of a pro-life crusade, but I have had plenty of time to assimilate my thoughts in jail. I will answer your question this way: There are so few who will take a stand because when it comes to abortion, courage wilts. Civil liberties unions ought to protest the violation of the rights of unborn people, but they don't. Evolutionists ought to fight against doctors tampering with the evolutionary process, but they don't. Animal protection groups ought to object to abusing unborn animals since science classifies humans as animals, but they don't. Environmentalists should demonstrate against the pollution of the environment inside women's wombs, but they don't. Jews ought to scream against today's holocaust, but most don't. Children's Protective Services should fight against the violent and fatal child abuse dealt to unborn children, but they don't. Child advocates ought to extend their love to children in the sanctity of the womb, but they don't. Women's rights groups, who protest the sexual mutilation of young girls in Africa, should protest total body mutilation of baby girls in America, but they don't. The police ought to protect miniature people, but they don't.

All these powerful groups—where is their courage? Did it wash away in a flood of pressure from their peers?"

Grandypa continued, "All these groups and agencies are wilting beneath pressure to have lopsided views about women's rights. It makes no sense. The people who are against spanking children are for abortion. The people who are against capital punishment are for abortion. The people who try to discredit the Christian faith by pointing to the fanatics of the Salem witch hunts are for abortion. I'd like to see you have the guts to confront all them as you are doing me."

"Are you against abortion in early stages when there is only tissue?"

"Poppycock! That is modern science acting like an ostrich, with its head stuck deep in the sand. With modern genetics, medical science knows a baby when it sees one! Medical scientists, who do not admit that life begins at conception, are in denial. They can't admit tissue is a baby because that would make abortion obviously unethical. What if abortionists kill the scientist-to-be who would discover a cure for a deadly disease? How many geniuses are being destroyed? Those scientists need to get a grip and give a rip: Abortion is barbaric! Those who do it are barbarians! They might as well be throwing our grandbabies off cliffs to crocodiles! How is there any difference? Abortion is a relic left over from ancient times that we haven't matured beyond!"

In disgust, Grandypa rolled up the window, refusing to answer any more questions. He started his engine and drove slowly away.

The teens and reporters exchanged looks. Hope broke the silence with a challenging remark. "We'll be waiting to see how objective your reports will be!"

The reporters noticed the police chief approaching. An officer was with him. The chief said, "You people need to interview this officer. He is the one who filed the incomplete report. He can fight his own battles."

The police chief wasn't about to serve as a buffer between the officer and the public. He wanted the public to have a clear understanding of why he would be firing the officer. The police chief was a good man, and his goal was to build a force of integrity.

Microphones shot into the officer's face. Cameras crowded him for close-ups. The reporters were angry that they had been made to look like fools, and they pelted him with questions.

"Why didn't you tell reporters that no shots were fired by the police?"

"Why didn't you report that the elderly gentleman was shot by the executive director of the clinic?"

"Why didn't you report that the protester was not carrying a gun?"

In a macho manner, the officer answered, "When you reporters got it wrong, the clinic's executive director and I decided to let sleeping dogs lie. The more you stir some things, you know, the more they stink. Besides, I figured that the old man deserved anything he got. He was the one who was at the wrong place at the wrong time. He might as well take the fall."

Off camera, a disgusted reporter muttered, "Like his great-grandbaby was at the wrong place at the wrong time. They both got injured at the same location, but his grandbaby's injuries were fatal!"

The police chief spoke to the teens. "I respect what you've done. If any of you would like to consider a career in law enforcement, call my office and request an appointment with me. I'll tell my secretary to put you straight through to me."

Each teen shook hands with the chief of police and thanked him for his invitation.

The reporters made sure their new stories corrected earlier reports. The testimonies of the prostitutes and the interviews with the clinic's executive director, Grandypa, and the policeman all made noon and evening TV newscasts. Radio news carried sound bites from each, with appropriate explanations. A color picture of the Teens With Wisdom Society, with Dale and the prostitutes at the speaker's stand, was scheduled for the front page of two newspapers in Sunday's edition, introducing detailed stories.

SCENE 32

*Making sense
out of nonsense—
and
sorting adults*

THIRTY-TWO

THE LAST truck backed into place to complete the circle of three tailgates in the meadow. John backed his Mustang convertible in with them and put the top down so that kids could kneel in the backseat and face the circle. Brady and Fred were the only absentees. Ms. Gibson was there as the guest of honor.

Everyone was excited over a lot of good news. John had landed a new coaching position and a better salary. Their press conference had cleared Grandypa of any acts of violence. And several students at LHS had asked about joining the TWW Society. Everyone complimented Leilani on her wonderful speech at the pep rally.

The night was cool and crisp. Ms. Gibson was fascinated with the teenagers' secret meeting place—the tall pine trees surrounding the meadow standing at attention like giant soldiers, the country-fresh air inviting her to breathe deeply, the wildflowers peeking in from the darkness polka-dotting the ground with color and giving freely of their fragrances, the little unseen creatures making noises far too big for them, the flickering light of fires on the top of Tiki torches, arguing with the darkness.

The mood was sweet…but also sour. The teenagers knew they were saying good-bye to their wonderful friends, John and Maria Bright.

Hope passed out photocopies of the STRONG WILLS.

Terence said, "I'd like to welcome everyone to our meeting. Let's read the basic beliefs of our Teens With Wisdom Society."

Terence again waited for someone else to begin to read. He didn't like to read in front of everyone. He was afraid he'd mess up because of his dyslexia.

They read aloud together. Their voices joined the sounds of life in the meadow. "Our Teens With Wisdom Society is a fellowship of teens who have formed an oasis of friendship and support in a stressed-out and confused culture. Our purpose is to help each other muscle up and rise above his or her problems, frustrations, or mistakes, and build an invincible life. Our common goal is to be truly independent—to live quality-controlled lives based on the wisdom of Christ."

Terence asked John to read their theme Scripture. John read it and took it personally. "*'Do not let anyone look down on you because you are young, but be an example for the believers, in your speech, your conduct, your love, faith, and purity'* (1 Timothy 4:12, TEV)."

Terence continued to lead the group, "And now let us affirm our STRONG WILLS. These are the choices we each should be making now, and the ones we should always make."

Terence waited to read until others began to read. He added his voice to their voices as they made their pledges. "I will do right no matter what I think is wrong with my parents or guardians. I will be responsible for myself and not try to use my parents' or guardians' problems to excuse my own stupid sins. I will do well even if my parents or guardians have a lousy opinion of me. I will succeed even if I'm not favored for success. I will not give my brothers or sisters or my parent's significant other's children the right to ruin my life forever. I will not allow open-minded-but-narrow-minded professionals to judge me to be a wasteland and make me compromise my positive contribution in life. I will finally leave the sins of offenders in the past where they belong. I will make it through the storms and disappointments of family life. I will not allow rude comments, attitudes, or actions of teachers to turn me away from respecting myself and from believing that I can achieve good goals with my life. I will prove that insensitive teachers are wrong about me. I will not allow my peers to pressure me away from what I believe is right by hassling me, by putting down my parents or decent friends, or by threatening to leave me out if I don't conform to what they want. I will honor God's trust of me in our best-friends relationship. The opportunities in my present and future are God's gifts to me; how I succeed with those opportunities is my gift to God. God votes for me, the pull of sin votes against me, and I am breaking the tie by the way I am voting with each decision I make."

Terence looked up from his paper. Leilani thought they were going to leave out the last part. She read it loud and fast as if it were her personal vow for victory: "By making the above choices and living loyal to these choices, we teens will succeed in life, although bad things have happened to us in the past, although we've made mistakes ourselves, and although there are pressures on us now. Our STRONG WILLS are our life preservers.

"Yes!" Leilani exclaimed. Then laughing, "We are strong-willed!"

Leilani was so happy that Grandypa was back home and out of jail that she was feeling better in spite of John and Maria's leaving.

Hope had been waiting to say something. "We need to make a STRONG WILL about things not turning out fair."

As Kaprice opened Hope's laptop computer to add the new STRONG WILL to the list, John muttered, "You mean, when doing right turns out wrong?"

Dale agreed with John. "That whole board meeting thing stunk worse than the back alleys of the projects. The school board chickened out. The fear of lawsuits put their tails between their legs like scared dogs, and they looked pathetic. What's happening to the adult world?"

"How would you like to word your STRONG WILL?" Maria asked, her pencil hovering over her clipboard, and Kaprice's fingers waiting above the laptop's keyboard.

Kyong Suk rubbed the bottom of her upside-down ribbon between two fingers, saying, "It needs to have something about the Judgment in it. It looks like that's our only hope for things to turn out right."

Her comment reminded Dale of something. "My Uncle Buddy, the one that has the therapy center, once told me that he thinks of the Final Judgment before God as the Great Fairness Adjustment where all injustices will be straightened out, where every wrong will be righted."

"Mercy! That's good!" John exclaimed as he looked around the circle. "God is going to right the wrongs for me...and for each of you! Most of you are also dealing with the trashy way people have treated you—Dale, Candace, Franco, Ray, Hope—"

"You!" Hope interrupted.

"I said me!" John reminded her.

"At my mother's funeral, Uncle Buddy told me that at every crossroad of life, you have to make a choice about whether you will get better or bitter. I've been trying to choose better. That's why my goal is to correct my limb on my family tree. Coach John, you need to choose better, too. So do you, Candace, Ray, Kyong Suk..."

"Whenever justice is bullied by injustice, I will choose to become a better person rather than a bitter person, and I will...what?" Maria asked, beginning to shape their conversation into a STRONG WILL.

Kyong Suk said, "I will, uh..."

Dale finished, "I will relax because all wrongs will be made right at the Great Fairness Adjustment where every knee shall bow before Christ. How's that?"

"Good, but it needs a little work," John said. "Maria, would you put in to words what you and Dale have said?"

Maria tried again. "I will always choose to become a better person rather than a bitter person when justice is bullied by injustice. I will remain strong because I know for sure that all wrongs will be righted at the Great Fairness Adjustment when every knee shall bow before Christ to receive His verdict."

"Great!" John exclaimed, applauding her to show how happy he was with her work.

"What about the Golden Rule?" Crisco asked in her little-girl voice. "Nobody would have been hurt if everybody had done the Golden Rule."

Maria turned to her and asked, "Can you tell us what the Golden Rule is?"

"Do unto others as you would like them to do unto you," Crisco recited.

"That's good, Crisco!" Maria congratulated.

Kyong Suk observed, "If Rumpley had done that, we'd still have John and Maria."

"If the school board had done that, we'd still have John and Maria," Dale emphasized.

Leilani said, "If the doctor and nurse had honored the Golden Rule with my baby, I'd still have him or her. Michelle or Michael would not have wanted to be aborted."

"You're so right, Leilani," Hope agreed, with pain in her voice.

Candace said, "If Gramps had done that, he wouldn't have violated me."

"And my dad wouldn't whip me until I have welts all over my legs, back, and butt," Ray said. "I'm sure he wouldn't like a giant to do that to him!"

Leilani spoke again, "If my father and mother had done that, I'd still be with them."

Franco thought a moment and took a turn. "If my mother would do that and if the men who intrude in our home would do that, Crisco would be safe, we'd have a home, and Mother would have children who respect her."

"If my parents had done that," Kyong Suk said, "maybe they wouldn't have fallen out of love."

"If I had done that," Hope said, eyes watering, "I wouldn't have rebelled against my family or insulted my dad's ministry or walked over my mother's tears...to get to the wrong crowd."

Daniel said quietly, "If I would do that, I would admit that my parents were right about my friends being the wrong crowd. We actually were. The meadow was where we hid out to have our nasty little parties. That was before we wrote our STRONG WILLS."

Terence heard Daniel and spoke right up, "I've always hated how strict my parents are, but I think I'll be a lot like them if I'm ever a parent. I'll try my best to protect my children from making mistakes that can destroy their futures. So, from now on I'm going to do unto my parents as I would like them to do unto me. I'm going to respect them for having rules instead of thinking they're bad. Hey, everybody! I have good parents!"

All applauded Terence's new and improved attitude toward his parents. At the same time, they were applauding the maturity they felt awakening within their souls.

John laughed, and everyone looked his way. "If the open-minded-but-narrow-minded professionals would follow the Golden Rule, they'd stop calling people bigots when they are less bigoted than them."

The kids cheered for him. "Right on, Coach!"

"Yea, Coach!"

"Tell it like it is!"

"And if I had a Golden Rule Trophy to give to someone," John shouted above the cheers, "it would go to Ms. Gibson!"

Everyone loudly applauded Ms. Gibson, and a few jumped off the tailgates to give her standing ovations. All three kids in the convertible stood and applauded. Kaprice clapped the most.

While Ms. Gibson smiled with embarrassment, John said, "At great personal risk, you did unto me like you would have had me do unto you. I will always remember you, and I will always respect you."

"Hope's dad should also be applauded!" Maria announced. "He had the position to tell the board members what you teens would like to have told them, and he represented your feelings well."

Everyone applauded again. The boys whistled with piercing shrillness.

As things settled back down, Hope seemed to be on a different wavelength. "Maria, we've got to make up a STRONG WILL for dealing with anger. Christian or not, Dale is going to hurt someone if he doesn't cool down his hot head."

"John and I have a couple of hearts to cool down, too. Others of you also carry grudges."

Candace said, "I'm not mad at Gramps. I'm just hurt."

"That's because you are such a sweet and caring person, Candace," John noted.

"Well, I'm mad!" Ray exclaimed. "Just the thought of that perverted old geezer makes me mad. Just like the sight of my father makes my blood boil. When I get as big as he is, and he starts to beat on me, I'm going to show him how it feels. I'm going to beat him until he begs me to stop!"

"Well, I've got a different problem," Hope said. "What do you do when you are mad at yourself? I dragged my father's name through the mud and told lies as if they were family secrets to professional therapists, and I exaggerated my parents' faults so the social workers would think I had good reasons for being rebellious. I cursed my mother while she was crying and praying for me. How do I forgive myself?"

Leilani moved close to Maria and began to cry softly. Between sobs, she said, "Brady's going with another girl! He wrote me. He just wants to be friends."

Kaprice moved from the computer to Leilani's side to comfort her.

"What a major jerk!" Ray declared.

"No big loss!" Kyong Suk said in disgust. "I never would tell you this before, but Brady had sex with me. After we did it, he said he just wanted to see what it was like to get it on with an Asian. He said he had read about it on the Internet and seen it on a video from Fred's library. I'm sorry, Leilani. I wouldn't have done it if we hadn't been drinking. That's why I thought I was pregnant. That's why I went to the abortion clinic with Platypus. Will you forgive me?"

"Leilani, you need to kick that playboy to the curb, if you know what I'm sayin'," Kaprice admonished.

As Leilani wept softly and tears fell in her lap, John asked, "What are we going to do with all this hurt that so many of us are feeling?"

"We need a STRONG WILL," Kyong Suk said.

Dale responded, "Uncle Buddy told me that I needed to take the Lord's Prayer seriously where it says, 'Forgive us our trespasses as we forgive those who trespass against us.' He says it's like the forgiveness of Christ reaches clear through us to others, and that gives us double relief."

"Double relief?" Terence quizzed.

"Yeah. We are relieved of guilt and doom by asking God to forgive us for our sins. And we are relieved of grudges and anger when we forgive others of their sins against us."

"If you know so much about it, Dale, why haven't you done it?" Hope asked in a no-nonsense manner.

Dale shot back, "Well, what about you? Have you gone to that CPS worker, that therapist, that child advocate that you lied to about your dad and told them the truth? Have you made things right for your dad? Have you told them that your dad is a very good person, and it was just you wanting to get out of the house to be a party girl?"

"Whoa! Aren't we defensive!" Hope said, secretly wishing she had approached the subject differently with Dale.

"It's not like I haven't done anything positive," Dale said. "I've asked for forgiveness for my sins."

"But your heart is boiling like a volcano, always about to erupt."

"Okay, you're right. I haven't felt like forgiving. It's been, like, stuck in my heart, and I've been holding it in, and it's been souring like the bottom of a stinking Dumpster...I've been choosing bitter instead of better in that area of my life."

"John, Maria, what can Dale do?" Hope asked. "He needs to forgive but doesn't feel like it. Well, for that matter, what can most of us do? I guess we're all in Dale's shoes."

Dale didn't give John or Maria time to answer. "Uncle Buddy says that you don't have to feel like you want to forgive in order to do it. He says that we're thinkers, not feelers. He says that we can, like, legislate it, issue a decision for forgiveness to happen. He says our feelings will get in sync later. He says to start prayers of forgiveness with the words, 'I do hereby forgive.'"

Maria said, "By listening to Dale, it's clear that knowing what to do is not enough. Let's all join hands and make a circle."

Everyone came off the tailgates and out of the Mustang, forming a circle inside the circle of vehicles.

"Now, let's actually do what we all know we should do," Maria encouraged. "Let's forgive no matter how we feel. I'll start it. Let's pray.

God, I do hereby forgive Mr. Rumley for attacking my husband and hurting us. I forgive the school board for wimping out. I forgive Fred for rejecting our group."

John went next, "God, I do hereby forgive the school board and the teachers who sided against me. As much as I can tonight, I forgive Mr. Rumley, Mr. Platt, and Ms. Rouse. Mr. Means is a good man. Help him learn to stand up for what he believes."

Leilani prayed, "God, I do hereby forgive myself for doing things behind my grandparents' backs after they took me in when I didn't have a home. I forgive Brady for walking out on me when I needed him most. Help me want to forgive him for what he did to Kyong Suk. I forgive Kyong Suk. And I forgive myself for having the abortion. Help me learn to forgive my parents for dropping out of my life. I forgive the school board and Mr. Rumley...and Mr. Platt...and Ms. Rouse."

Kaprice said, "I do hereby forgive the school board for not being brave, and I forgive Mr. Rumley for causing us to lose Coach John and Maria...and thank You, God, for my mom. She was wonderrrrful at the school board meeting. Thank You for her new job."

"God, please help me forgive myself," Hope prayed and began to weep softly. "I do hereby forgive the guys who did me wrong, the girls who spread rumors about me so they could steal my boyfriends. And, God, help me to make things right with my mom and dad. Amen."

With her head still bowed and eyes still closed, Hope said, "Leilani, we need to talk. I'm dealing with some of the same guilt that you've been dealing with. Everyone here knows I've had two abortions."

"Sure," Leilani replied.

Ray looked up at everyone and asked, "Do you think it would be okay for me to kill my dad, and then forgive him after he's dead, and ask God to forgive me for killing him?"

No one was in the mood for Ray's comment, and no one liked it. Ray said, "Look, I'm not ready to hereby forgive him. Okay? He may beat me up again tomorrow. You guys aren't facing that."

"Ray, your dad won't abuse you again," John announced firmly. "I reported the abuse to Children's Protective Services today. They will be getting in touch with your parents."

Ray's face drew a blank. "Coach?!"

"Trust my coaching on this one. I met a worker I trust. They're not all bad. There are good people in every field of service. That's something every one of us must learn. The twenty-first century will be a century of sorting to find good people. Let's go ahead with our prayer time now, and you and I will talk later. Okay?"

"Okay," Ray said, wanting the privacy of bowing his head. He was scared to death. He needed time to think.

Candace prayed next, "God, I do hereby forgive my gramps for molesting me. I do hereby forgive my mother for not knowing it was going on and not stopping him. I forgive Gramps for the pain I'm going through right now while I wait to take my HIV test."

Candace stopped praying and looked up. "Actually, I don't forgive. Really, I don't forgive them. Please don't be disappointed in me. I'm being honest. I can't forgive yet. When I prayed just now that I forgave them, I was only saying words that I don't feel. It's not this easy, and I can't act like it is. I'm sorry if I'm disappointing you guys."

"Consider it a start in the right direction," Maria said. "That's all God would expect of you. You'll need professional assistance. As John said, there are good people out there. God will put a wonderful therapist in your pathway. I'm sure of it."

Part of the problem was that Candace wasn't completely through the trauma of being molested. She was having to wait the waiting period to take her HIV test. It was always on her mind, constantly torturing her emotionally. She needed immediate and ongoing therapeutic attention. Hope suggested that she go to her family's new therapist. She said she believed that her dad's church would help with the cost.

Crisco's wee voice returned everyone to prayer. "God, I do forgive my mom for drinking when I was, uh, inside of her. Help me to make better grades."

Dale's time had come. He began to cry, his handsome, muscled-up six-foot frame trembling in grief. Everyone felt for him. The circle formed around him, and everyone began to encourage him.

After a long time, Dale spoke, "I am so-o-o ready to forgive. God, I do hereby forgive the corrupt people who have been in my life—the johns, the hundreds of johns that killed my mother."

For a few seconds he couldn't speak through his sobs, then he prayed, "God, I do hereby forgive my mother for dying and leaving me. God, I forgive my mother for being a prostitute. God, I forgive the gang that killed my little brother. God, I forgive my little brother for joining the gang."

The meadow was dark except for the Tiki torches highlighting the little huddle of teens and their friends, all bonded together before God. The crickets were competing with Dale's sobs.

Dale continued grieving and forgiving. He said, "God, I'll work on forgiving the psychologist who molested me. I forgive my mother for selling me to him...God, I forgive every straight person who labeled me bad 'cause I'm from the street. I forgive them for not letting me up. But, oh, God, help them see that I'm trying to rehabilitate my limb on my family tree!"

Dale sobbed louder. The rejection of good people seemed to hurt him as much as anything. "God, I do hereby forgive the people who were supposed to be good, the people I admired that set a lousy example in front of me. I forgive Mr. Rumley for trashing me. And I forgive the school board for saying stuff that makes no more sense than the stupid noises that the crickets make in this meadow."

Dale stopped again and turned to Hope. He placed his fingers under her chin, lifting her head from its bowed position. "Would you forgive me for hating you? I hated your guts because you had a good home, and you wouldn't stay in it. I was so jealous."

With tears streaming down her face, Hope responded, "Dale, I'm going back to CPS to tell my social worker and my counselor and my child advocate, everyone, the truth about my dad—that he *was* a good father, that he *is* a good father, and that my problems were my fault. I'll even ask them to forgive me for manipulating them."

"Good. I'm proud of you."

Dale turned toward the group, "Daniel, Terence, would you forgive me, too? I was jealous of your homes and the parents you used to gripe about. Coach John, Maria, you need to forgive me, too. I was jealous of your happiness together. I haven't had anyone close to me in a long time...maybe not ever."

Dale kept pouring stuff out, emptying his heart of all its grudges. The others did the same.

Some grudges seep back in like polluted water, Ms. Gibson thought, *but this is a great start for everyone here. Each time they forgive, there'll be less and less seepage.*

After all had forgiven the people who had hurt them, the group, still holding hands, prayed around the circle, asking forgiveness from God for their own sins.

Maria said, "Now, even after you have asked for forgiveness, you may have feelings that seem like guilt feelings, but they can't be guilt feelings since you are forgiven by Jesus Christ."

"So what are they?" Leilani asked.

"They are feelings of regret. The better you become, the more you are going to regret what you used to do wrong, and the yuckier it will appear to you as you look back on it. Regret is a good thing, though. It means that your old wrongs don't fit you anymore. You're better than that now. You have more integrity.

"So rename your guilt feelings. Call them regret feelings and let them remind you that you have become more mature. Okay? Remember this: God forgives us so that we can stand erect before Him again. Through forgiveness, God returns dignity to us."

As they stopped holding hands and took their places on the tailgates and in the Mustang, Dale's face glowed. He had emptied himself of sin and filled himself with God's love.

Maria continued, "Here's something you can say to yourself. Say: 'Yes, I feel bad about the things I did, but those feelings don't mean I'm still guilty. They mean that I regret what I did, and they testify to the fact that I am a better person than that today.' How's that?"

Terence added, "We definitely need a STRONG WILL about asking for forgiveness and forgiving others."

Kyong Suk got it right the first time. She said, "I will always feel welcome to seek forgiveness from Christ, and I will seek to be like Christ by forgiving others." As a second thought, she added, "Forgiving others and dumping grudges."

SCENE 33

Did right turn out wrong?

THIRTY-THREE

THE MEADOW grew quiet for a few moments. It was nearly time for good-byes.

John broke the silence, "I've tried to think of what I would say at this moment, and here it is: By faith, I am believing that no matter what has gone wrong, we can make it. I am an adult, and the STRONG WILLS were made up for you guys, but I've discovered that I need them as much as you do. I am taking them with me into my new job.

"Going through this whole mess with Mr. Rumley and the school board, rethinking my past, and watching what you young people have to deal with have made me see beyond a shadow of a doubt that the earth is not a fair place to live. Life here is an obstacle course. That's why we need to reach for heaven with all our hearts. Heaven is where everything will be fair and just. When you do right, it should turn out right. If it doesn't on earth, then certainly it will in heaven."

"And God shall wipe away all tears from their eyes..." Maria began to quote the Bible verse from Revelation 21:4 that talks about how life will be in heaven. *"And there shall be no more death, neither sorrow, nor crying, neither shall there be any more pain: for the former things are passed away."*

Hope held up a recorder/player that had been sitting on her lap. Everyone's attention shifted to her. She asked, "Is it okay if I play a little bit of my dad's sermon at True Life Church from Sunday? It's on the subject that we're talking about."

Kaprice said laughingly, "I wish Mr. Rumley was here. He loves recordings!"

Maria said, "Easy, Kaprice. Let's act in harmony with forgiveness now. Some of you forgave Mr. Rumley, don't forget."

The player came on, and Hope turned up the volume. Her dad was preaching.

Most of you know that our family has been through some tough times. Through it all, God has taught me something I'd like to share with you, my congregation.

In the days of the Old West, pioneers traveled across the country in wagon trains, searching for the land of their dreams. As they journeyed, things went wrong. A family member might have died or been killed. Perhaps they lost some of their belongings in river crossings. Maybe they had to repeatedly patch up broken wagons.

But what did they do when they reached their destination? Did they sit down beside their wagons and feel sorry for themselves for how hard the trip had been? Did they sink into depression? No! They got up and celebrated what hadn't been lost and began to build log cabins and break new land.

Well, each of us has arrived at his or her place today. What will you do here? Will you hate the past? Feel sorry for yourself? Sink into depression? Or will you celebrate what's still right with life and begin to break new land and build?

Hope stopped the player. She put her dad's words in her own. "Let's celebrate what's still right with life, and let's break new land and build new dreams."

"Let's get better not bitter," Maria summarized, smiling at Dale.

"Speaking of better," Dale said, "our STRONG WILLS have made me sure that I really can revive my limb on my family tree. These principles are my ticket to rising above the way I was raised."

Everyone applauded softly.

"That is, if my HIV report comes back negative when I'm tested. Everyone keep my and Candace's HIV tests in your prayers."

Dale ran his hand through his hair and excitedly repeated once more the commitment that he carried as his vision and dream for his future. "If I don't have HIV, my goal on earth is to redeem my limb on my family tree. I will raise my children right. They will raise my grandchildren right. Then they will raise my great-grandchildren right. And none of us will ever live on the streets again. None of us will be on welfare again.

"No one has to stay a victim. We each can control our destinies with the choices we make. Our choices are our tools of correction, our method of resurrection. Choice by choice, we can rise above our problems. Our destinies depend on our present choices, not our past problems. Our destinies depend on the choices within our STRONG WILLS."

With a thumbs-up gesture, Dale continued, "I'm moving off the streets. I'm moving in with Uncle Buddy. I want to be his apprentice. I want to become a therapist who counsels with correct values. I'll have to leave you guys, but I promise to write letters back every week for you to read in your meetings here. I'll get my uncle to help me do the writing so that they will be good enough to share with other Teens With Wisdom Societies. I'm going to organize one in Uncle Buddy's community."

As Dale handed out his handwritten address on the backs of beautiful sheets of paper, John said, "I'm beginning to see what has happened here. All I wanted to do was to keep my job and be the gladiator who conquered Mr. Rumley and his police-state tactics. But God had a higher purpose, and He answered our prayers in a bigger and better way. God's favorite thing is to bring good out of bad. In fact, I'm so excited about what God has done in us that I no longer have thoughts of suing the school district. I have something in which I'd rather invest my energy. Like Dale, I plan to organize a TWW Society in my new community. Then there'll be three societies. If we hadn't gone through all the injustice, the new societies wouldn't already be in the making. God's plans are always superior to ours...If we do right, will it turn out wrong? No, not if we will stretch far enough to see things from God's point of view. In God's sight, things have turned out right."

Ms. Gibson urged, "You should make that into a STRONG WILL— one that says there is always hope. I will, let's see, I will always remember that God's favorite creative act is to bring good out of bad."

"To grow flowers out of poop!" Kaprice wised off, bugging her mother as she returned to the laptop.

John smiled at Kaprice and continued, "God grew flowers out of waste. Through the pressure of our problems, He created your STRONG WILLS. They are His gift to you teens and to all generations of teens that come after you. Thousands of teens right now need help in dealing with stubborn problems; yet, like you, they can't afford to hire or may not be able to find a trustworthy therapist. Somehow, someway they have to survive. The STRONG WILLS give them the way to survive...but to do more than survive—to thrive! Let's lead the way. Right now, let's each make a decision, a personal commitment, to live by your STRONG WILLS."

The kids were itching to ask Dale to explain what was on the fronts of the beautiful papers he had handed out. Dale was hoping they would ask.

"My favorite uncle gave them to me to share with you. Could we read it aloud together?" Dale led. "Jesus Christ was a healer. He still is. Since I am to follow Him, I must be a healer, too. Therefore, I will monitor my every attitude and action with this question: *Will this heal?* (Will this help? Will this inspire improvement? Will this preserve good?)"

John immediately remembered his drinking. His drinking wouldn't have passed the test question of: *Will this heal?* He thought, *If I had asked the question, it would have saved me from that whole humiliating mess.*

Ray caught on quickly and took a brief tour of the past by asking a lot of questions of the group. "Will smoking pot heal? Will doing drugs heal? Will drinking heal? Will shoplifting heal? Will watching X-rated videos heal? Will having sex outside of marriage heal? Will having an abortion heal? Will shacking up with someone in front of your children heal? Will telling your child that one-night stands are smarter than he is heal? Will being a prostitute heal? Will having sex with a prostitute heal? Will having sex with her ten-year-old son heal? Will having sex with your stepgranddaughter heal? Will beating your child heal? Did Mr. Rumley's scheming control-freak plans heal?"

Franco concluded Ray's tour, "We have all been hurting because we or our significant others have been sinning—living out of sync with the healing personality of Christ. That's as clear as clear can possibly be."

Daniel was fascinated. "So this is what people mean when they say Christ is the answer! His way works! It is authentic! That's why it's called *The Answer!*" Speaking slowly and thoughtfully, he made a classic statement: "If we keep ourselves in God's will by only doing what will heal, we flow with the promises of God, and life is guaranteed to work right, and that makes Christ *The Answer.*"

"Think about it," Dale encouraged. "Teenagers have to disobey God to go to detention, and adults have to disobey God to go to jail...unless, of course, they aren't guilty. Those facilities would be practically empty if people didn't ignore God. Uncle Buddy was once in juvy jail talking to seventeen teenagers. He asked them what kids could get arrested for. They had fun telling him since they wanted to impress each other with how streetwise they were. He wrote the list on the chalkboard in front of them. The list was made up of crimes like...

assaulting a teacher

assaulting a student

assaulting a parent

ditching school

running away

breaking and entering

burglary

theft

shoplifting

stealing cars

possession of drugs

possessing paraphernalia

public intoxication

driving while under the influence

breaking into a computer system

writing hot checks

credit card abuse

carjacking

murder

rape

"Uncle Buddy then asked them which ones God wanted them to do. There was total silence for several moments. Then a kid shyly said, 'None of 'em.' Then Uncle Buddy made his point, 'You mean you have to disobey God to go to jail?!' He asked, 'What would happen if you gave your lives to God and began to live like He wants you to?'

"There was no answer because of the peer pressure in there. He helped them out. He motioned toward the list on the board and almost screamed, 'You'd be free! Free of all this! Do you see that obeying God will make your life work? God loves you, and He gives you commands to protect you.'

"Uncle Buddy says, 'It's like God has an umbrella and the part you hold onto makes a J for Jesus. Hold onto Jesus, and you'll be under God's umbrella of protection, and you'll stop getting rained on by the consequences of your own new sins.'

"He's right, guys. God gives us His way to protect us from getting ourselves into trouble. *Christ is The Answer!* That bumper sticker will mean more to us now."

Maria started to say something, but Dale didn't notice. "One time, Uncle Buddy was in the adult jail, and an inmate walked up to the bars and said to him, 'If you can prove that God exists, I'll accept Jesus Christ right here and now.'

"He replied, 'Think back over your life. When you obeyed God, how was it? Were you more honest? More understanding? More responsible? A better son to your parents? A better husband to your wife? A better father to your children?' The man answered, 'Yep.'

"Then Uncle Buddy asked, 'When you ignored God, did you remain that way?'

"The man backed away from the bars of the cell, opened his arms wide to display the jail, and exclaimed, 'I'm here, ain't I?!'

"Uncle Buddy responded, 'God loves you, and He is trying to protect you from all this. But He can't unless you give your life to Him and start obeying Him and start synchronizing your choices with what He wants for you.'

"The inmate became loyal to Christ right then and there."

Maria tried again. Again Dale didn't notice. "Oh, there's another story Uncle Buddy told me. He was in jail visiting with an inmate. Some guy told him that he didn't know why it was God's will for him to be in jail. He said he didn't know why God wanted him there.

"Uncle Buddy asked, 'When you were arrested, were you doing God's will, or were you doing something against God's will? Were you obeying God or disobeying God?'

"He answered, 'I was doing something against God's will.'

"Uncle Buddy then helped him solve his riddle. 'Then God didn't want you here. God didn't want you in trouble. If you had obeyed Him, He would have protected you from this terrible experience.'"

Maria spoke quickly. "But we aren't merely keeping a bunch of rules," she asserted. "We are following a warm person—the hero of heroes, the hero of morality—Jesus Christ. That's what makes Christian faith a warm and an exciting journey."

"The celebrity above all celebrities," Leilani said, remembering her speech.

Crisco looked up at her big brother and asked, "Does asking *Will this heal?* mean that I can't get upset when kids at school tell me that I need the oil drained off my brain?" Franco hesitated, seeing that Kaprice seemed to want to answer Crisco for him.

Kaprice took her eyes from Crisco and answered the child's question for the whole group, "Asking *Will this heal?* before you do things doesn't make a wimp out of you. Mom confronted Mr. Rumley hard, and it healed the school of bad leadership. He's no longer there!"

Ms. Gibson followed, "Coach John and Maria did the healing thing when they rebelled against the tyranny of Mr. Rumley and met with you young people in spite of his objections. Healing has come out of those meetings. You now have the successes you've experienced together, and you now have your new STRONG WILLS."

Hope said, "When you didn't know to ask or if you forget to ask *Will this heal?* before you do something, you can ask: *What will heal now?* That way you can fix any mistakes you've made. That's what I'm doing in my family."

"That's what I've been doing ever since Grandypa was arrested," Leilani agreed. "Without knowing the exact words, it's like I've been asking *What will heal now?* And I've been acting on the answers...and that's why my family is healing."

"I'm glad you are resurrecting from all that and asking God to help you forgive yourself, Leilani," Dale encouraged. Then affirming her, he added, "Will wallowing in guilt heal, Leilani? Will self-criticism heal?"

Leilani obviously agreed with Dale and appreciated his words of encouragement.

"I'm liking this!" Hope exclaimed, feeling really positive. "Asking *Will this heal?* is a way of counseling ourselves without adult input. Maria, you need to add it to our STRONG WILLS...And now dear, dear, Dale," Hope teased, "you have to ask *Will this heal?* before you whip out your switchblade! Remember that Jesus said if you live by the sword, you'll die by the sword."

"I'll do that," Dale agreed, "and it will be even better than counting to ten to cool down my hot temper before I react."

Hope didn't respond to what he said. Her mind was racing with a sudden burst of insight on another subject. "My dad's preaching makes sense to me now. The word *saved* means that I am saved from the self-destruction of sinning and ignoring God...and I'm saved to be God's daughter and to share an inheritance with Christ. Born again means that my values have totally changed for the better. I have stopped rebelling against my God and my parents, and now I am rebelling against Satan and the wrong crowd. Conversion, that's what it is. I have converted from going the wrong way in life to going the right way in life, from wanting to be with the wrong crowd to wanting to be with the right crowd—a complete change of mind-set. My dad's sermons weren't so bad after all!"

Having another revelation, Hope suddenly exclaimed, "Baptism! It's like your party boat sinks, but it's God to the rescue! He resurrects you! He raises you from the drowning crowd!"

Dale loved hearing Hope talk that way. "Think of the words that describe the party lifestyle—*stoned, wasted, trashed, plastered, bombed, destroyed.* The words fit so well. Just hearing the words ought to wise people up. God's not against us having fun. He just knows that our futures are in our choices, and He's against anything that compromises our abilities to make good choices, our abilities to live by the principles in our STRONG WILLS."

John asked them to bow their heads for prayer. He prayed, "Our God, the wisdom of the ages, these teens have put their minds with Yours, and You have given them their STRONG WILLS. I pray that You will now help each of them, all of us, adopt them and build our lives upon them."

John stopped and said to his circle of friends, "I want to give you a few moments of silence to pray to God and tell Him that you will sincerely try to live by your STRONG WILLS."

Silence.

Kyong Suk spoke up, "I promise!"

John said softly but loud enough for everyone to hear, "No, don't promise. That sets you up for radical temptation and for despair, if you fail. Just repeat after me: God, I do hereby accept...the STRONG WILLS... as the way...I will seek...to live my life."

Ms. Gibson wanted to add something. "You need one more STRONG WILL. At school, they're always talking about having a good self-image. They say that many problems that students have can be traced back to poor self-esteem. You need a STRONG WILL to help you have a healthy self-image."

"But how?" Leilani asked.

"Yeah, how?" Kyong Suk echoed.

Terence chimed in, "If I could make a better grade in math, I'd have a better self-image. Ms. Gibson, could we work together? I'll help your son practice soccer if you'll tutor me in math."

"That's a wonderful idea, Terence. I've been praying for someone to be a male presence in my son's life, and I'd love to help you with your math."

"Ms. Gibson," Ray said, "look around this circle. How are we supposed to have good self-images?"

Kaprice's mother had touched a raw nerve. She knew what they were thinking. John had been rejected by the school board. Leilani and Hope had hurt their families. Leilani's mom and dad had chosen chemicals over her. Franco and Crisco's mom had chosen guys over them. Kaprice's father had deserted her. Candace and Dale had been sexually molested. Some of the kids were in the grip of dysfunctional families.

Ms. Gibson said, "You don't get your self-image from what's gone on around you. You stretch as Coach John said. You stretch from here to heaven, and you get your self-image from Christ. God created us in His image, we lost it in the fall of humankind...but Jesus offers it to us again. Jesus Christ is God's image afresh. When we accept Him into our hearts, God's image begins to return. God forgives you to return His image to you and to return your self-respect to you."

"How shall we word it?" Maria asked.

Hope thought and said, "I will help Christ return God's image to me by living as best friends with Him, and I will feel secure because my citizenship is already in heaven, and no one can touch that."

"For real," Leilani said, "no human can interfere with that!"

Kaprice entered it into the computer.

"That's very good," John said to Hope. "I'd like to suggest that we adjust the one about open-minded-but-narrow-minded professionals judging me to be a wasteland and making me compromise my positive contribution in life."

Dale said, "Don't adjust it too much. I've already used that STRONG WILL. I think we'll all need it throughout our lives."

"Good point, Dale," John said. "Let's only add 'or people in authority' after professionals."

John bowed his head to pray again. "God, I thank You that these teens have the maturity to accept their STRONG WILLS. As they honor them, I'm completely sure You will support them. Thank You. Amen."

"Could I add one more, although we've already prayed?" Dale asked, unfolding a piece of paper he had taken out of his shirt pocket. "I think we need to end our STRONG WILLS with one that will help us sort things out in this corrupt culture. I wrote it when I went back to the streets after the board meeting: I will keep myself enCOURAGEd by sorting my way through life—flushing what is wrong and highlighting what is right."

With sparkling eyes, Maria, said, "That makes eighteen Strong Wills. You guys are so sharp! So cool, I mean. Your discoveries and these times together have truly been blessed by God." As an afterthought, Maria mused, "I wish there were nineteen. Then there would be one for each of your preteen and teen years."

Crisco asked, "Is it okay to give the Strong Wills to Mom? I think they will help her."

"I'm sorry, Crisco, but that is not what you or anyone else should do," Maria answered gently. "Your mom will be bothered by some of them. To really, really understand the Strong Wills, people have to know our story, and they have to have a heart change, too. That's why the Strong Wills should never be separated from the drama within which they were born."

SCENE 34

An exciting new quest begins

THIRTY-FOUR

JOHN LOOKED up and said, "I think the best way to close this meeting is to join hands and pray for the hundreds of teenagers who will become members of Teens With Wisdom Societies in the future."

As the teens slid off tailgates and stepped out of the convertible and re-formed their circle, Hope caught Ray's eye and borrowed his line, "Welcome to the world of teenagers where God answers prayer. God answered my parents' prayers. God answered the prayers of the parents who prayed that their kids would stop hangin' out with the wrong crowd." Then smiling mischievously, "Terence and Daniel are now running with the Teens With Wisdom Society—doesn't that daze you and amaze you, guys?" Again more serious, "God answered our prayers for Leilani and her family. And for Candace. And for Dale to have a real home. And—"

Ms. Gibson added, "I'm not a teenager, of course, but God answered my prayer to get out from under Mr. Rumley's control without getting fired."

"God didn't answer my prayers for Mom," Crisco protested.

Dale was quick to answer her. "That's true, Crisco. And God hasn't answered Ray's prayers for his mom and dad or Leilani's prayers for her parents or Kaprice's prayers for her dad. And this is where a lot of kids get disappointed with God, but they shouldn't because they are asking God to do what He has already promised He won't do. He won't normally interfere with a person's choices. To answer those kinds of prayers, God would have to invade the control centers of people's minds and make robots out of them, and God won't do that. Remember, He didn't keep Adam and Eve from making wrong choices.

"But it's not God who is failing. The persons who are making bad choices are failing...Actually, God has already answered your prayers, Crisco." Dale looked up and said, "And those of Ray, Leilani, and Kaprice. He has already given your parents the answer. Like the Bible says, they should repent of doing wrong and begin to do what's right. God has already done His part; now they must do their parts. They must complete the circuit. Without their cooperation, it ain't gonna happen. Does everyone understand what I'm sayin'?"

No one seemed to need further explanation. The group was quiet for a moment as if thinking over what Dale had said.

"Prayer is...," Daniel began to speak suddenly and firmly. Everyone quickly looked at him because he hadn't had much to say. Seeing that everyone's attention was on him, he started over. "I was getting the wheels realigned on my truck the other day and it hit me: Prayer is taking my heart to God on a daily basis for realignment with His heart and His will. I wrote my thoughts into a STRONG WILL. It goes like this: I will pray often to realign my heart with God's heart and God's will."

"That makes nineteen STRONG WILLS," Maria observed, winking at Daniel.

"I know," Daniel said, smiling back at her.

Maria jotted it down and said, "Let's do that now. If anyone doesn't feel comfortable praying aloud, just squeeze the hand of the next person."

Leilani surprised John with a question. "Who is Mat?"

John slowly repeated her question to buy time to think about how to answer it. "Who...is...Mat? Let me just say that Mat is short for the word *maturity*."

They laughed a little because they all thought Mat was a person.

"Okay, I have a question, too," John said, smiling. "What on earth does FAFF mean?"

Kaprice happily replied, "Friends are friends forever!"

They lifted their hands high as Ms. Gibson said, "That's true! That's true no matter how many miles come between us!"

The teens prayed around the circle. They prayed that God would bless each and every teenager who reads and lives by the STRONG WILLS— the strong choices—that came from their secret meetings in the meadow.

Terence closed the prayer, "And, God, I pray that we, and the teenagers who come after us, will use our STRONG WILLS to rebel— to rebel against the wrongs of this crazy, mixed-up, and corrupt culture. Amen."

As Terence said amen, Ms. Gibson began to sing from the depths of her soul. Her voice filled the meadow. "Amazing grace! How sweet the sound!"

Softly, Ray said, "Welcome to the world of teenagers, where we are returning to the image of God."

"That saved a wretch like me!" she sang. "I once was lost, but now am found; Was blind, but now I see. 'Twas grace that..."

Ms. Gibson stopped singing and said, "Your STRONG WILLS are complete now. I'd love to hear them read together."

The teens let go of each other's hands and returned to their places.

Kaprice returned to Hope's computer, copied Daniel's STRONG WILL from Maria's notes, and pressed print. The portable printer came to life and began feeding out several copies. Kaprice said, "I hope you don't mind, but I rearranged the STRONG WILLS in the computer to follow a better order and to read more smoothly." The group waited patiently while the little printer worked hard for them. Kaprice handed out the new edition.

Terence again waited for someone else to take the lead. Kaprice did. The group read the title in unison: "The STRONG WILLS of the Teens With Wisdom Society—Our new standard for cool."

They read their purpose. "Our Teens With Wisdom Society is a fellowship of teens who have formed an oasis of friendship and support in a stressed-out and confused culture. Our purpose is to help each other muscle up and rise above his or her problems, frustrations, or mistakes, and build an invincible life. Our common goal is to be truly independent—to live quality-controlled lives based on the wisdom of Christ."

They read their theme Scripture. "'*Do not let anyone look down on you because you are young, but be an example for the believers, in your speech, your conduct, your love, faith, and purity*' (1 Timothy 4:12, TEV)."

Then the teens read their STRONG WILLS slowly and passionately, giving each one the attention it deserved.

"I will do right no matter what I think is wrong with my parents or guardians.

"I will be responsible for myself and not try to use my parents' or guardians' problems to excuse my own stupid sins.

"I will do well even if my parents or guardians have a lousy opinion of me.

"I will succeed even if I'm not favored for success.

"I will not give my brothers or sisters or my parent's significant other's children the right to ruin my life forever.

"I will finally leave the sins of offenders in the past where they belong.

"I will make it through the storms and disappointments of family life.

"I will not allow rude comments, attitudes, or actions of teachers to turn me away from respecting myself and from believing that I can achieve good goals with my life. I will prove that insensitive teachers are wrong about me.

"I will not allow my peers to pressure me away from what I believe is right by hassling me, by putting down my parents or decent friends, or by threatening to leave me out if I don't conform to what they want.

"I will not allow open-minded-but-narrow-minded professionals or people in authority to judge me to be a wasteland and make me compromise my positive contribution in life.

"I will always choose to become a better person rather than a bitter person when justice is bullied by injustice. I will remain strong because I know for sure that all wrongs will be righted at the Great Fairness Adjustment when every knee shall bow before Christ to receive His verdict.

"I will always remember that God's favorite creative act is to bring good out of bad, to grow flowers out of waste. There is hope—always!

"I will always feel welcome to seek forgiveness from Christ, and I will seek to be like Christ by forgiving others and dumping grudges.

"I will honor God's trust of me in our best-friends relationship. The opportunities in my present and future are God's gifts to me; how I succeed with those opportunities is my gift to God. God votes for me, the pull of sin votes against me, and I am breaking the tie by the way I am voting with each decision I make.

"I will help Christ return God's image to me by living as best friends with Him, and I will feel secure because my citizenship is already in heaven, and no human can interfere with that.

"I will pray often to realign my heart with God's heart and God's will.

"I will guide my life with the Golden Rule by doing unto others as I would like them to do unto me.

"I will follow Christ by asking *Will this heal?* before proceeding with my attitudes or actions.

"I will keep myself enCOURAGEd by sorting my way through life—flushing what is wrong and highlighting what is right."

Kaprice led them in reading the last paragraph in unison.

"By making the above choices and living loyal to these choices, we teens will succeed in life, although bad things have happened to us in the past, although we've made mistakes ourselves, and although there are pressures on us now. Our STRONG WILLS are our life preservers. We are strong-willed!"

Kaprice returned her eyes to the computer monitor and her fingers found the right keys. "I need to add a place for people to sign their names and fill in the date."

John said, "But you don't want to make it a promise. You could word it, uh, I accept the STRONG WILLS as my ideal for living life…"

"And I will seek to live true to them," Kaprice quickly finished as something else demanded their attention.

They all turned toward the sights and sounds of a car and a huge truck invading their meadow! Lights were flashing on the roof of the car! It was a police car! Blinding headlights appeared to be blinking as the vehicles dodged through the trees. The secret entrance to their secret place had been discovered!!

"Oh, no! What's happening now?!" Leilani exclaimed, not wanting anything else to go wrong.

No one answered. All waited. Doors slammed. The lights on the police car continued flashing. Two policemen, adjusting their gun belts, walked over to the group. Another man followed them. Without saying hello, the man said, "Do you people realize you are trespassing? The police are here to usher you off my property and warn you that I'll press charges if I catch you out here again!"

One of the policemen began to recognize the teens by the flickering light of the Tiki torches. "You are the young people who were at the school board meeting!" Then beginning to shake hands with the teens, he said, "You guys did a great job at the press conference in the police station this morning! Congratulations!" His partner began shaking hands, too.

The landowner was disgusted by the way the policemen were sucking up to his trespassers.

As the lead policeman shook Dale's hand, he said, "Young man, I apologize for singling you out and searching you in front of everyone. The principal of your school was worried that you were carryin' a weapon. After I watched the quality performance you young people put forth at the school board meeting, I felt badly for you. What happened there wasn't right."

"No, it wasn't right!" the landowner exclaimed tartly, losing patience. "Mr. Rumley was railroaded out of his job!"

When he stepped near a Tiki torch, Ms. Gibson recognized him. "Aren't you Viola Jeffries's husband?" She asked the question to clue in the others on who they were dealing with.

"Yes, and my wife and Mr. Rumley are very close. He's at our house now, and Viola is helping him prepare for his new position. No thanks to you." His eyes drilled holes in Ms. Gibson. "He has found a higher-paying job in a better school district. One that will respect his authority." Getting louder and addressing everyone, "Now snuff out your torches and get the heck off my land before I press charges!"

Kaprice popped off, "Your wife and Mr. Rumley may be a little too close if you know what I'm sayin'!"

"Kaprice!" gasped Ms. Gibson.

Kaprice didn't shut up. "Mr. Jeffries, your biggest problem right now is not who is on your property but who is with your wife!"

"Kaprice Gibson! What are you doing?!" her stunned mother asked.

"I'm sorry, Mom," Kaprice replied, "but it's right that he should know…and Mr. Rumley can't hurt you now. Besides, I'm sick and tired of adult corruption! Since adults expect us kids to act right, they've got to act right, too!"

Then to Jeffries, she bluntly explained, "One day your wife went into Mr. Rumley's office wearing one outfit, and presto chango, she came out wearing a different outfit! Either it was magic or hanky-panky. If I were you, I'd hurry home, park a block away, slip in real quietlike, and check things out for myself. I think you'll find that you are being played for a fool."

"Young lady, you had better watch your mouth!" Jeffries retorted. "Slandering someone's character is a very serious matter!"

"Kaprice! Say no more!" Mom sternly warned.

The policeman, ignoring the alleged affair, demanded the landowner's attention as he gestured toward the teenagers. "Your suspicions were wrong about these kids. This is not a drug party or a meeting of the occult. This is the start of something positive! Something extraordinary! Something huge! You need to hear the document that these kids read to the school board members. One day you'll be proud that it started on your land. Do you kids have a copy that you can show him?"

The teens nearest him tried to hand Mr. Jeffries a copy of the STRONG WILLS.

Refusing to extend his hand toward theirs, he impatiently responded, "Don't bother! I won't read it. I won't be impressed. This whole thing will fizzle. You kids will forget about it. You'll go back to partying. But I won't be providing you the place! You're trespassing! Get off my land!"

Whirling around, he stomped angrily toward his one-ton truck. Secretly, he was worried about his wife and Rumley. He had seen a few signs that had made him wonder if something had been going on between them, but now something concrete had been said. However, he wasn't about to let his concern show; he wanted the girl to be wrong.

Kaprice called after him, "Remember to approach your house as quietly as a mouse!"

Jeffries turned around long enough to give her a dirty look. "I will!" he exclaimed with aggravation. "And my stealth will prove you wrong!" Turning toward his truck, he stomped on. His engine roared louder than necessary. He slammed his vehicle into gear, and taillights disappeared through the trees. He was gone. The meadow was quiet again. The lights on top of the police car continued flashing.

The teens returned their attention to the policemen. Hope explained their side to them. "Officers, we used to party out here, but we don't now. We don't need to hide anymore. We are no longer proud of what we should be ashamed of. We are more mature now. We are ready to come out into the open and make our contributions in life. As we leave this meadow tonight and drive out of the woods, our expedition begins."

FAFF

CHARACTER REFERENCE: To make it easy to stay in touch with characters.

————————TEENS *(Listed alphabetically by first names):*————————

Bo Langley: Slipped date-rape drugs to Hope and Maranda.

Brady: Leilani's boyfriend. He says his parents are stupid and easy to fool.

Bruce: No-dorks-on-board motorcyclist. He rides a killer Ninja.

Candace Thornton: Victim of ongoing sexual assault by her stepgrandfather (Gramps).

Copperhead: Tattooist and member of the Reptile gang.

Crisco Russo: Franco Russo's eight-year-old half-sister. She flies in on weekends to see her mom and Franco.

Dale: Orphaned and homeless street kid. His mom, a prostitute, died of AIDS-related diseases. His younger brother had his head blown away in a turf war.

Daniel: Quiet comedian. He believes his parents are too nosy, too strict, try to pry into his business too much, and try to choose his friends too often.

Franco Russo: Student depressed because his mother's sleepovers or live-ins sometimes beat her in front of him and his little half-sister (Crisco).

Fred: Self-appointed porno librarian and Internet pornography tracker and informant. He says he has to parent his parents.

Hope: Minister's daughter who reported her parents to Children's Protective Services and was removed from their home.

Jock, the: Nameless smart-mouthed guy who helped Coach Bright deal with a nasty problem.

Kaprice Gibson: Head cheerleader for Lincoln High School. She is Ms. Gibson's daughter and best friends with Leilani.

Kathy: Party girl.

Kyong Suk Song: Teen sandwiched between her parents in a bitter divorce battle and blaming herself for their problems. (Her first and middle names are pronounced Kiong Sue and are said together.)

Lance: Party guy.

Leilani Summers: Cheerleader for Lincoln High School, Brady's girlfriend, and Kaprice's best friend. Leilani's grandparents won custody of her when she was seven years old due to her mother's cocaine addiction and her father's alcoholism. (Her first name is pronounced Lay-lawn-ee.) Nicknamed: Princess Leilani of Hawaii.

Maranda Donnell: Gang raped after she was slipped a date-rape drug by Bo Langley.

Princess Leilani of Hawaii: Nickname for Leilani. See Leilani Summers.

Python: Member of the Reptile gang.

Rat: Member of the Reptile gang. His name is short for rattlesnake.

Ray Beavers, Jr: Hyperactive and socially clumsy guy from a very dysfunctional family.

Terence: Popular guy with dyslexia. He says his mom and dad are trying too hard to be good parents, and they supervise him too closely.

Zack: Party guy.

————————ADULTS *(Listed alphabetically by last names, unless none was given):*————————

Beavers, Ray, Sr.: Abusive father of Ray Beavers, Jr.

Brain, Rump: Nickname for Mr. Rumley, the principal of Lincoln High School. See Rumley, Alfredo Henry.

Bright, Coach John: Young new coach at Lincoln High School. He fights the principal, Mr. Rumley, for the right to "be there" for teens.

Bright, Maria: Coach John's sharp wife.

Bundik, Donald: Secretary of the school board and Mr. Rumley's golfing buddy.

Burleson, Mrs.: Science teacher at LHS. Dale and Candace had her for Biology.

Chairman of the Department of Psychology, Memorial Hospital: Psychologist who is forced into a winner-takes-all battle with a teenager. He is referred to as *Doctor*.

Chester: School counselor. See Rouse, Evelyn.

Face, Rump: Nickname for Mr. Rumley, the principal of LHS. See Rumley, Alfredo Henry.

Falderal, Jimmy: Fanatical TV evangelist.

Gambino, Winston: Teacher at Lincoln High School. He lives in John's apartment complex and helped him with a nasty problem.

Gibson, Ms.: Mr. Rumley's secretary. Kaprice Gibson's mother. A discreet and wise woman.

Gramps: Child molester and Candace's stepgrandfather.

Grandestmother: Leilani's grandmother.

Grandypa: Leilani's grandfather. Leilani says he's smart, watches CNN and C-SPAN, and is handsomer than the gentleman on KFC boxes.

Grizzly: Leilani's pet name for Hank. See Hank.

Hank: Criminal manipulator of the legal system.

Jayla: Prostitute.

Jeffries, Mr.: Viola Jeffries's husband.

Jeffries, Viola: School board member. She attends the same church as Mr. Rumley and is his flying instructor.

Knight, Dr. Weldon: A doctor at the Women's Clinic.

Means, Robert: President of the school board. He is also president of Carlton and Means Investments, downtown, and Mr. Rumley's golfing buddy.

Molester, Lester the: Candace's stepgrandfather. See Gramps.

Moss, Dr. Conrad: Therapist at Memorial Hospital.

Myrna: Prostitute.

Platt, Cris "Platypus": School nurse. He orders condoms for the students in school colors.

Platypus: School nurse. See Platt, Cris.

Rouse, Evelyn "Chester": School counselor. She arranges abortions for students.

Rumley, Alfredo Henry: Principal of Lincoln High School. Mr. Rumley, fifty-nine, sees himself as a progressive thinker and his school as a perfect example of modern educational trends.

Rumpley: Students' nickname for Mr. Rumley, the principal of Lincoln High School. See Rumley, Alfredo Henry.

Rutherford, Estelle: School board member. She serves on a Chamber of Commerce committee with Mr. Rumley.

Simmons, Elaine: School board member. She attends seminars with Mr. Rumley.

Stone, Ginny: Nurse at the Women's Clinic.

Summers, Samuel David: Leilani's grandfather. See Grandypa.

Wycoff, Bill: School board member. He is in the Lions Club with Mr. Rumley.